On th

Mike Parker is a writer and broadcaster. His books to date include *Map Addict* and the *Rough Guide to Wales*. He writes for publications including the *Guardian* and the *Sunday Times*, and presents on radio and television.

Praise for *On the Red Hill*

'[An] extraordinary, ambitious, many layered memoir ... its scope is immense ... [A] turbulent energy stirs the book out of any nostalgic pastoralism in which it might have luxuriated. [Parker's] re-creation of the lives of Reg and George, ultimately crowned in happiness and fulfilment despite the constrictions imposed on them by society, is exemplary gay social history, of a kind we deeply need.'

Simon Callow, *Guardian*

'A fascinating account of queer lives in rural Wales over almost five decades ... It holds a mirror up to the often hidden gay lives of the past century ... The result, in prose as swooping as the birds that teem about the house, is an important study of everyday gay life before and after decriminalisation ... An intimate account of the stunning natural beauty of this part of Wales, and its proud history ... It is through this unusual book, a lovely hybrid of memoir, panegyric and queer history, that Parker too ... seems at last to find his own *noddfa* – sanctuary – and with it a sense of belonging.'

Daily Telegraph

'Mike Parker's elegant pastoral is an unflinching but tender story of gay love and inter-generational friendship. What emerges is a beautiful and often overlooked kind of family portrait.'

Laurence Scott, author of *Picnic Comma Lightning*

'A perfectly balanced blend of memoir and biography set within the beautifully portrayed Welsh countryside. An evocative and moving examination of just what it means to find a place to call home.'

Neil Ansell, author of *Deep country*

'A praise-poem to adventure, belonging, the power of nature and, above all, to the resilience of human beings and the love between them. Parker's great strength and passion is in illuminating certain hidden strata of these islands, in the unearthing and re-telling of stories silenced by the forces of political history ... A beautiful, immersive and – in these testing times – vital and necessary book.'

Niall Griffiths

'This is such a delightful book about beauty, joy, love and home ... Any book which pulls the two meanings of "gay" back together is welcome; a book that achieves this fusion this in an isolated but loved and lovely green Welsh valley is to be celebrated and read.'

Sara Maitland

'An intricately woven celebration and acknowledgment of life in modern rural Wales, always gripping, often romantic but never sentimental ... The seasons colour the pages in vivid greens and deep russets, and the closeness to nature is raw and honest. The footpaths, streams and trees that surround the house are ever-present ... In turn fascinating, funny, moving and touching ... This is the truest version of modern Welsh life I have ever read.'

Manon Steffan Ros

'A tender account of love, life, language, a beloved landscape.'

Gillian Clarke

ALSO BY MIKE PARKER

On the Red Hill

Where Four Lives Fell Into Place

MIKE PARKER

WINDMILL BOOKS

3 5 7 9 10 8 6 4

Windmill Books
20 Vauxhall Bridge Road
London SW1V 2SA

Windmill Books is part of the Penguin Random House group
of companies whose addresses can be found
at global.penguinrandomhouse.com

First published in Great Britain by William Heinemann in 2019
First published in paperback by Windmill Books in 2020

www.penguin.co.uk

A CIP catalogue record for this book is available from the British Library.

ISBN 9781786090492

Typeset in 10.97/13 pt Cambria
by Integra Software Services Pvt. Ltd, Pondicherry

Printed and bound in Great Britain by Clays Ltd, Elcograf S.p.A.

To Reg and George,
Penny and David,
with gratitude and love.

CONTENTS

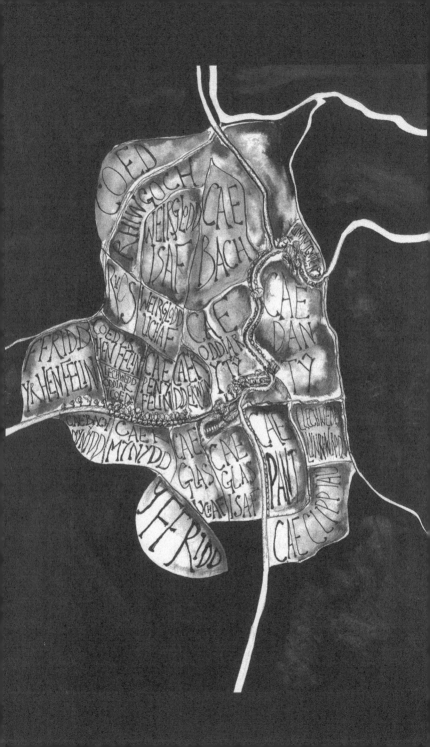

PARISH OF DAROWEN.

LOT 4.

THE COMPACT HOLDING KNOWN AS

RHIWGOCH,

ying close to the village of Talywern, and in the occupation of Mr. Richard Jones, at an annual rental of £43. is is a very useful mixed farm. The land reaches to the river Ednant on the north, from which it rises wards and is intersected by the parish roads to Machynlleth and Melinbyrhedyn leading past the homestead.

The Farmhouse, which stands in an elevated but convenient position, and has had a new part added it within recent years, contains Kitchen, Dairy, Back Kitchen, 2 Pantries, and 4 Bedrooms. Immediately jacent are **The Outbuildings,** which have been overhauled and are in satisfactory order. They comprise whouse for six, Hayhouse, Wainhouse with Granary over, Store Cattle Shed, 2 Piggeries, another Cattle Shed ings for six, Stabling for 4 horses, Barn and 2 Bays, all stone-built and slated; together with a detached three-y Hayshed built of timber with corrugated-iron roof.

Sale catalogue, 1911

Men of my sort could take to the greenwood.
E. M. Forster, *Maurice*

PROLOGUE

Thursday, 2 February 2006

The Powys registrar was visibly relieved that her first same-sex civil partnership ceremony had gone without a hitch. 'Well, you know what I always say?' she trilled in our direction as the ink dried on the signatures. 'G-A-Y – what does it stand for? Good As You.' She carefully put down her regulation fountain pen and smiled beneficently at the four of us, seemingly expecting if not a round of applause for her generous liberalism, then at least a heartfelt thank you.

I glanced sideways at Reg. He might have just married the man he had been living with for nearly sixty years, but he still didn't want anyone, least of all a pen-pusher from the county council, calling him A Gay. His face had tightened into a polite grimace. Occasionally, he'd get as far as saying 'the G-word', but even that was only ever whispered sotto voce, as if its velvet softness might still conceal the iron fist of bigotry that had so shaped his life. I once tried to explain to

3

him why many of us were happy to rehabilitate the word 'queer'. His eyes bulged alarmingly, and I didn't try again.

Municipal register offices are rarely the most appetising of environments, and Machynlleth's is no exception. Wintry beams filtered through the muck crusting the solitary window, while a smell of musty cardboard hung heavy in the half-light. A suitably baleful atmosphere to register a death, perhaps, but woefully out of kilter for a birth or marriage – let alone this great legal landmark.

Legislation allowing the first state recognition of same-sex relationships reached the statute books in December 2005. First to tie the knot were two men in Worthing, who'd had the fortnight waiting period waived because one of them was terminally ill with cancer; he died the day after the ceremony. It took another two months for this brave new world to arrive in our small Welsh market town, which may well be something of a record. Fashions normally take at least a decade to reach us.

Emerging outside, we took some photographs and walked up the street to Preds' house for a celebratory high tea. On the way, I nipped into the Co-op to buy a bottle of bubbly.

'Champagne on a Thursday afternoon?' said the girl on the till.

I explained the occasion.

'Oh, those two old men, you mean? The ones who come in on market day?'

I nodded.

'They're lovely; always so tidy and polite. How beautiful that they can get married now.' She looked as if she might cry. 'Oh, give them my love, and say congratulations.'

Reg was quite the blushing bride, downing a glass of fizz and turning nougat pink as a result. George enjoyed himself in his usual polite and faintly detached way, with a keen eye, as always, on his wallet. His diary for the day:

> Rang Mike re taking photos of Reg and I at ceremony. He has a Digital – will bring. 1.45pm Prebb [sic] came in his car & took us to Mach – solicitor by the clock and at 2.30 to have our GREAT moment 'CIVIC RIGHTS PARTNERSHIP'. Wonderful gathering.
> (Paid £47.00).

*

If the countryside appears at all in gay histories, it is usually only as a place to escape from, and as swiftly as possible. For many of us, this is a pattern that never fitted. Since childhood, the green places have called us the loudest, and although we did the urban thing to burst from the closet, the lure of the rural soon overwhelmed the anonymity of the city. It didn't even feel like a choice, but something intrinsic that would have been dangerous to resist, like the act of coming out itself.

So it was for George Walton and Reg Mickisch, an elegant couple of demobbed Londoners who fell in love in the post-war ruins and moved to Bournemouth. In 1972, just five years after the decriminalisation of homosexuality, they upped sticks to the sticks: a tiny Welsh-speaking village in the hills of Montgomeryshire, mid Wales. They remained in the area until their deaths, five weeks apart, in 2011, aged ninety-four and eighty-four, respectively.

Although the search for the queer rural is more mainstream today, there was no well-grooved path to follow in 1972. They bought an old village pub near Machynlleth, and spent a year knocking it into shape as a guest house. According to their visitors' book, the first guest, C. W. Brook (Mr), stayed in October 1973 and found that he 'enjoyed every moment with good company' and 'excellent service'. Three years later, they relocated to a more solitary property, and then returned to the original area in 1980, setting up the B&B in its third and final incarnation at Rhiw Goch, 'the Red Hill', an eighteenth-century farmhouse on a quiet lane with no immediate neighbours.

I understood the unconventional urge that had propelled them here, for my leap into the rural Welsh unknown had also been far from textbook. Sharing the same Worcestershire childhood horizon as poet A. E. Housman, I was equally bewitched by its 'blue remembered hills', the slumbering giants of the borderlands and the mountains beyond. I seized every opportunity to visit Wales, and ached to live there. In my twenties, I bagged a dream commission of writing the inaugural *Rough Guide to Wales*, spending months touring the country with a hire car, a tent and an insatiable itch. No mere job, this was deep research for a new life. That, though, seemed to depend on finding the man to share it with – and he was proving highly elusive.

Tired – in truth, bored – of waiting for him, I jumped alone, aged thirty-three, with almost no work and just my dog Patsy for company. The moment I knew that it was happening came during a Snowdonia holiday in the first months of the new millennium: a switch quietly flicked in my head, and I was on my way. I rushed back to Birmingham, gave notice on my house, and began hunting for a place in the west. Though the budget stretched only as far as a granny flat a few miles north of Aberystwyth, a home so diminutive that Patsy and I had to take turns moving around it, nothing could dent my excitement at finally being a resident of rural Wales. From decision to relocation had taken eight weeks.

Even in that short time, I had acquaintances from all corners of my life lining up to tell me I was making a dreadful mistake. As a gobby gay Brummie, they said, the best I could hope for in Llan-nowhere was to be ignored and to die a lonely old queen. At worst, they thundered, I'd be hanged like a hillbilly Mussolini from the nearest lamp post.

Without knowing quite why, I was sure they were wrong. On my travels in Wales, even out into its wildest corners, I'd often sniffed a queer cunning in the air. A quiet tolerance too – not from the tick-list of minorities fast becoming the political imperative of the day, but something softer and deeper, embedded in ancient rock. On moving, there was no shortage of comradeship, and before long, my man

7

duly turned up in the shape of Peredur, or Preds, the youngest son of a local hill farm.

If the naysayers were so vehement in their condemnation of my move, what must Reg and George's family and friends have had to say in the early 1970s? However portentous the warnings, they would have made little difference to George. He would have lost no sleep over the reception they might get in Wales; he approached their coupledom with the same well-mannered confidence that underpinned all areas of his life. By sheer force of personality, he would drive it through.

Reg, though, would have been terrified. Excited, yes, but absolutely terrified, especially as the plan was for George to continue running his photographic studio in Bournemouth, while Reg – who was severely dyslexic, couldn't drive and had never lived outside of a city – alone oversaw the work on the house and its genesis into a B&B, which he would also then be fully responsible for running.

Gentle, sweet, troubled Reg, who combined porcelain sensitivity with steely strength. His was by far the greater burden, but his too was the greater contentment – and legacy.

Their sixty-two years together encompassed the full gamut of society's attitudes. For the first eighteen years of their relationship, its very existence was illegal. Yet they were together long enough to go from being outlawed by the state to being married by one of its officials.

Thursday, 2 February 2006, was a red-letter day all round, and proved to be a milestone for us, too. Although Preds and I didn't know it at the time, the occasion sealed our place as their successors, for Reg changed their wills in our favour soon afterwards. In us, he saw themselves, and the feeling was mutual. Despite the half-century age difference, we'd recognised each other the moment we'd first met, and had fallen overnight into a well-worn friendship. Preds and I became regulars at Rhiw Goch, helping out with the house and garden, hanging out over cake and the fruitiest of gossip, and, when the time came, easing Reg and George as softly as we possibly could towards the end.

After their deaths, we inherited their house, their thousands of books, photographs, paintings and plants. In short, we inherited their lives, and the challenge was – and is still – to live them. To live *with* them, as well. For Preds, who fell in love with Rhiw Goch when he first passed by at the age of six, there is a seamless destiny at work. For me, though, always a mule of a man, it is a challenge that sometimes drags me to the edge of my sanity, for there has been no choice in the matter. Lines from *Hamlet* that I crammed for A levels thirty years ago – 'There's a divinity that shapes our ends / Rough-hew them how we will' – repeat on me, like a meal that's taking an age to digest.

Had someone drawn me aside at the age of twenty and asked me to imagine my improbable dream for a quarter of a century hence, I would have hesitantly talked of Wales, of an old stone house, of night skies and open fires, of a man I loved and who loved me back, of a dog and walks and swims in cool green waters. It all happened, yet amidst such luminous good fortune, I can at times only see the dark. And the darkness at Rhiw Goch, five hundred feet up in the swollen green hills, can sometimes be suffocating.

*

I face east, and wait for sunrise, and for spring.
In they sweep on the chatter of the morning breeze,
an air scented with the dwindling sap of youth.

The day, the year, a life: they swell so soon
into the noonday fire of summer, before fading, just
as fast, on their return to the cold earth and the
silent night.

The circle turns; the compass wheel too.
Should balance be struck, and held, the prize is
magnificent – nothing less than a homecoming.

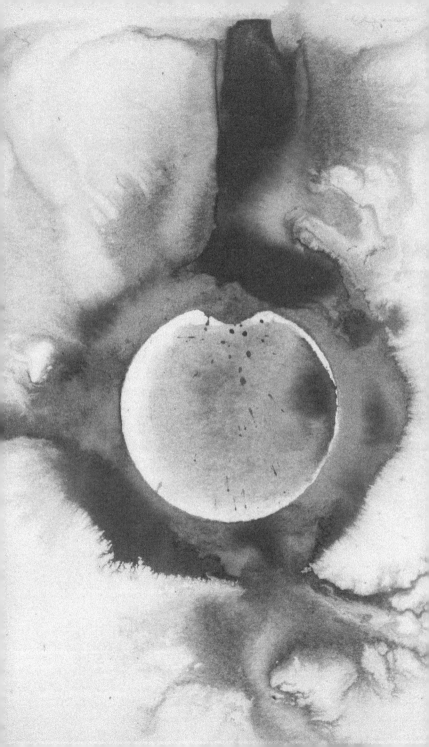

FIRST QUARTER

The Element of
AIR

❖

The Season of
SPRING

❖

The Direction of
EAST

❖

REG

AIR

For a few weeks sometime between March and May, the *gwynt traed y meirw*, the 'wind of the feet of the dead', blows in to rattle windows and nerves. It is an old name for the east wind, from when corpses were interred with their heads in the west and feet in the east, so that come the day of judgement, when they stood free of their graves they'd be facing paradise. The name drips with Gothic melancholy, so very Welsh in every respect, though so too does the phenomenon it describes. The spring east wind is deeply unsettling.

A *gwynt traed y meirw* does not suit the old farms and cottages in this corner of mid Wales, where everything was constructed or planted for protection from the prevailing south-westerlies off the Atlantic. Rhiw Goch is no exception. The house was built precisely on the strength of three factors: a freshwater spring only yards away, a solid plug of bedrock on which to sit, and a hill that provides natural shelter from the south-west. By contrast, to the east and north of the house are open fields spilling down to a valley far below, so that any wind from that direction has ample time to accelerate across the moors before funnelling up our valley and slapping us face-on. It is a harsh and dry wind, a Siberian blast, turning mud-rutted tracks to dust within days, bleaching grass, slamming doors and loosening slates, making fires sputter anxiously, desiccating skin, lips and spirit.

Often it brings late frosts, which scythe through the blossom and first leaves. It can even bring flurries of snow and hail, and with it a chorus of piteous bleating from the lambs, unable to believe that their new world has suddenly turned so cruel. The only creatures celebrating are the birds of prey as they cruise the gusts and home in on the tiny and the vulnerable. The crows are the most heartless. They work in teams, crowding round a struggling lamb and keeping its panicking mother at bay. The lamb may die of fright, but dead or not, the crows will peck its eyes out and have their fill. The bigger predators, the hawks, buzzards and kites, watch from a distance, waiting their turn. With so little traffic on the lanes, roadkill is a rarity, so the birds' beady attention stays focused on the fields.

From the heart of this carnival of death comes much new life; it is spring after all. As the daffodils shoulder their way up through cold clods, I mutter my annual prayer that our red kites will once again nest in the wood below the house. They did so seven springs ago, at the end of our first full year at Rhiw Goch, piling up sticks and twigs in the crook of an oak branch. From a vantage point in the field opposite, we had a perfect view down into the nest, and spent hours watching the parents incubating the egg, then later the rapid growth of the chick from fluffball to gangly adolescent.

Thanks to his unusually yellow wings, the male is instantly recognisable, even amongst the dozens of kites that pass us daily. We see him regularly throughout the year, but come the beginning of March, the search is on and he'll appear above the fields, gliding on the thermals, then suddenly plunging to fight off other kites, buzzards or crows in dare-devil aerial acrobatics. I hold my breath, silently willing him back to our wood, though it is probably a lost cause. They've not settled there since that first year, and I fear it's my fault. I was so excited by their proximity that I crept far too close. Fastening the binoculars on to the nest, my gaze was met by yellow eyes blazing straight back at me. Kites teach their young to play dead if a predator comes too close, but this was before the egg had hatched, and I was the one being willed to die. I scuttled away, feeling both blessed and cursed.

If I did scupper our kite's nesting site, he's not short of qui-eter options. Off he soars, catching a current and floating around the still-skeletal trees along the river below, before twirling higher up and over the thousand-foot whaleback hump of Fron Goch, the 'Red Breast', crowned with the gorsy palisades of an Iron Age fort. Skylarks rise in noisy protest, but he freewheels by and is rewarded by the glitter of sea, a dozen miles away to the west. Doubling back over Darowen village, he follows the trees along rutted holloways that radiate out from its circular churchyard, dark with yews.

The village, a mile and a half away on the other side of the valley from Rhiw Goch, looks far more Devon than Powys. Most Welsh settlements lie tucked away in valleys and gaps, but Darowen occupies an elevated plateau with views in all directions. It is where George and Reg first landed in 1972. They'd been looking for a place to move for a couple of years, and were on many estate agents' mailing lists in the further-flung corners of the country. George, already in his mid fifties by then, was impatient to get going, and jumped at the chance to buy Cefn, a stout stone property in the centre of the village. Though it was damp and dilapidated, it was also cheap and had plenty of room for conversion into a guest house. It had closed as Darowen's pub – the Red Lion – just over half a century earlier, after a policeman had disguised himself as a labourer one Sunday and cajoled the landlord into serving him an illegal beer. The sting was all that had been needed to get it shut down – an outcome celebrated in gloating handbills by the local chapels.

Our red kite rises higher, and I envy him the view as he scans below for a suitable tree in which to build this year's nest. From up there, this patchwork of fields and farms and fences is boundless, the steep tracks between them just the lightest of scratches. He orientates himself along the wooded valleys that gouge through the high ground like claw marks, their streams trickling from the great sump-mountain of Pumlumon. Joining forces, they rush north-westwards and into the River Dyfi, the traditional divide between mountainous north and rolling south Wales. It is a border too for the red kites, one that they rarely cross. Before moving to Rhiw Goch, I lived for ten years in a village north of the Dyfi, and never saw a kite there. Now, only six miles away but on the other side of the river, I see them hourly.

From above Darowen, if the kite flies just a few hundred yards further, he has the pick of dense, old oak woods that rarely see human footfall, or, for even greater solitude, the conifer plantations marching across the lower slopes of our nearest proper mountain. That, though, is the buzzard's habitat, and the kite is shy of intruding. Back on this side of the valley, he cruises the twin peaks of Bryn-y-Brain, the 'Hill of Crows', above us, but never settles. The sunken drovers' track that climbs it from our front door is studded with ancient trees, but aside from a few owls, it is, as the name suggests, home mainly to corvid gangs who guard their territory with noisy belligerence.

One pearly April morning, I walked our old sheepdog Taff through the wood on the north-facing scarp of Bryn-y-Brain. The copse was once farmed for its dense Montgomeryshire oaks, but it's long been abandoned to the kites and is largely impenetrable, just as they like it. Aside from the path I was on, skirting the wood's uppermost corner, there are no rights of way through; the only other walkable track far down the slope is overgrown and peters out by a mysterious stone well built like a giant hearth into the hillside. On this occasion, we were trailed by cadres of cocky young crows, bouncing from branch to branch and crawking furiously at us. In the trees, fresh smears of white excreta down the sides of every old kite nest showed that they had been squatted – and the squatters had been partying hard. Taff and I scurried through, heads down, as if trying to pass unnoticed through a particularly lairy town centre on a Saturday night. It was a genuine relief to get out of the wood's dark umbra, screeches echoing behind us.

Although unnerving, the experience piqued me, and I decided to walk the same route a couple of mornings later to see if it really was quite as menacing as my memory was having it. I reached the wood and found a silence that made my skin prickle. If anything, the absence of sound was even spookier than the raucous croaking of a few days earlier. The nests were filthy and trashed, but abandoned. Where had the crows gone?

Three weeks later, Preds and I took a May Day walk along the other side of the river, through an avenue of monumental oaks that once formed the main approach to one of the district's oldest houses. At the other end, the path fades into a larch plantation, and as we climbed the gate, I was hit by a strange, sickly smell. At the same moment Preds exclaimed and pointed to a sticky black heap. It was a pile of dead crows, dozens of them. The young thugs I'd met in the wood had been rounded up and shot, for they had been terrorising the lambs – with considerable success, I felt sure, recalling their blood-drunk swagger. Six months on, Preds returned to the spot and came home with a bag of bleached crow skulls, which he wove into an elegantly grisly wire chandelier that hangs in our big barn as a mortal reminder. Every Beltane needs its sacrifice.

The crows have squatted the owl sanctuary too, high up on the shoulder of Bryn-y-Brain. A tumbledown barn on what was once the edge of the Rhiw Goch farmland, it was given a plastic roof and an outsized nesting box fifteen years ago by the local wildlife trust. Barn owls came, but the crows soon took over. They placed a nesting box in our side barn too, and to Reg and George's delight it was used for a while, though it's long been empty now. The owl man still comes round on his tour of duty every summer, checking the boxes. Ours is invariably quiet, though numbers are up in the district as a whole, he tells us, and there are plenty to be seen nearby.

Heard too: from twilight onwards, there is almost always hooting somewhere in the trees near the house. The sound is soothing, mesmeric, though it also makes me blush as I remember my very first night as a citizen of Wales, almost twenty years ago, in that tiny granny flat near the sea. Before turning in at the end of a very long day's move, I took Patsy out and as I gulped the unfamiliar sweet air, a *tu-whit-tu-whoo!* wavered out of the gloom. A hot streak of fear shot through me, and without processing it I bolted back to the flat. Who was out there, making owl noises? What were they up to? Was it a signal, and if so, to whom? Not until I was safely barricaded back inside, adrenaline surging, did it occur to me that it was far more likely to have been a real owl. I had a long journey ahead to shake off the city.

Our red kites are all descendants of the last few native pairs – the oak woods of mid Wales were their final redoubt forty years ago when they faced extinction. In the early 1980s, they were down to only a dozen or so nests, one of which was on Preds' family farm three miles down the lane. Numbers have steadily built since then; in a nearby village, the sky is awhirr with kites cruising and swooping for the hunks of meat that Mr Evans hurls into his garden at two o'clock sharp every afternoon. They are creatures of habit, even in their strict feeding order: the very old first, then the young, and then everyone else. Red kites have been successfully reintroduced elsewhere, notably in parts of Scotland and the Chilterns, but those were bred from birds imported in 1989 from Spain. With a touch of local snobbery, and a possible hint of xenophobia, we like to think that the difference between native and Spanish kites is much the same as that between a demure native bluebell, its colour so deep you could drown in it, and its beefier, blander Spanish sibling.

Exuberant bird life is the single greatest joy of Rhiw Goch. At every turn of the year, our skies teem with life. Even in the dead of winter, you'll find clouds of starlings rolling through the fields, before taking off and pirouetting as one. Driving home on a late-spring afternoon, you will almost inevitably be escorted along the lane by a wagtail dip-dipping its way ahead, like a pilot boat bringing a tanker into harbour. A few hours later, your headlights might catch a sudden flare of white as a barn owl takes flight from the hedge, its ghostly silhouette powering away into the black.

While the constant shrill of kites, buzzards, crows, ravens and owls fills our wider horizon, around the house itself is a Disney cast of other birds living with us, swooping and singing, peering in at the windows and often bursting in through open doors. In the wall of the original longhouse, redstarts, wrens and thrushes flutter in and out of improbable cracks to reveal glimpses of wide-stretched baby beaks eager to be filled. There are more hungry mouths out front, in a raggedy pussy willow by the stream; the succession of holes neatly drilled into the trunk mark it as the woodpecker's favourite nesting haunt. Or cast your eyes up to the eaves of the house itself, where baby martins squint hopefully from muddy bowls.

Swallows are our most treasured house guests. The vanguard, usually two or three, appear in mid April, before the rest pour in a day or so later. Weighing less than an ounce, they've flown here from southern Africa, yet still have the energy to start dive-bombing the cat the moment they arrive. With their silky flight and flashes of petrol blue, the swallows ooze class, even in their choice of nesting place: they colonise the high beams in both barns, possibly the oldest things at Rhiw Goch. The house is eighteenth-century, its precursor, the adjacent barn that was the original stone longhouse, at least a century older, probably more. The mighty oak beams spanning it were likely recycled from even earlier buildings, taking us – and the swallows – back as far as the Middle Ages. They certainly sweep in and out of the barn as if they have long owned it.

Towards the end of their stay, after a second brood in late summer, the swallows from all over the district converge daily on the electricity wires in our field. It's the best vantage point around, looking out across the valley to Fron Goch and up the passes through the hills, the best spot to ascertain wind speeds and directions and the coming weather. Every morning there are hundreds, nudging each other for space on the sagging wires and chirruping excitedly as they decide if this is the moment to start the long journey south. On the day the decision is finally made, the atmosphere changes and a sense of collective purpose charges the air. It is always a bittersweet day, though not for the cat. She can walk taller than she has for months. Until next spring, anyway.

*

When we first moved into Rhiw Goch in the spring of 2011, the gwynt traed y meirw had just switched to a more regular south-westerly. With that came a warm, breezy front, letting us throw open the doors and windows for weeks on end. The poor house, musty as a mausoleum, was desperate for air. No one had lived there over the winter: George, vanishing into dementia, had been moved out in the autumn of 2009, and Reg, following yet another major stroke, had gone into a care home in November a year later. It had been a dreadful decision for us all to make, but we didn't think he'd survive a winter there alone. Indeed, only days after we'd moved him, a cold front from Greenland swept over Britain, bringing the widest snowfall for nearly twenty years and the coldest December since records began.

Much of the house's fustiness came from the thousands of books piled high in almost every room. Television only arrived in Rhiw Goch on the eve of the new millennium, and as radio reception is so poor (to this day, the only reliable option is longwave), it was books that filled their lives, George's in particular. As far back as you can go, his diaries record every book purchase, every WHSmith sale for miles around, every book club joined. Prices are faithfully recorded for each transaction.

They'd been read, too, most of them: from thumping biographies of wartime generals and cases of ancient Egypt, Athens and Rome, to galaxies of pulp sci-fi, a blood-bath of Christies and Rendells, and one hundred and eight Edgar Wallaces. There was not much Welsh literature beyond Thomas Firbank's classic *I Bought a Mountain* and some of its many breathless imitators. Little gay literature either: amongst the novels, E. M. Forster was the sole, reluctant flag-bearer. Even then, it was *A Passage to India*, and *Howards End*, the saga of inheritance and destiny in an 'old and little, and altogether delightful' country house. Forster's posthumous gay romance, *Maurice*, was nowhere to be found.

Often George would record at the back of a book the date he read (and sometimes reread) it, together with a snap review. In some there was also 'Reg read' and another date, usually soon after the first. I can picture the scene: George turning the last page and handing the book straight to Reg, who'd then dutifully tackle it. Reg trusted George completely to make that sort of decision for him, a symptom of his chronic lack of confidence in his own intellect. Their annotations spell this out: George's in fluent phrases and smooth handwriting, Reg's 'V GOOD' in the childish lettering and random punctuation of his dyslexia.

As a spring breeze billowed through the house, I should have been sweeping, swabbing and painting, but instead, most days saw me cross-legged on the floor of one room or another, sneezing from the dust and cobwebs as I attempted to sort books into those to keep and those to get shot of. This was never going to be easy. I have thousands of my own, and find getting rid of any almost blasphemous. A few were obvious candidates: a set of 1960s *Encyclopedia Britannica*, a ton of *Reader's Digest* condensed classics, numerous austere volumes about the Second World War, and – strangest of all – shelf upon shelf of doorstop biographies of minor nineteenth-century European royalty. Even allowing for any possible change in my tastes over the years ahead, I was confident the evening would never come when I'd want to sit by the fire and immerse myself in a starchy hagiography of Princess Stephanie of Hohenzollern.

Many of the books were known to me already, old friends from the shelves of my maternal grandparents' house of thirty years earlier. They too had books crammed into every corner, up staircases and entire walls, squeezed on to insufficient shelves; to the younger me, they had been as much a comfort blanket as a library. It was a sour contrast with my dad's house, where I had to live, its one lonely bookcase home to a Middle England read-by-numbers: a *Complete Works of Shakespeare* in the tiniest type, alongside the complete works of James Herriot, Jeffrey Archer and Giles the *Daily Express* cartoonist. Around them swirled five children, from four different sets of parents, and a havoc of animals, adults and addictions.

The familiarity of so many books only cemented a growing realisation that in becoming such close friends with Reg and George, I'd been conjuring up the indelible spirit of my grandparents. They were all born around the First World War, and there were so many crossovers in their life stories, attitudes, travels and interests. As with George, I'd always been slightly in awe of my irascible grandfather, and could only communicate with him through the medium of our common intellectual interests. As with Reg, I'd been loved and listened to without qualification by my grandmother, and made to feel fed and warm in ways that eluded me elsewhere. In both houses I've owned in Wales – a quarryman's mid-terrace and then Rhiw Goch – so many visitors have overflowed with happy memories of their own grandparents' homes, which I take as the highest compliment. Preds is in similar thrall to his mother's parents, whose farmhouse near Bala set the standards for so much of his life. Rhiw Goch is a homage to them all: Dick and Nancy, John and Mary, Reg and George.

*

While bookish tastes came from my mum's side, with housing it's always my dad's opinion that has mattered most. A retired estate agent, he was keen to help in any house deliberations, coming over from the Midlands to see a few places when I was first looking to buy somewhere and escape the claustrophobic confines of the rented granny flat. On inspecting the Victorian slate terrace that I eventually bought, he stood outside on the brow of the hill, looked down over the grey huddle of the village, and sighed, 'How on earth do you think you will ever fit in here?'

I had no answer, only a kernel of stubborn faith that this was where I needed to be. People kept telling me that I'd know the right place when I saw it, a theory that had been robustly challenged by a year of seeing dozens of houses across mid Wales, none of which had clicked. I'd passed this one after an evening in the village pub, and had known immediately. Though it had been past midnight, I'd stopped on the way home to press my nose against the estate agent's window and pore over the particulars by the orange glow of a street lamp.

Despite my dad's concern, the tall terrace in the old quarry village was a fine fit for a decade, especially in my single years. When Preds and I got together, and he gallantly gave up his house in town to join me there, it was clear that it could only be a relatively temporary option. We are both so bullish in our sense of place that in order to succeed as a couple, we would need somewhere entirely new to us both.

Somewhere like Rhiw Goch, for instance? The question hovered in the air, sharpened by the urgency of Reg and George's decay. If we bought their house, they could afford the best care for the rest of their days. For Preds, it was clear: not only would it help our dear old friends, it would secure us his dream home, the place he'd loved for decades. But I was struggling to see it. Though I knew we had to move, I liked life in a post-industrial mountain village, somewhere that had absorbed outsiders since its inception, somewhere with rushing streams, a pub and a regular bus service. I liked too that I had chosen it, and that I'd been right.

Remembering my dad's ambivalence over that choice, I called him to come and take a look at Rhiw Goch. If I was expecting – perhaps even hoping for – another disparaging assessment to confirm my doubts, I was to be disappointed, because there was no prevarication this time. He was so enthusiastic that something inside me shifted, and for the first time I believed that we could live there, and, more to the point, that I might want to. We began the process of buying it, encouraged by the confirmation from George and Reg's neighbour Penny that we were to be the beneficiaries of their wills. The news – simultaneously humbling, thrilling and more than a little unnerving – stoked our heightened unreality, the sense of being on a runaway train of events. Either way though, it was clear that we could move straight in.

Until hearing my dad's verdict, I had not been able to see Rhiw Goch as anything other than a place in sad and terminal decrepitude. Every corner was filled with the accumulated weariness of two old men sliding towards death, and it overwhelmed me. Reg's bedroom, in the small parlour by the front door, was the worst. His lumpy single bed was surrounded on all sides by piles of books two and three deep, tottering on makeshift shelves that could have given way at any moment and buried him alive. It left me gasping for air.

In came the spring breeze, though, and out went the bed and, box by box, the books. Up came the threadbare rugs to reveal pristine quarry tiling that sparkled in unfamiliar sunlight. Upstairs, friends pitched in with brooms and paintbrushes, even axes. The three B&B rooms were choked with heavy Edwardian wardrobes, all dark wood and pompous flourishes, but with little actual storage space. To George they had been 'exotically Moorish', and well worth the effort of taking out the sash windows to move them in thirty years earlier, but they were reduced to kindling in no time. The house – and I – began to breathe once more.

The exterior required urgent surgery too. Everything was inevitably overgrown, but the real problem was that they'd planted hedges and bushes far too close to the house. In the kitchen – a Victorian extension added to the Georgian house – the front window was completely hobbled by an unruly hedge. Preds spent days digging it out, unveiling a fine view of a stone wall and mature ash trees beyond. At the other end of the kitchen, the back door couldn't fully open as it was part blocked on the inside by a wardrobe, and on the outside by yet another hedge. It was foliage as net curtains, an incursion of suspicious suburbia into the hills. Our mission was to open the house up once again, and to replace it gently back into its landscape.

Most of all, Rhiw Goch was rescued by gales of laughter, as friends, family and neighbours swept in with plants, cakes, cards and wine. It yawned and stretched, blinking in the brass-bright dawn, and opened its arms wide. Every time we have a gathering here, the house and garden sing, for it is a place of sweet liaison and feasting in magical shadows, and always has been. As the only house for miles along the old drovers' road, it almost certainly functioned as a *cyrfdy*, an informal wayfaring station offering food, ale and pasture. The stone-flagged hallway into the kitchen echoes like an old country tavern. Communal, convivial excess is its lifeblood.

Reg and George kept an orderly home, for themselves and their paying guests, though it had its own solicitous bacchanalia. In the visitors' book, almost everyone mentions Reg's sensational cooking, achieved on a temperamental oil-fired range and electric hob; as one regular guest put it, 'always done with love. You never saw Reg panic.' Sherry and wine were dished out by George, and totted up on the bill. Open fires, deep baths, hot water bottles and bedtime cocoa all helped to cosy their visitors in. One French guest wrote, 'George and Reg have in their heart the sun they haven't outside.'

In the dusty swirl of our early weeks at Rhiw Goch, it was good to read the overflowing enthusiasm of guests' letters and the large, scarlet visitors' book. We'd only got to know them long after their B&B days were over, when the house and garden were in genteel but steep decline. Far less picturesque was the decline of Reg and George themselves. As we moved in throughout April, they were both ailing terribly, Reg in a care home in Machynlleth, and George in a nursing home twenty-five miles away in Newtown. Accidents and relapses added hospital stays – in Shrewsbury, Aberystwyth, Newtown and Machynlleth – into the bewildering mix.

They were mirror images of each other: George with his mind wiped clear but his athlete's heart thundering on, Reg crumbling to dust physically, and agonisingly aware of every dip. In the final few months, the strokes came thick and fast, wiping out almost all Reg's powers of speech. Each time I saw him, he looked imploringly at me through damp, pink eyes and croaked one word: 'Home'. Penny the neighbour had power of attorney, and I pleaded with her to let us take him up to Rhiw Goch and see us breathing new life into it. We could, I said, give him a perfect day at home, and let him slip away, with us by his side. It would, I was sure, allow him to let go in peace.

Penny was having none of my soap-script fantasy. An ex-nurse of formidable clarity and kindness, she told me very firmly that taking him there for a visit was impossible, and not to let Reg have the tiniest intimation that it had even been considered. 'I am praying so hard,' she said, 'for God to take him to heaven, and I absolutely believe that he will.' We bumped into each other in the Co-op the next day, and continued the conversation in urgent whispers, before both beginning to cry quite helplessly.

Nine days after he was moved into the same Welshpool nursing home as George, Reg died. We'd returned home after a night away to a phone call telling us that bronchial pneumonia had set in and he had only hours left. We raced over there and sat by his bed, holding a papery hand each and talking quietly to him, telling him how much we loved him and thanking him for all that he'd given us, while a diamorphine drip eased him away. I nipped out to make a call, and when I returned he had gone. In his very final act, and with no discernible consciousness, he had chosen to die with just his darling Preds by his side.

Penny arrived minutes later, and was devastated to have missed him. As we stood around his body – and how quickly it had become just a body, a husk – she talked with fierce tenderness about how much pain and struggle Reg had known, how hard he had always had to fight it. We wept and hugged, and gathered ourselves to go and tell

George, in the dementia unit on the floor below. For well over a year he and Reg had been in different locations, yet they had ended up for those last nine days only feet apart. It seemed cruel that they never got to see each other, but perhaps proximity was enough.

Penny took George's hand, and told him that Reg had died, that he had always loved him to bits, and that he was going to heaven. Despite the fog closing down his mind, something went in. A momentary flash in his eyes told us everything, though he said nothing.

Coming back that night to Rhiw Goch was strange. The house felt different; it knew. We sat outside drinking tea, candles burning steady on the stillest of starlit summer nights, as owls hooted in the trees. Twice in the previous few days, while walking to the front door I'd caught a glimpse in the corner of my eye of what appeared to be a tall, slender, greying gentleman standing by the living room window, looking steadily out. When I'd turned to look properly, there had been no one there. 'So he did make it home,' said Preds when I told him, and we cried again, for Reg and for the life he'd given us.

Five weeks later, Preds was driving to Wrexham for a day at the National Eisteddfod. Shortly after passing Welshpool, he was walloped by severe stomach cramps and forced to turn back. As the cramps eased, a small voice told him to visit the nursing home. At the moment Preds walked into his room, George sighed deeply, shuddered and took his final breath.

SPRING

As Reg and George's stories were drawing to a close, I was sat on the cool tiled floor of their home, hunched over their diaries and wondering just how much history might be repeating itself. A note from the previous year, written in Reg's quavering hand, swam before my eyes: 'Prebbs [*sic*] and Mike Good Soul's, Me and George +50 yrs!!!' It was uncannily true, and something we had joked about too. I am fifty years and a month younger than George; Preds forty-eight years and two months younger than Reg. Like Reg, Preds is the artist, the landscaper and plantsman, the homemaker, the youngest child, the quiet man brimful of kindness. No wonder Reg had responded so deeply to him, gushing into his diary, 'seems as if I have known him for years. You might say I love him!!! 83 to his 35!!'

That seemed like sweetness itself, for there is no one with a bad word to say about Reg, nor indeed Preds, but I was uneasy with the notion that I was therefore some kind of reincarnation of George. It was obvious why anyone might

35

make that connection: both of us map-addled travellers, bookish, opinionated and driven, outwardly confident and socially deft, especially next to our less assertive partners. For all his many admirable – and familiar – qualities, though, there was something distant about George that had often left me slightly discomfited. I'd decided that it was probably his dementia showing earlier than we'd realised, but that wasn't the full picture. Reading his diaries and letters gave shape to my hunch, as I winced at the vanity and indifference to others. The main exceptions to this were various young men, who received the full-beam glare of George's attention, and not, I felt sure, in ways that were necessarily welcome. It read like a warning.

Outside, the gathering spring only exacerbated my unease. Even after ten years in a mountain village, the greenness of Rhiw Goch was on a whole new scale. It drenched me. Green everywhere I looked, and in an infinite variety of shades, from the feathery lime of the beech in first leaf to the dark, army camouflage of ivy in sunless corners. Green so luminous that it tinged the sky. I had never known such green, an endless rippling sea of it crashing in all directions. It gave me the unsteadiness of sea legs too – chlorophyll as chloroform.

Paradoxically, the murkier the skies above, the deeper the green seemed. On a bright day, the glowing patches drifting across the fields and the playful, dappled sunlight in the woods were phosphorescent in their loveliness, but in a way that danced across my vision with fairy grace. Going out under leaden skies, or at dusk, and the depth of the green sucked me in like quicksand, holding me under and allowing no escape.

In the spectrum of colour, green lies in the middle, between the colder shades of blue, indigo and violet, and the warmer tones of yellow, orange and red. That seemed to fit, too. Having hovered on borders and boundaries, on the fold in the map, for most of my life, our new home sat firmly in the middle; there were no edges to hang on to for safety. It lies in a plump, settled landscape whose identity has remained unperturbed for centuries. And green, the middle colour, the still place at the heart of the spectrum, is its natural shade.

Green is good, we know that. Green is clean, fresh, bright, natural, sustainable. We hear it all the time: 'for the sake of the environment', a phrase that has become almost as hollow and inverted as 'for your safety and security'. But green is also nauseous or naïve, and moving here, I felt both. Friends admitted their jealousy at our new place dug deep into its glade; they too were green, with envy.

I've sometimes joked that my love of Wales was ignited at birth, when Tom Jones was at the top of the charts for a month and a half with *Green, Green Grass of Home*. I imagine that on that Sunday night, a week before Christmas half a century ago, I emerged in a Midlands maternity hospital and somewhere in the distance The Voice was booming out of a tinny transistor: 'Hair of gold and lips like cherries / It's good to touch the green, green grass of home.' Destiny was set, and it had brought me here. Here on the red hill, I was desperate for my lights to flick effortlessly to green, but instead I was stalled on amber.

The dislocation of that first spring has eased, but it remains the season that I approach with greater caution than any other. This is so deeply alien to my younger self, who, come the March equinox, couldn't wait to emerge like an excitable pupa, ready to squeeze every last drop of sunshine, sex, partying, travel and nature out of the light half of the year. It was all new life and boundless possibility, the sauce and sizzle of *Under Milk Wood*.

Now, though, the first day of strong spring sunshine brings me out in heat rashes and blood blisters, making my nose look as if I've downed a bottle of port for breakfast. Itchy scabs on my scalp scold me for the thousands of sunscreen-free hours I spent baking under fiery skies. And in the fields and lanes, the lamb and badger carcasses, dead birds and ransacked nests chime their doleful reminder that for there to be life, there must be death, and in spades. Go outside on a foul night in late March and there will be will-o'-the-wisp lights dancing in the fields all around, as Eifion, Wyn, Emrys or Rheinallt, our farmer neighbours, struggle through howling winds and rain to keep their newborn lambs alive. Like Walt Whitman, we 'yet shall mourn with ever-returning spring'.

Only a few generations back, March and April were the months of greatest privation in the countryside, the food that had been bottled, pickled, preserved and salted the previous year gone and the new season's green shoots yet to yield a bounty. Many people express incredulity that suicide rates peak so dramatically in the spring, since it seems counter-intuitive. Not to me. If you are deep in depression, the winter months act as a projection of your inner self: dark, lethargic and almost comfortably locked in stasis. As the days lengthen, the skies brighten and the chorus of birdsong swells to a crescendo, the gulf widens with alarming speed, and suddenly it can no longer be bridged.

David Hockney, at his elfin best, helped me through the second spring at Rhiw Goch. It was the year of his block-buster *A Bigger Picture* exhibition at the Royal Academy, an 'ebullient to the point of jubilation' (the *Observer*) evocation of the seasons in his native Yorkshire. One morning, I heard him interviewed on the radio about the processes behind the work, the dozens of canvases and films in particular inspired by the landscape of Woldgate, an ancient ridge track to the west of his home town, Bridlington. When I'd taken my mother, a Yorkshire exile, to the exhibition, these were the pieces that had tugged me furthest into their depths, the spring ones especially. In the interview, Hockney spoke of how he'd been studying in detail the annual cycle of Woldgate for seven years now, and how many details within the flora, fauna and landscape only revealed themselves after several cycles. You needed countless trips around the rotating seasons to work with them, to enjoy the expectation just as much as the realisation.

By contrast, I thought of a ruralist painter I'd known, a peacock of a man who loved to believe himself the son of Graham Sutherland and John Piper, yet found to his intense irritation that most of his work sold only as postcards. Unable to stay still in the landscapes he claimed were his inspiration, continually moving house and chasing a muse condemned to remain eternally out of reach, he became possessed by a furious control-freakery that destroyed his art, and eventually his life.

It is a clear division. There are those for whom the cumulative effect of the passing years only augments their love of the land. Then there are those for whom the pleasures fade year on year, and horribly fast. A law of diminishing returns rules their existence; they are forever sulking that their neighbour's grass appears so very much greener than their own. That too felt like a warning.

After seven springs at Rhiw Goch my list of the season's highlights is fattening nicely. There are the headline-grabbers: the cascades of snowdrops, daffodils, primroses and bluebells that calibrate the spring from its earliest whispers to its thunderous finale. They all appear, and nowhere lovelier, along the towering banks that line the old holloway, now the steep and winding lane down to the hamlet below us. There too in the quickening run-up to summer come tiny violets and speedwell, celandines and forget-me-nots, saxifrage, sorrel and campion, cow parsley and lady's smock, each taking their bow before sidling from the stage. As I watch Preds break his back to bring the garden to precisely ruffled perfection, I can't help but mull over the flawlessness of these hedged banks, so deep and ancient, yet untouched year on year by human hand.

Many of the season's finest moments come if not un-expectedly, then certainly unannounced. There's the morning when I clomp down the stairs, thick with sleep, and am walloped afresh by the sight of plump pussy willow catkins backlit by the rising sun. Or the dog walk down to the boggy dingle below, my skittering thoughts suddenly melted by a sunburst of marsh marigolds wink-ing from the gloom. Or the wide early-morning view from a gate on the knuckle of Bryn-y-Brain, just before the gwynt traed y meirw turns and the greenery explodes, when the hills growl with latent power. A phrase I've only heard since being in Wales is '*duw*, it's a strong spring', usually said to excuse sudden physical or mental fatigue. The image of this primal force gathering pace around us, sucking us dry of strength and sense, fits perfectly, and is one I confidently expect to use regularly as I grow older.

Spring is *harddwas teg a'm anrhegai*, 'a fair and beautiful youth bearing gifts', according to Dafydd ap Gwilym, the fourteenth-century mid-Wales bard of all that is green and lusty. It is the tickle of anticipation. We count down the days to the evening sun first flooding the long passage between the back of the house and the big barn, the old longhouse; that this happens at the spring equinox only deepens our certainty that we live on an omphalos of sacred geometry. We brave the winds to sip an al fresco sundowner, and talk about how good it will be when we can do so without having to muffle up in fleeces and hats. I splash up and down the pond, dreaming of the day when flowers once again titivate its edges and my skin isn't bruised purple by the cold.

Some of the finest foreseeable joys are the tiniest. There are no flowers that give me a greater rush than the soon-to-bud blackthorn blossom, tight little snowballs in a crown of black spikes, or the inflorescent buds of the hazels, minuscule flamenco skirts in a shameless pink. At my sister's house one bright March morning, I startled even myself by announcing that I was eager to get home as it felt like the first day of the year to hang the washing outside. It was a thought I'd never consciously processed and it came out of nowhere, but, once voiced, I realised it was a diamond-hard truth. Hauling the laundry basket to the top of the orchard, pinning the clothes out on the line strung between a budding apple tree and a hawthorn, and leaving them to billow in the soft breeze is the purest of pleasures, and you must take those wherever you find them.

No two springs are the same. One year, March brought us sulphurous skies and snow that lingered into April, piled up in the hollows and whipped into crusts across the high fields. The following March saw a heatwave, a bright blue, smoky miasma hanging over the hills as we went picnicking and swimming in lakes and rivers. When there is a late cold snap that delays the flowers, one warm spell brings them all out together in a firework cascade of colour.

The season catches up with itself by the end of May, when spring imperceptibly slides into summer. The leaf canopies snap shut over the bluebells in the woods, foxgloves and ferns unfurl on the hedge banks, and a shimmer of buttercups rushes across the hay pastures with the speed of a teenager's blush. From my desk, the view of Fron Goch vanishes for another six months behind the trees, its reassuring presence just a promise. Knock-kneed lambs are now tubby bruisers, barging into their mothers' weary teats and chomping everything in their path. The dawn chorus mellows into day-long song, as nests are finished and eggs laid, while the scent of warming earth is punctuated with sudden wafts of rose, honeysuckle and the post-coital musk of hawthorn blossom. There's no more wild garlic for salads, the nettles have become too gritty to eat and what's left of the rhubarb is drooping.

Spring ends on the day that a gin and tonic can be laced with cordial squeezed from the first elderflowers. It is the best drink of the year.

*

In Reg and George's time, spring came early to Rhiw Goch. It would begin as soon as February, on the first day that George was able to strip off and catch some rays in the shelter of the front porch. It made Reg terribly nervous. He was blasé about George basting himself in the back garden, away from prying eyes, but never quite got used to him splayed out on the front doorstep like a slab of slowly barbecuing topside. While busying around the house doing his chores, Reg would keep a weather eye on the lane for any passing traffic. There never was much, and still isn't today, but there must have been the odd tractor driver lumbering by who copped a surprise eyeful.

Having spent his working life behind the camera, George was just as fond of being on the other side of the lens. Using mirrors, he was a pioneer of the sculpted selfie, often tucked into a G-string (if that). His diaries are full of admiring notes about how hard his muscles have become, how good his legs are looking and, most of all, how bronzed a tan he has. Knowing winks, often in saucy French – 'sunbathed "complet"; 4hrs in the garden (Altogether!); sunbathed 7 hours – sans!; sunbathed nu in conservatory!' – record the many occasions when he let it all hang out. From the first sunbathing sessions of the year, as snowdrops still quivered in the breeze, he grabbed every hour of tanning potential in order to spend half the year the colour and texture of a well-polished desk.

Although he'd always been mindful of presenting a tidy face to the world, this preening and primping was all quite new. In photos from the 1970s, George is jowly, waxy even, with greying mutton-chop sideburns, a hangdog expression and a paunch. Next to the porcelain-pretty Reg, he looks more like his father than his lover. Moving to Rhiw Goch in the autumn of 1980 unleashed something volcanic in George: a long-delayed adolescence, the power of a second spring, and it flowered fiercely.

A whirlwind of factors collided. Their second Welsh house, where they lived for four years between Cefn and Rhiw Goch, had gone badly wrong, a dispute with neighbours having spiralled out of control and left George in a state of despair. After that, the freedom at Rhiw Goch intoxicated him. He turned sixty-five in 1981, and was able to claim his pension, thus ending even the theoretical possibility of a return to photography, the profession that had quietly died as the B&B business boomed.

Most importantly, he took up cycling again, for the first time since the war, and soon became utterly obsessed by it. The date – 18 March 1983 – when he first got back on a bicycle was an anniversary that he never missed, even when he'd sometimes forgotten Reg's birthday a month earlier. That cycling also made him far fitter and stronger, and introduced him to a band of much younger friends, only fuelled the fantasies that he was truly reclaiming a lost youth. With the cycling, the weights and the sunbathing, and the not-always-judicious use of chestnut hair dye, came a whole new wardrobe of skintight tops, crotch-clinging shorts, silky blousons and Roman sandals.

George's goal was the uncluttered horizon of youth, as filtered through the highly selective memory of a pensioner. As for so many of his generation, whose own springtime had been stolen by the Second World War, the pre-1939 days took on a prelapsarian glow that he was forever chasing. His hankering for rural solitude, the urge that ultimately brought him to Rhiw Goch, was born in numerous cycle tours of Scotland, Wales, the Lakes and the West Country taken throughout the second half of the 1930s.

He had needed to escape the cramped Hackney courtyard in which he'd grown up, the eldest child of a stern and struggling shopkeeper. George had been a studious, dutiful son who'd progressed steadily through school and into a clerical office job, but once he'd glimpsed the world beyond London's wintry slums, there was no going back. In 1935, at the age of eighteen, he and a couple of old school friends began taking off for the weekend on their bikes, initially into the countryside around the city. Like ripples on a village pond, they spread further out and, instead of camping, took to using the brand-new network of youth hostels.

To George this was a revelation, and a revolution. In the common rooms and dormitories of the YHAs he found his people: square-jawed chaps with firm handshakes and the breezy confidence of the middle classes. He began to dress in their uniform of blazers and baggy shorts, over knee-high argyle socks held up by garters. Enthusiastic

We climb Ebbor Gorge from Wookey Hole   June 20th.

postcards home sang the praises of stout comradeship, nature rambles and high teas.

Mixing in such company also inspired him to believe that perhaps he could make a living out of his hobby, photography. He used every scrap of holiday to explore and photograph the wild places, mailing the completed films back to his father, with explicit instructions about where and how to get them developed ('Take them as soon as you can because I want them when I get home', before signing off with 'Your soon to be Prodigal son, George'). The best of the finished results were sent to photographic agencies in London, with covering letters requesting an interview. In August 1939, at the end of an idyllic fortnight's tour of north Wales ('Wish you could get a house here!' he wrote to his parents), he was invited to talk about a potential commission by one agency. Weeks later, Hitler invaded Poland, the war began in earnest and George's ambition was stalled.

Even putting aside the poignancy of smiling young faces that wouldn't survive the oncoming carnage, George's pictures of those heady few years are mesmerising. From Llanberis to Polperro, Thanet to Skye, he captures the big views, the tiny, telling details, the architecture and roadscapes, the light and shadow of the land. There are action shots, frozen moments of larky fun in youth hostel kitchens and along empty roads, groups of grizzled locals and sightseers in tourist honeypots, and, throughout, impish cameos from donkeys, dogs, ducks, cows and cats.

There also is a shy, sometimes sly, homoeroticism that rang bells of recognition in me. Lads in home-knitted swimming trunks are captured bursting from the briny,

NORTH WALES TOUR

Hostellers at Gyffylieg Y.H.   July 18th.

Rounding a bend

Marine Drive
Great Ormes Head
Llandudno

The Headland

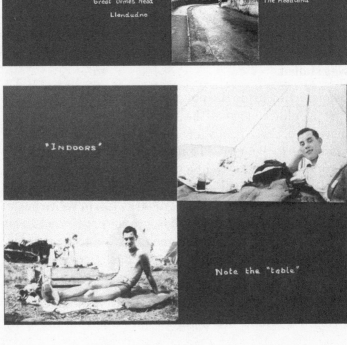

"Indoors"

Note the "table"

their muscles rippling with unselfconscious pleasure. Towards the end of the albums, one particular friend – a dark, wiry boy with a beguilingly goofy smile – appears in almost every sequence. The final series, just a week before the outbreak of war, are of him and George alone on a camping holiday at Canvey Island. We see inside their tiny tent, its bedding coyly ruffled, and are invited to admire their makeshift camp kitchen, constructed outside around an upturned packing crate. It is both the ersatz domesticity of a child's Wendy house and the carnal heat of a Henry Scott Tuke painting; I'd recognise it anywhere, and remember it well. As it was for George, it is my default erotic depth charge, one so electric it can short-circuit sense.

By the time he was demobbed in May 1946, George was almost thirty. Six years in the Royal Fusiliers and Somerset Light Infantry had made a man of him. He'd served in Northern Ireland, England, France, Belgium, the Netherlands and Germany, had seen death at close quarters and escaped it himself by inches. He'd also grabbed romantic encounters with comrades, had his heart broken, and gained a regular lover in the shape of a sharp-suited wide boy from Bournemouth named Stanley.

On first returning to Britain, George lived for a couple of years with his family in a Hackney basement flat. The cramped conditions gave him even greater impetus to resume his pre-war wanderings of the Lakes, Wales and the West Country, often with swarthy young men whom he'd photograph against stirring backdrops of crags and valleys. This was what he had won his war for. He was impatient for the good life, for the fruits of battle, so although George had ended their relationship, when

Stanley invited him to move down to Bournemouth, he leapt at the chance. Wasting no time, he found an elevated brick-built lock-up near the central station that became both his home and his new business venture, the Garret Photographic Studio.

*

If the springtime of George's life was the full trumpet of mid May, all sturdy shoots and grassy plateaux, then Reg's was much more late March, a time of trembling, tentative growth in pitiless winds. Even so, spectacular flowers bloomed.

His involvement in the war was mercifully brief. Turning eighteen in February 1945, he was called up to present himself at a barracks near the family home in north-west London. The official portrait of the slim slip of a lad in an oversized army uniform is heartbreaking, for he looks like a child in fancy dress. Unlike dutiful George, Reg was not cut out to be a soldier. Delicate, nervous and yet to start shaving, he was immediately identifiable as not being like other men, and the thugs circled. His life would have been hell had it not been for a sympathetic commanding officer, who shielded him from the most onerous tasks and warned the bullies off. Reg was never sent to the front line, and was released from military service soon after VJ Day, seven months after his eighteenth birthday.

His short army career was even more of a strain on his mother. After a Luftwaffe bomb had exploded behind their house in early 1941, she'd suffered a nervous break-down, and remained desperately unwell. Teenage Reg, the youngest and by far the favourite of her three children, was her main carer. He needed no encouragement to bunk off school, since he hated it. To the teachers, his chronic dyslexia was just plain stupidity; to his fellow pupils, Reg's gentle manner, his stammer and his German surname ensured the worst kind of attention. As the war progressed, it became increasingly difficult to carry the name Mickisch in suburban north London. Reg's father, a piano maker

who'd run an eponymous music shop in Dollis Hill for twenty years, changed its name shortly before the war, so hostile and so frequent was the abuse. This haunted Reg for decades; well into the 1970s, he was using a middle name, Lewis, as his surname for official purposes, including as the proprietor of their new Welsh guest house.

The one reward from his ostracism at school was a life-long friendship with a fellow outcast, another gay boy called Reg, or Little Reg as he became known next to the six-foot Mr Mickisch. Once the war was over, Little Reg dragged him down to Chelsea and Soho, to the bars and hotels of the queer demi-monde. Having felt so worthless for so long, Reg discovered his voice – literally so: his stammer vanished as he jumped headlong into the chat, the mercurial flitting and flirting and the high-velocity repartee. He also possessed the ultimate currency on the scene: willowy, movie-star good looks, and dazzling youth. It was in the Salisbury, the Swiss and the A & B[1] that Reg received his real education.

His early lovers included a Conservative MP, who wined and dined the wide-eyed Reg before taking him back to the West End flat that he kept especially for his gay encounters. In 1948, as he turned twenty-one, Reg gained a regular boyfriend, Norman, eight years his senior and a timber merchant from Hampshire. Reg was smitten, making the regular train trip down to Peters-field and even taking him to meet his mother. Norman lived in a tied cottage on the Ashford Chace estate at Steep, a pretty Georgian house that forty years earlier had been the home of poet Edward Thomas and his young family.

Gay London in the late 1940s was a great deal livelier than is often imagined. War had blown the lid off the city in more ways than just its obvious physical destruction. Barriers of culture, class and nationality had been broken down, and, to some extent, those of sexuality too. The ubiquitous proximity of death focused intent and broadened horizons, even if only briefly. When the sirens rang out, and people scuttled for the safety of an Anderson shelter or a Tube station, many men would head instead in the opposite direction to make the most

---

[1] Arts and Battledress Club, Wardour Street.

of the blackout and the confusion. Every city had its places for illicit gay sex at such times, and they teemed with action. As Quentin Crisp had it in *The Naked Civil Servant*:

> As soon as bombs started to fall, the city became like a paved double bed. Voices whispered suggestively to you as you walked along; hands reached out if you stood still and in dimly lit trains people carried on as they had once behaved only in taxis.

Although homosexuality was still illegal, it wasn't until the re-election of a Conservative government in 1951 that the authorities really started cracking down on it once more. For a brief few years after the war, there was some comparative freedom, if you managed to find a discreet entrance into the underground scene that lurked beneath the rubble. The pluralist spirit of wartime lingered on there, although great caution was still needed. Blackmail was a real threat, and Reg, ably taught by Norman, soon learned the code: be careful of using your full name; memorise addresses rather than commit them to paper; keep all hints of affection out of your love letters, and destroy them regardless after reading. Ironically, poor Norman was himself destined to become one of the grim statistics, after being imprisoned in 1953 for indecency, a counter-charge brought against him by a young man trying to escape a conviction for burglary.

For the 22-year-old Reg, 1949 was a pivotal year: he met George and lost his mum. He and George clicked immediately when they met in a London club, but both were involved with someone else, and content to keep it that way. Reg's mother died shortly afterwards, in the final month of that blood-soaked decade. She had never fully recovered from her wartime breakdown, and even if her passing came as no great surprise, it devastated Reg, always Mummy's boy. His agony crippled him for the next couple of years, by which time he and George had lost contact.

In the summer of 1952, Reg surfaced from the doldrums of grief with a sudden determination. Although still in mourning, he couldn't help but be infected by the optimism of what they were calling the New Elizabethan age. Ever the ardent royalist, he was agog with excitement about the new Queen, and admiring the dignity with which she had overcome her father's death, was determined to follow suit. Realising that he had let his soulmate drift away, he dug out George's phone number at the Garret. One Tuesday in late July, he called, terrified of the possible reaction, and thrilled when it transpired to be unqualified delight. That weekend, Reg took the train down to Bournemouth for the very opposite of a brief encounter. On the Sunday, they took the ferry over from Sandbanks for a day on the beach at Shell Bay. By that evening, when George walked him to the station for the return train to London, they had made plans for Reg to move down and join him.

He went back down to Bournemouth the following weekend. His mind was so made up that he even brought his widowed dad with him to give this potential new life the once-over. That would be unusual enough now, but in 1952 it was so sweetly subversive. To Reg's father, it was clear that the older, urbane George made his boy feel safe, and that was enough for him. Inevitably, George laid it on thick, even going so far as to ask for his formal consent to Reg relocating to Bournemouth. He was effectively asking for his hand in marriage.

Gustave Mickisch, known to all as Gus, a worldly and kind man who knew full well that his youngest son would never 'find the right woman', gave his blessing without hesitation. Within a couple of months, Reg had moved, and found a job in the menswear department of one of the town's grand stores. His and George's sixty years together had begun.

EAST

The *gwynt traed y meirw*, that cruel spring blast from the east, has another, more pejorative, nickname hereabouts: *gwynt milain y Sais*, the 'vicious wind of the English'. The inference is clear: like so many other baleful forces in Wales, it blows in from across Offa's Dyke, gathering its cold spite as it whips across Middle England. It would seem to be a toss-up as to which is worse: the rotting feet of corpses, or the rotten influence of the English.

Reg, George and I all made this same journey, blowing into Wales from the English flatlands. We are far from unusual. In the 2011 census, 21 per cent of the Welsh population was born in England, more than double the comparable figure for Scotland. While a fraction of this is accounted for by borderland births in Hereford, Shrewsbury or Chester, the bulk are those seeking some version of the downsizers' dream. Since the 1960s, the number of escapees from urban England into rural Wales has ballooned, attracted by the space, scenery and relatively low property prices.

The headline figure tells only part of the story, for the pattern of distribution is uneven, with a far higher proportion of incomers in the Welsh-speaking rural areas of the west, north and middle. There are very few heading to the former coalfields of the Valleys.

If you walk down Machynlleth's wide main street on a bank holiday, it is not the windows of the craft shops or antiques emporia that most tourists are clustered around. It is the estate agents. 'For Sale' signs popping up in hedges is as reliable a portent of spring as the first daffodil, since only the most stubborn of dreams is likely to be ignited in the mud and murk of January. The point is even more pertinent when you remember that many of the houses on sale have no direct sunlight in the winter, some for months on end, or are wringing damp through the dark half of the year. Such places reappear on the market every second or third spring, in a pattern as fixed as the movement of the stars. You buy in the spring or summer, are horrified by the first winter but almost manage to forget it as the light returns and temperatures rise once more, before the second winter crashes in to break what's left of the spirit. Back on the market goes the house, while the same estate agent dusts off the particulars and happily takes his commission from the next batch of starry-eyed hopefuls.

The Welsh rural idyll, feverishly marketed by newspaper property sections and daytime TV shows, fades very fast for some, especially those for whom it is nothing more than the cheapest option. They'd far rather be in Devon or Dorset, but the cost of a small semi there will buy an old farmhouse here: it is no contest. Some grow to appreciate the differences in their new locale, though too many don't: these profound differences – language, culture, history, politics, an entire world view – become increasingly irritating to them as they retreat ever further into their bunker.

Even for those of us who actively chose Wales, and who view its chippy distinctiveness as a bonus rather than a drawback, there is often a slow puncturing of initial enthusiasm, as dreams curdle in the heat of everyday reality. Romantic Wales, the land of crags, castles and ancient culture, has long excited a particular English sensibility. It was there at the very outset of the Picturesque movement in the 1780s, when revolutionary turmoil cut off the Continent for young cubs looking to undertake their gap-year Grand Tour. Instead, they turned their gaze to the rugged bits of their own island, and sallied forth clutching copies of Gilpin or Coleridge, who wrote of Wales that he had found 'the wild-wood scenery [to be] most sublimely terrible . . . it surpasses everything I could have conceived'. For striding Victorian polyglot George Borrow, the high priest of Celtic Romanticism and author of *Wild Wales*, this was 'a truly fairy place'. It's a perception that endures, reconfiguring itself for each new epoch.

A lofty gadabout is one thing, but when incorrigible Romantics become so inflamed that they move to Wales, it can end in bitter recrimination. Poet Walter Savage Landor, enraptured by the Picturesque estates developed across Wales at the turn of the nineteenth century, breezed into the Black Mountains in 1807, determined to create his own. As William Condry wrote, 'he spent £50,000, planted many trees, quarrelled with every one in sight then departed'. Many of his problems were self-inflicted, such as planting species that locals rightly told him would never grow there. On his departure from Llanthony, Landor fired off an angry letter to the Bishop of St David's, one of many with whom he'd fallen out: 'If drunkenness, idleness, mischief and revenge are the principal characteristics of the savage state, what nation . . . in the world is so singularly tattooed with them as the Welsh?'

Throughout the last half-century, there has been a steady and growing stream of English idealists escaping to Wales. The godfather of them all was John Seymour, who bought a farm in Pembrokeshire in 1964: 'I was back in a peasant society where people still brewed beer and killed pigs and we were no longer freaks,' he later wrote. Seymour was the original good-lifer – quite literally, as it was the success of 1970s BBC sitcom *The Good Life* that pushed sales of his books *The Fat of the Land* and *The Complete Book of Self-Sufficiency* into orbit. In the late 1980s, he too flounced out of Wales, declaring that it was by then 'insufficiently authentic', whatever that means, and resettling in Ireland.

Reg and George were an unlikely part of this new wave of incomers. In our very first conversation, Reg proudly described himself and George as 'pioneers', and though I flinched at the inference that rural Wales was some sort of Wild West dustbowl, I soon came to see that he was right, more so perhaps than even he realised. Many of their English contemporaries moving to the area in the early 1970s were young straight couples, mainly well-heeled hippies with small children who soon went merrily feral. Not only were Reg and George gay, they were respectable, conservative gentlemen, lower-middle-class sons of London shopkeepers and already middle-aged. No one else moving into the area looked quite like them.

For George, whose love of the wild places had been ignited on those pre-war bicycle tours, his spiritual cohorts were Shelley, Wordsworth and the Romantics, rather than John Seymour and the back-to-the-land brigade. In their first couple of years at Cefn, when Reg was there full-time but he was only an occasional visitor, George started writing a poetry collection under the title *The Secret Land: Poems and Songs of Powys, Mid Wales*, walking the paths and commons around their new home as he chewed over its verses. This was the first time he'd attempted to write poetry since the war. The rustiness is evident in this opening poem, as is his powdery take on their new manor:

Criss-crossed with lost valleys
Lies the Secret Land.
Green, secret, slumbering under ancient skies
Lie the ancient hills . . .

. . . Hallowed Secret Land, God-given
Nurtured and cherished by God-fearing men
Lineage-linked men, born and reborn
From the ashes of their forebears
Buried time and again in their Secret earth –
Reborn to walk proudly their heritage
To speak proudly the noble tongue
Of this Secret Land.

Placing himself and Reg into this landscape, he wrote a
poem titled 'The Intruders':

We walked that day in long-forgotten fields,
Disturbing the gossamer of lost dreams,
Losing our present thoughts of peace and ease
In reveries of other days than these.

The lonely hillside murmurs still
Of voices that they heard –
The breeze that weaves midst falling leaves,
Of brook in spate and song of birds.

But then another voice there, bids us stay,
That speaks of other memories, other voices,
Other ways, in those dead days
That long, long since, have passed away.

Secret, lost, long-forgotten, lonely, slumbering, dead: words that invariably spring forth when English eyes first sweep across rural Welsh landscapes. In truth, those fields are anything but long-forgotten; they are named, tilled, grazed, fenced, improved and fought over every time the tenancy agreements come up for grabs. When I first met the farmer who rents our field from us, as his father had from Reg and George, he told me in hurt and urgent tones how his uncle had done the dirty by outbidding him on some other parcel of land. From the way he talked, I thought this was something that had just happened. Only later did I discover that it was a couple of decades ago.

To an English Romantic – and it's a label crowning me just as snugly as it did George – the mythological allure of Wales, his 'Hallowed Secret Land', tends only to pall on closer inspection. Nothing real can live up to its seductive half-light. The challenge, then, is not to do a Landor or a Seymour, ricocheting loudly to the other extreme in disappointment, and sounding like a petulant lover who declaimed his passion from on high or afar, but on moving in with the object of his adoration is horrified to find that they leave toenail clippings in the sink and never put the bins out.

Ennui is an occupational hazard, especially if your livelihood depends upon peddling a version of the dream that first brought you here. It was certainly the case for me: on moving to Wales, I quickly lost interest in the guidebook version of the country that had kept me engaged for most of the previous decade. I wanted to dig deeper, down into the dirt and shale, rather than repeatedly buff the shiny surface. George, also trying to cash in on the dream in a B&B, went in the opposite direction. His last poem is dated October 1974, the month that he sold up in Bournemouth and moved to Wales full-time, some two years after Reg. He never returned to *The Secret Land: Poems and Songs of Powys*, because more prosaic, and sometimes far harsher, realities were soon to intrude.

During those two years alone, Reg had taken to Darowen village life with unexpected gusto. Though he had been thrown into this new world, the urbane gentlemen's outfitter from the upmarket south-coast boutique shape-shifted remarkably. He surprised himself, and George too, by co-ordinating the renovation work on the house superbly, despite being unable to drive and stuck there alone for weeks on end, the village phone box (Cemmaes Road 250) his only line to the outside world. George kept a tight hold on their finances, negotiating hard and paying the bills from Bournemouth, and allowing Reg no independent income. On his fortnightly visits to Wales, George brought just enough food to tide Reg and any B&B guests over until his next appearance.

All the same, Reg swiftly became a much-loved neighbour. His kindness and curiosity, together with a rare talent for listening, won round those quite startled by his and George's arrival in the village. Even in the chauvinist early seventies, rural Welsh-speaking Wales was very much a matriarchial society; the women gave Reg the nod and their menfolk fell dutifully into line.

George did not quite know how to react to Reg's success in establishing himself so well within the community. It was something he found impossible to emulate, partly because he was only there every few weekends, but also because of his generally stiffer character. By the time he moved there fully, it was too late to catch up. He appreciated the friends that Reg had made, but the only people he really liked were an English couple who lived half a mile away, in an ancient house buried deep in a wood. 'What a revelation—!' flutters a starstruck George after their first invitation to lunch. He is wowed by their 'fifteenth century Cruck Hall House (1480) with later additions 16th & 17th century, filled with wonderful old oak furniture mostly 17 cent.' There, they 'stayed to lunch, served in the kitchen on a gorgeous 17th century oak refectory table, with home made sloe wine'. Though the wine, the house, the furniture and the company all intoxicated him, still it wasn't enough.

George had been living full-time at Cefn for only a year when he announced that they had to move. It devastated Reg. He'd supervised the extensive renovation of the house, and had applied his flawless taste to its furnishing, and all on the tightest of budgets that George allowed him.

From nothing, he'd built up a successful guest house, and was already welcoming back enthusiastic regulars. He'd made real friends in the area and loved exploring it with Andy, his dog. Most of all, he'd discovered in himself unknown depths and strengths, something George perhaps found as challenging as he did pleasing. He presented their need to move as a natural and inevitable product of Reg's success: somewhere bigger! An old farmhouse! No neighbours! More customers! But they both knew that wasn't the full reason, nor perhaps even the main one.

Of course, George got his way and in 1976 they moved twenty-five miles back towards the English border, into an old farmhouse named Penhempen. It was a disaster. Although they had no immediate neighbours, they shared a drive and an antiquated water system with the farm that their house had once been part of. A dispute erupted between them and the farmer within six months of their arrival, and got steadily worse. It drove George to distraction, and killed any last traces of his *Secret Land*. Wales, he now knew, was not lost or slumbering; it was clocking his every move and plotting. From then, the tone changes markedly in his diaries. 'Welsh' often becomes a compound term of derision: 'that Welsh communist!', 'Mrs Welsh Big-mouth' and so on. It is never used as a compliment.

External events only compound his indignation. At just the time that things were coming to a head with their neighbours, the Meibion Glyndŵr[2] campaign of burning down holiday homes erupted. The first came on a midweek night just before Christmas 1979, when four

[2] 'Sons of Glyndŵr', from the fifteenth-century rebel prince Owain Glyndŵr.

cottages – two in Pembrokeshire, two in Gwynedd – were set alight. The arson campaign reaches George's diary seven weeks later: 'Toll of burnt down cottages in Wales now 18! You can thank the Welsh Nationalists for this – *whoever* actually does the dirty work.'

By the end of 1980, Reg and George had managed to sell Penhempen ('So happy to be away from Satan!') and buy Rhiw Goch, a mile and a half across the valley from their first house, Cefn. Although they were both thrilled to be back in the district, it was here in the Welsh-speaking heartlands that the arson campaign was strongest. It was, some of their old guests have told me, a regular topic of conversation, though Reg and George always insisted that they weren't worried, because it was only empty holiday cottages that were being torched. Even those nearby who did have weekend cottages, such as their new neighbours Penny and her husband David, were not unduly concerned. 'We had four children and were so looked after by our neighbours,' Penny told me. 'They took the registration numbers of cars anywhere near [their house], they would not have let anything happen to it. It didn't even worry us.' Those watchful eyes that had become such a problem at Penhempen were now a real advantage at Rhiw Goch, the sign of a scattered but supportive community, comfortable with its mixture of inhabitants, rather than a fragmented or fractious one. It still rings true today.

When we had been living at Rhiw Goch for only a few weeks, Preds startled me one evening by saying how good it was that Welsh people 'had got this house back'. It was, he continued, quite a widely held feeling in the area amongst the locals. The apparent harshness of the sentiment blindsided me, but I soon understood it. Before Reg and George, the house had been a London family's holiday home, and before that a Buddhist monk's retreat. It was last farmed in the 1960s, as a small dairy unit, by another English rat-race escapee. For the first time in over half a century, the old walls were echoing regularly with Welsh, in an area where it is still the mother tongue of half the population.

All too often, on both sides of the argument, the debates about the shifting identity of rural Wales get stuck in the bald statistics of language. To those most exercised about its survival, it's an existential crisis where Welsh will expire if they take their eyes off it for a second. For the virulent anti-Welsh brigade, banging on about being 'forced to learn a dead language', it should be abandoned like a mouldering ruin in the bracken. Both positions thrive on each other's hyperbole. Both have been around for the best part of two hundred years. And neither is true.

Reg's dyslexia made learning a new language impossible, though he was delighted to use the Welsh versions of their names – Rheinallt and Sior – when he could. George's early poetic effusions to 'speak proudly the noble tongue' did not extend to learning it; it was ineluctably part of the romantic dream that had long since soured.

His disdain spread like a stain into other areas of his life. For a man so literate, it is remarkable how few works of Welsh literature, even in English, I found on those over-crowded bookshelves, nor Welsh music in his many drawers of tapes. He adored the landscape, but cut himself adrift from the culture woven through it like silk thread. When after a couple of years at Rhiw Goch he got the cycling bug, it was to Shropshire, Herefordshire and the

Marches that he most often turned for all-day rides. Given the choice, his eyes always turned east.

*

The best Rhiw Goch sunrise of the year is the winter solstice, a handful of days before Christmas. It is not just that it marks the returning light, though that is always welcome, but that it is perfectly aligned for maximum impact. The house faces south-south-east, so that by the time the sun climbs free of the surrounding hills, its first rays hit us square-on. The stone porch at the front door becomes a cauldron of light; the front windows dazzle with promise.

My previous house in the quarry village lost its sunlight behind a mountain between November and February; after ten winters of that, Rhiw Goch was a literal eye-opener, and a paradox too. The low angle of the winter sun, combined with the leaflessness of the surrounding trees, means that in the depths of the darkest season the house is often far brighter than in the dog days of June.

Visiting Reg one luminous early spring day, I told him how the sunlessness of my house for a full quarter of the year was really beginning to grind me down. It was such an extreme place to live: a tall south-facing slate terrace that baked in the summer sun, and was then plunged into a Narnian winter. Cold, china-blue days were the worst; not only did the sparkling light all around seem to mock our shadow, it never touched the frost that stubbornly refused to melt, leaving the path to the front door an ice rink.

'Oh, we get the sun all year round here,' Reg replied. 'You'd like that, wouldn't you? It would make all the difference.'

He gave me a curious, knowing smile, which I didn't know how to read. This was the only time he intimated to me even slightly that we were going to inherit Rhiw Goch – something he had ensured by frogmarching George down to the solicitors' in order to change their wills. It was a moment of imperial regime change in their long relationship. George's lights were slowly dimming and, for the first time, he abandoned decision-making and left it all to Reg, aided by Penny. It was she who pushed them into a reluctant civil partnership. 'George said, "We don't need it,"' she told me, 'but I said, "You do. If anything happens to you, Reg will be absolutely vulnerable." George was a lot older and all power; Reg was nothing, and I really worried about him.' They did as they were told. Penny can have that effect.

The wills were changed in mid 2006, a couple of months after the civil partnership ceremony. We had no idea. Looking back, there was only Reg's oblique comment about winter sunlight that had given me pause for thought; similarly for Preds, there had been just one fleeting moment of wonder when helping Reg in the garden, and being told to plant it to his taste, not theirs.

Only towards the end did Reg spill the beans, and then only because he had to. After George had been placed in a care home, and Reg had returned home after his first stroke, Preds tried to talk to him about the options available. Although there were friends and neighbours keeping a close eye, Reg alone at Rhiw Goch was worrying us all. Why don't you think about selling up, Preds gently asked him one day, and use the money to buy a small place in town? After repeatedly rebuffing the question, Reg tearfully let on that he couldn't do that, because his dearest wish was to leave us the house, intact and debt-free. And that he hadn't wanted to tell us because he hated the idea of it making us feel beholden to him. His stoicism and suffering – so that Preds could have his dream house and garden, and I could be free of crippling winter blues – are there in every glorious sunrise. They're there, too – perhaps even more so – on the far greater number of mornings when dawn limps in only as the gradual lightening of a grey eastern sky.

Although it took me so long to accept it, at forty-five, well into the second half of my life, it was high time that I moved to somewhere more sunrise than sunset, and as equally winter as summer. In the words of nineties 'Cool Cymru' band Catatonia, I'd always 'chased the sun out west' in pursuit of the party and whatever nefarious promises the night might bring. It was time to get to bed early and rise for the dawn, to celebrate the day's sober discipline rather than collapse into its dissolute fall. Preds is even more locked into this pattern. In the spring, he's usually up at five, pottering around the garden in his dressing gown and soaking up the precious silence, before I crash through it like a startled warthog.

For the month around midsummer, dawn breaks behind us, to the north-east. On the longest day itself, the sun inches up over a standing stone four fields away, on the other side of the valley. This is Carreg y Noddfa, the 'Stone of Sanctuary', a seven-foot monolith squatting at the top of a field, its lichened sides square to the cardinal points of the compass.

The stone is both haughty and homely. It commands our landscape with a steady, imperious gaze, while its worn base in a circle of scuffed earth tells of centuries of sheep and cattle snuggled into its lambent warmth. Despite its

solitude, Carreg y Noddfa is one of triplets. Its sibling stones lie a couple of miles to the north and to the east, though the latter was broken up in the 1860s for walling. The triangle of territory between them served as an officially designated *noddfa*, a place of safety and sanctuary to those fleeing persecution. In the pre-Norman era, this was a common secular concept in Wales, later codified as an ecclesiastical one. By the Middle Ages it had become the title of our township, or tithing district: Trefddegwm y Noddfa, the 'Township of the Sanctuary', a name still in use into the twentieth century.

According to the idiosyncratic 1969 *Shell Guide to Wales*,

> the two surviving sanctuary stones lie on a direct line passing through the site of [Darowen] church and bearing accurately on one of the Five Heads of Plynlimon ... From this point the eye is led, again in direct line, to the cairn, [suggesting that they] form part of a complex of pointer-stones whose remains are widely spread over the Plynlimon moorlands, and that Darowen itself was originally a principal place for controlling the system.

Glorious though the idea is, it seems to be the perspective of one man with a map, a ruler and a vivid imagination, rather than any hard evidence. Even his ruler was a little wonky; the 2.7-kilometre line drawn between the stones runs well over a hundred metres east of Darowen church. No other source that I can find mentions the idea.

Archaeology dates the sanctuary stone opposite us as Bronze Age, from the second millennium BCE. The surrounding field is known as Cae'r Hen Eglwys, the 'Field of the Old Church'; it was common practice amongst early Christians to build their churches at sites already venerated as sacred. In the 1911 *Inventory of the Ancient Monuments in Wales and Monmouthshire*, the farmer recalls ploughing near the stone decades earlier and striking masonry, which turned out to be the foundations of 'a solidly constructed building'. These were removed 'so as to plough easier'. His grandson renovated the ancient farmhouse in 1992, and found in a chimney breast a bricked-up chamber containing a horse's skull and a dozen children's shoes, a tradition that dates back to the fourteenth century. As the piece of clothing uniquely moulded to the shape and soul of the wearer, shoes were thought to be traps for evil spirits.

I once walked the perimeter of the *noddfa* triangle between the three stones – from our front door, a journey of eight or nine miles. It was soon obvious that the sacred land feature on which they are oriented is not the great mountainous bog of Pumlumon (today's more common orthography for Plynlimon), but something much closer: Fron Goch, the elegant swell of a hill that tops out at just under a thousand feet. Both of the surviving stones are pointed at it and, even more remarkably, clearly mimic its shape.

Ever since first coming to visit Reg and George, Fron Goch has bewitched me. They honoured it too; it was one of Reg's favourite walks, and its summit is where George chose to bury Toby, the first of their dogs to die in Wales. From the hill fort on its bulbous peak, a long ridge stretches seawards, giving it the appearance of a landlocked Ynys Enlli, or Bardsey, off the tip of the Llŷn peninsula. The holiest spot in Wales, Enlli is known as the 'Island of Twenty Thousand Saints', from the sheer number of pilgrims who voyaged there to meet their maker.

With no other hills crowding it, Fron Goch's modest height belies its swagger, and more than any other feature or building it is the heart of our scattered community. Every year, we celebrate Gŵyl Fron Goch, 'the Fron Goch Festival', a neighbourhood party usually held in someone's barn or outhouse. One year, it took place on the summit of the hill itself on the night of the summer solstice, a bon-fire-beacon crackling into the skies as we drank and chatted and laughed, while the farm youngsters tanked around us on quad bikes.

Every time I've climbed Fron Goch, it has left me euphoric. In its anonymity lurks an archaic power, something that could be said too of the district as a whole. And like the sanctuary stones, we are all aligned to it, Rhiw Goch especially so: from the field opposite, the long frontage of the house is framed precisely by its smooth hump, our central chimney a finger pointing straight at the summit. At the back door, the eye is drawn through the garden and up towards its dome of a peak, at times as pretty and playful as a stately home eye-catcher, at others a penitentiary wall hemming us in. Occasionally, it vanishes altogether, wrapped in plumes of morning mist or growling invisible behind curtains of driz-zle. One autumn, a friend staying in the back bedroom said that when she opened the curtains, the first rays of sunrise on the rusty bracken of Fron Goch made it look as if a new red planet was rising at the end of the garden. It's an image that stuck, and we are all tiny moons in its orbit.

Aside from his questionable sacred mathematics, the author of the 1969 *Shell Guide* often hit the mark. In an echo of George's excitable take on his new neighbours in the fif-teenth-century cruck-hall house, this district is, he wrote,

typical of a Welsh countryside that the 20th century has
barely touched . . . houses sheltering their Tudor and
Stuart construction under immemorial oaks can, if the
visitor is permitted access, tell him much of the old stones
of Darowen, and offer wines – dandelion, elderberry,
parsnip, rose-hip – that are seductive but dangerous.
Here is the traditional Welsh hamlet, as yet unspoilt and
unknown.

In the tumultuous half-century since, change has swept
through even this backwater, but his description still holds
true. Most of the holdings around us have been in the same
family for centuries, those on the farm around the sanctuary stone since the 1660s. A retired farmer up the road told
me that he considers himself something of an interloper, as
his people had farmed here for only nine generations. He
was only semi-joking. Preds too: though he grew up on a
farm just down the road, his parents moved there from
'away', twenty or thirty miles to the north, across a county

divide and numerous other invisible borders. To some, he is almost as much of an incomer here as I am.

Even within a Welsh context, such a degree of settled depth is rare. All the more intriguing then that the area receives such scant attention in books and articles. This is a nation able to spin a myth out of thin air, yet of the dozens of volumes about Wales on my shelves, the eccentric *Shell Guide* is pretty much the only one even to notice us – in English, anyway. Looking through Welsh-language texts, there is far more, particularly about the many quiet revolutionaries that this place has spawned – from the parish priest whose eight children were all leading lights in nineteenth-century cultural, religious and educational movements, to the pioneers of a radical health service developed for local lead miners. There is much too about the area as a sanctuary, its softness, and its separateness from the world beyond.

In his instinctive way, with precious little Welsh, Reg got this, and was eager to understand more. He pumped Preds for insight into local culture and his upbringing, and fired questions at me about history, language and lore. His was a hunger that had never been wholly sated by George's cerebral hand-me-downs, but as George's aloofness hardened towards the culture around them, and then as he faded away mentally, Reg's appetite only quickened. In creating such successful B&Bs at Cefn and then Rhiw Goch, Reg tapped deep into its sense of sanctuary. He ran with the grain, even if he could not give it the intellectual ballast of louder, loftier voices.

That spirit endures, and still in the shadows. This patch remains blissfully ignored by guidebooks and tour promoters. There are no campsites, no caravans, no designated tourist attractions, no brown signs pointing towards the standing stones, the hilltop church of St Tudyr or the Iron Age hill fort on top of Fron Goch. The labyrinth of paths, byways and bridleways are rarely walked or ridden by anyone other than locals.

If it helps preserve the peace, we're happy to be ignored, and happier still to have people assume the worst, as they have for centuries. In his *Descriptio Cambriae* (*Description of Wales*, 1194), the clerical sycophant Gerald of Wales railed against designated places of sanctuary like this, claiming that many

> abuse this immunity and far exceed the indulgence of the church ... From their place of sanctuary they sally forth on foraging expeditions, harass the whole countryside and have even been known to attack the prince.[3]

Sabre-rattling and scaremongering are always the main ingredients of lickspittle authority-worship. It has no place here.

This is Y Noddfa. Sanctuary lies deep in the bones, and still calls to outlaws.

---

[3] Translation by Lewis Thorpe, from the Penguin Classics edition of 1978.

REG

While George wasn't especially bothered about having a civil partnership, Reg was actively horrified. 'He just didn't like the thought of it at all,' Penny told me, 'and that was nothing more than him being deeply ashamed of being gay. He was so uncomfortable in his skin, sadly.'

They reluctantly went ahead with it, 'only because I said they had to', but invited just Preds and me to the ceremony. 'I was really hurt that they didn't ask us,' continued Penny, 'and I asked Reg why on earth not. He said, "Because you're not like us." And by that, of course, he meant gay.' Even a state-sanctioned celebration of their lifelong love was something to be kept behind closed doors.

Most people who have grown up gay struggle with deeply internalised homophobia, but with Reg it had seared so hot that it seemed to have cauterised his being. All his life, the fragile self-confidence so painstakingly built up could be deflated in an instant, and even when he knew that the right response was indignation, scalding shame often got in there first. He could never forget how Norman, his first boyfriend, had ended up in jail for indecency, his name and reputation trashed; nor the simmering bigotry that had faced them at Penhempen; nor even how in the eighties he'd gone to see the doctor in Machynlleth with a sore throat and been forced to have an AIDS test. There was forever a tiny part of him that held such humiliations to be justified.

A mind so compromised is inherently lonely, and unable – or unwilling – to spot comrades. In the early days of getting to know Reg and George, I lost count of the number of times Reg said that he couldn't believe I was 'y'know . . . like *me*' (blush), because I seemed 'so *normal*'. He had a very strong sense of normal, and in his own mind he always fell far short of it.

Penny once asked him when he had first known that he was different. He replied that his dad had told him, when he'd refused to let Reg join the Boys' Brigade. 'It wouldn't be suitable for you,' Gus had said, 'you're not like the other boys.' What had been intended as a kindly intervention, something to save his son from ridicule and bullying, was instead turned inwards to fester, sending the already iso-lated Reg deeper into his own purdah. His difference was not just in his sexuality; it was in his Polish-German ances-try, his fluttering demeanour, his stammer, his dyslexia and hypersensitivity.

Ironically, given the stout Victorian Christianity espoused by the Boys' Brigade, being kept away from them pushed Reg's own religion to extremes. In the hands of a highly strung teenager, it became a bloody crusade of self-flagellating literalism. Reg and I talked about this adolescent fundamentalist phase, since it was one that I had gone through too, as did many other gay friends. It took different forms but always for the same reason: a desperate last throw of the dice, a fervent, solipsistic prayer that God will rinse you free of the feelings that are becoming daily more evident and troublesome. 'PRAY THE GAY AWAY', as a recent headline had it.

My teenage flirtation with the evangelists soon melted in an inferno of booze and boys, and although Reg's fervour cooled too, he remained besotted with High Church frills for the rest of his life. After all, this was his family's central European heritage, and his devotion to it only intensified on the early death of his mother. Although the saints' icons, rosaries and prayer cards gave him strength, they also exacerbated his sense of living at the margins, of never quite belonging. By contrast, George's simple Anglicanism positioned him foursquare in the mainstream, a place he liked very much. The Church of England was one of his pillars – as were its political wing, the Conservative Party, the military, and the self-made ethos drilled into him by his father. The Church's hymns and prayers sang out English infallibility, one so unequivocal that even his homosexuality failed to dent it.

In this regard, I am much more a Reg, peering in from the outskirts, than a George. Although I grew up swaddled in the same damp, aspirational Anglicanism as George, it choked me. I needed light and air, and so gravitated towards a faith rooted in the outdoors and the divine within, in the elements and seasons, and in the urge to honour them. Its holy scriptures are poetry, music, art – and Ordnance Survey maps.

This heathenism had always been my driving force long before I could give it a name. Even as a child in the English suburbs, it was the spirits of place that called, and not just in the prominent locations, the hill forts and henges, for they were found too on patches of scrubby wasteland, or at the bottom of the garden. In Wales, they were everywhere, and in full voice. This is a land where Christianity, even at its most muscular, has never managed to dislodge older, deeper beliefs. Whatever my faith was called, I knew from my very earliest encounters that Wales was its home.

Accepting with good grace the gift of Rhiw Goch showed me how rusty this faith had become. Any belief system is boosted by signs as affirmation, and they all pointed unequivocally in this direction. This was the house that Preds had wanted since childhood, ten minutes away from his widowed mother. To raise the funds to buy it, we managed to sell up in the middle of a recession, to exactly the right people, and without even having to go through an estate agent. And then, at the very last moment before buying Rhiw Goch, Reg and George both died and we came to inherit it instead.

Confirmation came in even the tiniest of details. Chiselled into the boulders of the old granary building destined to become my study is an Ordnance Survey benchmark. Its flared triple prongs are identical to the *awen*, Iolo Morganwg's symbol of Druidic wisdom and the poetic muse. The benchmark's horizontal grid reference is 9,998 metres, so that two metres further north lies the zero line dividing two principal blocks of the National Grid. This cartographer's ley line therefore lies straight along the path between the back of the house and the barn, along my daily commute from kitchen to office and along the trajectory of the sun at the March and September equinoxes.

Could there have been clearer signposts? Yet still I fought them. A few months after moving, we drove over to my old village for dinner in the pub. As we began the drive back to the gaunt solitude of Rhiw Goch, the beer and bonhomie soured, leaving me belligerent and mournful for what I'd given up. We were chasing Preds' dream, not mine, I sulked silently. My mood darkened as we neared home, a word I was still struggling to fit to our new surroundings. Preds took one look at me and went to bed, wisely leaving me to stew in acid self-pity.

Mawkish tears prickled. In truth, I'd been leaving my old village since Preds had come to live with me years earlier. I was part of a bigger unit now, and could not – and should not want to try to – keep the old options open. The picture would become clear only as time elapsed; I needed to be trusting and patient. I told myself all this, but it only scratched the surface, and drew blood.

Fed up with my mood, the dog whined for escape. Heading outside, the stillness was thick as tar, the silence total. Autumn was on its way; there was a new sharpness in the air, and in the night sky too. In the fathomless black sparkled constellations clearer than I had seen for decades, crowned by the shimmering arc of the Milky Way. And just to underline the riposte, to make it so explicit that even I couldn't ignore it, as I looked up a shooting star scorched through the middle of my vision, hitting me like an electric shock.

I wish I could say that was the end of it, but there were so many other occasions when I succumbed to old habits. It made me reappraise Reg and the sheer sturdiness of his faith, for he too was led here by forces beyond his control, but never collapsed into the same sort of sullen indulgence that I did so well, and so often. To my lapsed heathen self, the tat and trinkets of his proto-Catholicism were pitiful, but they seemed to have given him a strength and depth that eluded me. I needed to reconnect with the simple beliefs that had first brought me to Wales.

The job was half done, for there was no ignoring the overpowering numen of the landscape, or underestimating the enduring potency of its status as a sanctuary. After the first full cycle of a year, the realisation crept up on me that there was a sense of balance here that I had never previously experienced. The seasons flowed with a seamlessness that was new to me. None stood taller than its fellows; they took their turn, then gently and generously ceded the stage. There was a new harmony here too with the elements. Of the four – air, fire, water, earth – we all feel instinctively much closer to one or two, and need to work at the others in order to bring them more into balance; if a place can help that process with its inherent symmetry, then so much the better. In the pagan traditions that speak loudest to me, each element corresponds with a season and a compass bearing: air with spring in the east, for instance, the first stop when calling the quarters to create ritual space. The directions are then invoked in clockwise order: fire and summer in the south, water and autumn in the west, earth and winter in the north.

As those circles turned, I caught glimpses of other wheels in perpetual motion: the sun, moon and stars, births and deaths, generational echoes in old houses, the farming calendar; rhythms of light and shade reflected internally and stronger with each passing cycle. The structure of this sprawling story, looping through time and place, presented itself.

Corroboration came when I considered how we all slotted in: four elements, four cardinal points, four seasons, the four of us. It could not have been clearer that Reg embodied the element of air, George fire, me water and Preds earth. The fit is uncanny. Air is the element of faith and divination, of things unseen and borne on the wind. It is the element too of gossip and conversation, of memory and mental agility, of bubbling laughter and wispy hunches. It is playful, flirtatious, quick and light. It is in the east, the dawn and the morning; in spring and youth. In all of these, it is Reg, that high-flying kite of a man bringing colour and joy to the skies, right to the bitter end.

Even in those dire last months, when his speech and mobility had deserted him, he could still provoke tears of laughter. In the care home in Machynlleth, where he'd gone after a second, more serious stroke, there was a light and a lightness still in him that had long since disappeared from his fellow inmates.

One March morning when I visited, he wanted to go from the lounge to his own room; the staff encouraged me to do the job of hauling him into a wheelchair. I made a complete hash of the task, and came close at one point to dropping his frail frame altogether. There was no murmur of recrimination, nor so much as a squeal of alarm. Instead, he fixed me with those still-gleaming blue eyes and rolled them theatrically, needing no words to tell me what a clumsy idiot I was. His eye-roll made us both laugh so hard – there in a place where it felt like no one had cracked a smile in months – that I nearly dropped him again. I managed to wrestle him into the wheelchair and push him back to his room, the corridor echoing with our laughter. Care assistants poked their heads around doorways to see what the commotion was, but seeing that it was Reg, they smiled indulgently and watched us pass.

He was only at the care home for a few months, and until the final few weeks his wit never abandoned him. He came up with pin-sharp nicknames for fellow residents and staff, just as he always had at home. One near neighbour, a sweet charmer who liked to overplay his gay-friendliness by giving us all a full-body bear hug every time we met, Reg nicknamed 'Kinky Boots'. Typically camp and faintly bizarre, the name fitted perfectly, stuck fast and, like so many of his little gems, has survived him.

Perhaps because he was so unsure of himself, all of the happiest periods of Reg's life came from contact with other people. His interest in others, even those he'd never met, was profound, and utterly genuine. More impressively, he remembered every detail. You could talk in passing about a friend or relative, then not mention them again for a year or more. But when you did, Reg would instantly recall how they fitted into your life and any other details you'd shared so long before. I have never met anyone with such a sharp, specific talent.

This was a skill both innate and polished from his earliest days. With two far older siblings, Reg's upbringing was intensely focused on adult company, only amplified by his frequent absence from school. After his brief few months of army training at the tail end of the war, he worked in a

Lyons Corner House in the West End, a job full of chatter and laughter that he adored; the insights he gleaned there into the importance of food and camaraderie were recycled decades later in their guest houses. On joining George in Bournemouth, Reg moved into menswear. He was a perfect retail assistant, diligent and discreet, his capacity for remembering faces, names and histories responsible for a great deal of repeat custom. In a parallel life, the ever-graceful Reg would have been modelling the clothes on the catwalk rather than selling them.

Beyond work, the early Bournemouth years were joyful. The war was won, living standards were inching up and foreign package holidays were yet to take off: Bourne-mouth boomed, preening itself as the country's classiest resort. Holidaymakers came from all over Britain to lie on the beaches and sit in the parks, lapping up dances and bands and concerts. Reg's dad, Gus, was a regular visitor throughout the twenty years that he outlived his wife. After the painful decade of her decline, he and Reg found a comfortable new happiness together, one that George slot-ted into perfectly.

Though the flavour of the town was genteel and avowedly orthodox, there was every kind of fun to be had if you looked hard enough, including bohemian elements that never made it into the official tourist brochures. Homo-sexuality remained illegal, and prosecutions rose through the fifties, but there was a large and supportive network of gay men in Bournemouth, many of whom ran or worked in its wedding-cake hotels and boarding houses. Some of their bars and function rooms hosted an underground gay scene, relatively easy even for visitors to find.

George and Reg were never great pub-goers; their social life revolved around suppers and soirées, picnics and classical concerts at the Winter Gardens. On summer weekends, they'd hook up with a gang of boyfriends and head down to the Sandbanks ferry for a day on the nudist beach at Studland. Willowy, beautiful Reg would happily whip his trunks off and strike coy starlet poses for George's roving camera. Often, someone would turn the camera on the two of them, and for good reason. The photos capture a radiant couple, pulsing with sunshine and lust.

*

Reg's talent for conversation and comfort was the making of their move to Wales. As well as a popular neighbour, he was an absolute natural as a B&B host. Though George was minutely aware of the financial imperative of their guest houses, he never much liked the social side of it, except with the few favourite regulars who shared his tastes in music, literature or politics. Reg became adept at smoothing over feathers ruffled by George's occasionally abrupt behaviour, from regular tellings-off of late-night revellers, to a party of Australians chided for taking too many baths (after which, a bath surcharge – 15p – was introduced). One guest remembered leaving a piece of bacon untouched at breakfast, and George snapping, 'You eat that – I'm not having you leave it on the side of your plate.'

The B&B operation at Rhiw Goch dwindled through the second half of the 1990s. They had long since stopped advertising, and relied on repeat bookings and word-of-mouth recommendation. George was still obsessed with cycling, and would disappear for the day once breakfast was done. Reg, with more free time than he'd ever had before, took Molly and Willy, a brother and sister pair of terriers, for long hikes or walked over to visit neighbours. Much of his time was still spent cleaning, cooking and pottering around the garden.

The new century saw their roles gradually reverse. George was deteriorating physically and mentally. His diary becomes a litany of health worries and appointments – knees, bowels, polyps, warts, teeth, prostate – and it is clear that his memory was beginning to fog. Although Reg was plagued by his own health problems, recurring anxiety amongst them, the final decade of his life proved to be one of his most contented; he was at long last free to make his own friends, on his own terms.

George had always exerted a powerful veto even over their social life. Most of the time it didn't show, because Reg was so used to falling in with whatever George wanted to do. But there were odd flashes of something undeniably darker. Throughout their first couple of decades together, the only true friend Reg had made for himself was Peter, a colleague from the Robert Old menswear store. He is still alive and still in Bournemouth, where I met him recently.

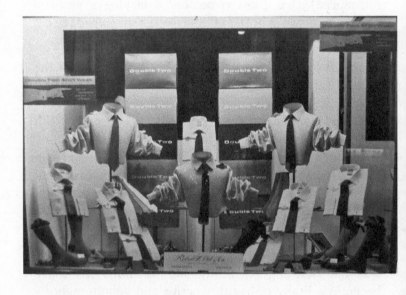

A dapper ninety-one, his memories remain sharp: 'It was lovely. I was mainly shirts and pyjamas, that sort of thing, and he dressed the windows. Reggie and I hit it off straight away. We'd chatter away, being of an age, and that much younger than George, we'd chatter away like a couple of girls, and of course we were in the same trade.'

It was Peter who helped them move to Wales in 1972. 'I remember the day we went,' he said, 'the furniture had all gone, and I loaded my car up with stuff, and George did the same with his. Reggie came with me in my car, and we followed George. But when we got into Wales, we lost him. Anyway, we found our way eventually. Of course, it wasn't Rhiw Goch then, they were in the village. I helped them settle in, that kind of thing, and I was there about a week.'

He returned regularly over the next twenty years, to all three of their Welsh houses. Although he was a close friend, and would invariably spend much of his holiday helping paint walls and outhouses, or doing even heavier labouring tasks, he was still expected to pay the going rate for full board.

George soon inveigled Peter into another kind of unpaid work: as a nude photographic model. It started in 1976 when he and Reg moved to Penhempen, the second house. Even as he turned sixty, the possibility of getting his – and others' – clothes off was a significant factor in George's urge for isolation and the holy grail of having no visible neighbours. He wasted no time in cajoling Peter to strip and pose, at first indoors and then out in the woods and streams. 'Reggie wouldn't have anything to do with it,' Peter recalled. 'He'd be downstairs housekeeping or getting a meal together or something, and then George would do these pictures of me. Sometimes we went out, he'd got his camera, so I had to take my clothes off and had pictures taken out in the open.'

Was George perhaps jealous of his friendship with Reg, I asked Peter. 'It might be,' he replied, 'but there was no need. I mean, Reggie had more reason to be jealous, because George and I were having, well, not sex exactly, but we were naked and frolicking around. I think Reggie did get a little bit upset for a time, but I said to him that there's no need for him to worry, that there was nothing between George and me. I just enjoyed the fun of it. Nothing else.'

Even if it was unconscious, this was surely manipulative behaviour by George, and part of a pattern. After seeing Reg strike up new and independent friendships with neighbours in the two years that he was alone at Cefn, George insisted they move away. On getting his way, he then hazed Reg's guileless best friend into becoming an occasional sex toy. And when that had run its course, and they'd moved house once again, George unceremoniously cut Peter out of both their lives.

'Eventually they moved to Rhiw Goch, and I went there for several years,' said Peter. 'I used to go usually in the early spring, I would write and say, "Can I come and stay?" and they'd say, "Ooh yes, do." That went on for some years. The last time, though [in the early 1990s] – I don't know why it happened, but it did – I was there, as usual, went for walks and things, and on the day I was coming back, George said, "Is there anywhere else you could go on your early spring holiday?" I said, "Well, yes, I suppose there is." He said, "Well, could you make other arrangements? Your coming here intrudes on our privacy." Yes . . . after all those years, they were not just friends, they were my best friends, and I was shocked out of my mind. And hurt dreadfully.'

Decades later, I could still see the pain on Peter's face. 'Did they ever mention me?' he asked at one point, in a tone so plaintive that it hurt to hear. Although phone contact was resumed some years later, he never saw them again.

So when, one late summer day in 2001, Penny knocked on the door of Rhiw Goch to ask if everything was all right, Reg seized the opportunity to make a new friend for himself. It was an unlikely meeting of souls. Penny and David had been Reg and George's nearest neighbours ever since they'd been at Rhiw Goch, twenty years by then, though contact had hitherto been minimal. Their old farmhouse, half a mile away over fields and a stream, was a holiday bolthole from frantic lives in the south of England; once there, they were 'reclusive', Penny told me, 'it's the only word I can use. We didn't know anybody in Machynlleth, we didn't want to know anybody. We lived a really busy life, David with his academic work, I was a nurse, we had four children and I was always tired. So when I was off, I really didn't want to see people.'

That changed on David's retirement in the late nineties, and his insistence that they relocate more or less full-time to Wales. 'I didn't want to,' she said. 'I was really, really unhappy – I wanted to live in England, near my grand-children. I was busy, as a school governor and charity trustee, but I didn't want to go to Wales. I loved it as a cottage, but I didn't want to live there. So I was bored and rather lonely.' That led to the knock on the door of Rhiw Goch, something she describes as 'one of my God-given moments'.

'We didn't know Reg and George for years and years, except to pass and say hello to – George more so, because he would stop in the lane, on his bike, in his Lycra, and was always delightful, always lovely. Then one day, I don't know why, I realised that I didn't know Reg, so I knocked on the door, and said I was Penny and thought I'd say hi. And he was as Reg as he could possibly be, said that if he'd known I was coming, he'd have taken his pinny off.'

As Preds and I were soon to find out, a friendship with Reg tended to go straight in at the deep end. Penny's did too. 'I said to Reg on that first meeting, "Are you all right?" and the answer was "No". So I said, "What can I do?" "Well, George needs to go into hospital in Shrewsbury, can you take us?" And I said, "Yes, of course I can do that." And from then on, really, I became their main carer. I went from not really knowing them, to knowing *everything*. George I can't say I loved, I was very fond of him, but I absolutely loved my Reg, who was as precious to me as any child. I found his vulnerability so striking. And his humour! He would make me cry with laughter, quite frequently. He would make me cry in all sorts of ways.

'Whenever I'm feeling a bit low, to cheer myself up I think of the time I took Reg to Wrexham hospital. David had put the satnav on, and as we came down the hill, the satnav said "turn left". "Who's that?" said Reg. "Oh, it's just a satnav." "But it's a woman, where is she?" "Darling, it's a satnav." When we reached the end of the lane, it told us to turn right, and Reg said, "She's spoken again!" When we got to the junction at Cemmaes Road, he was telling a story, and the satnav piped up, whereupon Reg said, "Don't interrupt, I'm speaking! She should at least have waited until I'd finished speaking." When we got back to Rhiw

Goch – George had stayed at home, and David had done his lunch – we went in and Reg said to George, "You'll never believe this – Penny's got this woman who sits in the back of the car and tells you where to go, but you can't see her!" Sometimes I put the satnav on, and I remember . . . oh, it was so beautiful.'

Daft as the story sounds, I can hear Reg in every word. He darted through ideas and topics, his conversation pirouetting like a ballet dancer in full flight, while his wide eyes scanned yours for feedback. Often his thought process would whip down a side alley of pure surrealism or deadpan observation, before whirling him back to the topic in hand. A chat with Reg was a vertiginous ride that left you dizzy, exhilarated – and exhausted. He'd spot a momentary lapse in my concentration, or I'd pause too long in reply, and his insecurities would rush back in. 'Oh, I'm talking too much, silly old fool!' he'd say, and really mean it. I'd reassure him that I loved our chats, and I hope he knew that it was true. Numerous times I told him that I wanted to tape a conversation with him, but it never happened. The strokes came and the loquacious tour de force was cruelly silenced.

Reg's conversation was curiously mirrored in his artwork: prodigious and prolific, naïve, vivid and intensely varied. In both, you never quite knew what might come next. Right to the end of his life, even after his later strokes, he continued to draw and paint. A speciality was bespoke cards for close friends; one arriving in the morning post was such a fillip, and we all have some stashed away. Mine were of trees, dogs, flowers, fairy houses and smartened-up versions of me, often annotated with

acerbic asides: '© Daft Old Ducks of Talywern', said one. The fluidity that escaped him with letters and numbers poured through his pictures, whether portraits (only ever of others), landscapes, animal studies, interiors, still life, even cubist and abstract experimentation. Sometimes, increasingly so towards the end, crucifixion scenes appeared amongst the colourful cartoon animals and flora, a head-on shunt between Enid Blyton and Salvador Dalí.

'He had a huge talent,' Penny said to me. 'What a pity he never had art lessons, he would have adored to have done that. But George didn't encourage anything in Reg except to be his domestic wife, to be truthful.' In that final decade, it was Penny's painstaking care and attention that freed Reg, as George quietly mouldered in his armchair by the fire. He'd had to give up cycling in 2002 at the age of eighty-five, and so much of him went with it. He could no longer keep on top of the bills and paperwork, and as Reg had no experience of that and was both dyslexic and innumerate, Penny took on the power of attorney for them both. 'So I did all the bills,' she said, 'and Reg just lived. He had this incredibly happy time when he was allowed to think for himself, and make his own decisions. He'd take taxis, pop into town, come and go as he pleased, and it was lovely.'

This was when Preds and I got to know them. We met them separately, shortly before we got together as a couple, and as it had been for Penny, the connection with Reg was instant for us both. I first met George and Reg at a flamboyantly Machynlleth wedding: on May Day, in a field, all homebrew, flowers and stilted dancing through arches of greenery. I'd seen them in town before; thanks to the rural jungle drum I knew that they were a couple who used to run a bed and breakfast, and was intrigued to find out more of their story. Beyond the odd smile and nod in the market, we'd never spoken, so spotting them at the wedding perched on a hay bale, I went over to say hello. George was polite and reserved, but Reg opened up immediately, and we gossiped and laughed as if we'd known each other for years.

At around the same time, Preds was working in the health food shop in Machynlleth, where Reg was a regular customer. Relishing his new-found freedom to mooch and shop at leisure, he'd try to hit the shop at a quiet time, so that Preds and he could have a proper natter, or even head off for a coffee break. At first alone, and then together, we were regular visitors to Rhiw Goch. George was only ever a background presence: unfailingly polite but enthused by very little except for my dog, the ageing Patsy, whom he'd fuss over joyously. Reg saved his fuss for us, and it came in waves.

Perversely, his first stroke in August 2009 proved to be something of a liberation for him, since it broke the spiral of terminal decline at home. George was receiving daily carer visits to help him wash and dress, but he'd often refuse point-blank to let them near him, and then take out his befuddled fury on Reg. By now, Reg had taken over writing the entries in the household diary; in his anguished, spidery notes, there is the inescapable feeling of a fuse about to blow.

When it did, Reg went to hospital and George into care. George never returned home, though Reg did, within six weeks, and in relatively good shape. He had bounced back from the stroke, had rested and been fed and looked after. Between then and a much larger stroke in July of the following year, he enjoyed a golden swansong. Though guilt was never far away –

24 January: I do miss George very much he was my life, I dare say I love to [*sic*] much, oh well.

16 February: I'm told I can't look after him, Im not much cop to him, Feel Iv let him Down

– he gratefully took every sliver of happiness on offer, from blowing £800 on a 'lift and tilt power recliner' armchair to falling happily into the role of Preds' other boyfriend.

Through that first half of 2010, Preds took him on regular outings, to National Trust properties and gardens, markets and tea shops. Despite nearly four decades in the area, Reg was seeing many of these places for the first time, and everything with a childlike glee. Perhaps his favourite date was when they went to see the film *A Single Man*, Tom Ford's stylised take on the Christopher Isherwood tale of a suicidal gay man in the early 1960s. It was the first time Reg had been to the pictures for thirty years, an especially poignant fact for one who adored the cinema and idolised its stars. Many of their trips out included calling to see George, by then settled into a care home twenty-five miles away in Newtown. Afterwards, Preds and he would go for bacon, egg and chips in a cafe, which in Reg's febrile imagination became a candlelit dinner for two.

The rationale for Penny's insistence on their civil partnership had been that if anything happened to George, a decade older, Reg would be unable to cope. By any conventional reading, that did indeed appear to be the case, yet perhaps it was the other way round. George, after all, had never cooked anything beyond a cup of tea, and it is impossible to imagine him knowing how to keep the house running, aside from the bare bones of its finances. George's strengths were all out there, businesslike, unquestioning and explicit. As he faded, so did they, and with startling speed. In Reg's deterioration came new reserves of strength and even inspiration, as was often the case for him in times of challenge and adversity.

For Reg's funeral tea back at Rhiw Goch, we pinned up dozens of his paintings in the living room. The cumulative effect was magical. Throughout the afternoon, the wall of colour and joyful energy drew everyone to it, and precipitated feverish recollection, tears and laughter. Guests were invited to take any pictures they wanted, and the remainder stayed up for months.

One in particular mesmerised both Preds and me; we framed it and moved it into a permanent place by the fire. It is a portrait in pastels, just two colours, black and blue. A svelte young woman stares out, her oversized eyes, the colour of forget-me-nots, grasp you in their soulful embrace. A thick mop of black hair bushes down to her shoulders. The lines are spare, strong and sure. We each separately came to the same conclusion: it is, without question, a self-portrait, the only one he left.

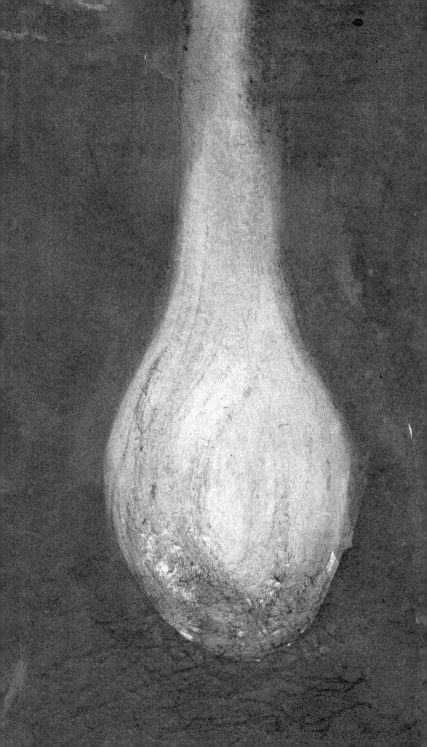

SECOND QUARTER

The Element of
FIRE

❖

The Season of
SUMMER

❖

The Direction of
SOUTH

❖

GEORGE

FIRE

The chandelier of crow skulls is lit, and we're off. Everyone coming into the big barn skids to a halt on spotting it. Many are intrigued and purr with pleasure, others a little freaked out by its ghoulish glow right at the heart of the action. A few of our more health-and-safety-minded guests – mainly the friends who had their children later in life – are clucking about the proximity of naked flames, ancient beams and soft furnishings.

Every time we have a party, Preds pulls something even more sparkling out of his repertoire of design skills. It's a running (and slightly barbed) joke that his dashing aestheticism is sometimes a *trompe l'œil* deployed to conceal piles of detritus, but today there is no quibble. The barn is looking magnificent. Aside from the candlelit bird bones, there are fairy lights through the ivy and strings of coloured bulbs animating dark corners. Outsized gunnera leaves hang from the eaves, giving the old stone walls a strangely tropical lift. Zinc buckets overflow with wild

flowers, next to sofas and armchairs draped in his extensive collection of Welsh blankets.

Our swallows have fledged and the stage is set for my sort-
of-fiftieth birthday party. 'Sort of' because there are still
four months to go, but I wanted the ease of an al fresco
late-summer do instead of the usual midwinter bash. As
Preds and I share the same birthday, a week short of
Christmas, we've had plenty enough cold, dark celebrations. The last time we lit the crow chandelier was for
Preds' fortieth, two years earlier. To help offset the
December chill, his theme was 'James Bond ski lodge,
Roger Moore era'. We partied through the night in salo-
pettes, wigs, greatcoats and Russian hats.

Today, I'm showing off my birthday present, the sixty-foot swimming pond spooned out of the bottom of our field by a neighbour and his mini-digger. It's been there only three months, but has already sunk into its contours, the frill of plants and clouds of flowers looking like they've been there for years. Many of the afternoon arrivals are jumping in, lobbing beachballs and being pushed around on a sagging lilo. The weather is smiling, and Rhiw Goch sings.

For those not swimming, I've laid a 1966-themed treasure hunt around the gardens and outbuildings, then up the bridleway that climbs Bryn-y-Brain, before bumping back down through the fields. An ulterior motive was to get people to explore the various spaces and find one that they might make their own. Pairing everyone with their optimum spot is the key to a good Rhiw Goch party, and planning this one, we were both taken aback by the variety available.

We've already reclaimed so many corners that were unused by Reg and George. Nibbled out of the field is the pool and, over near the house, a grassy hollow that was once the kitchen midden. We dug out shards of broken crockery and bedsprings, fenced it off, built a stone water trough, planted fruit trees, bushes and the almighty gunnera, and grandly rechristened it *y berllan*, the orchard. Alongside, on the plug of rock where the drovers' track begins its climb, Preds has landscaped its slopes, planted more fruit in the side soils, and carved a sinuous, secretive path through the beech trees to the nant, the stream, trickling down from the spring.

Another addition was forced on us the Christmas before. After a stormy night, we woke to a double calamity: poor Taff, our ailing sheepdog, on his last legs and so too a wartime Nissen hut, ripped free of its moorings and collapsing rustily. We'd talked about getting rid of it, as it blocked the evening summer sun from the back of the house, but had gradually filled it with so much junk that the decision had been quietly shelved. The storm made it for us, and has bequeathed a sunny and prolific veg plot – a *potager*, as Preds likes to think of it.

There are new indoor spaces too. On the side of the house is another stone barn, and beyond that slate steps climb to the old granary, now my workspace. The book-lined study with its wood-burner and wrap-around sound is the realisation of a thirty-year dream; I so wish that Reg and George could see it. Sometimes, when they'd let out every possible room to paying guests, Reg had to sleep on a camp bed in the granary – far less cosy in those days – and in the early years they'd occasionally sit up there, since it has the best view of all over the hills and sanctuary stone. There's also the milking parlour between the big barn and the lawn, which has been reroofed and turned into Preds' plant nursery: a sensual overload of fronds and flowers, chairs and throws, and another wood-burner. Today, for the party, it doubles up as the bar.

Even on a warm summer's day, some prefer to stay in the house. The living room is full of older locals chatting, and some playing Scrabble, both English and Welsh versions, while who knows what is going on in the TV parlour opposite, for the door has been clamped shut all day by the children who have taken it over as their den. The kitchen, of course, is never quiet.

A hog roast is served and the day slides into evening. In the bar, people are cackling as they mix rocket-fuel cocktails, while reggae pulses out of my study, a siren call to the smokers. Around the gardens, Chinese lanterns are lit, the main fire too, instantly drawing a crowd to its flickering dance. I wander over the lane to the camping field to round up any stragglers for the cabaret. The waxing moon, three-quarters full, is rising copper and sultry. Spirits are high.

By the time I get back, the cabaret is about to kick off in the big barn. People are crammed in, catcalling and hollering with laughter, and the only place I can squeeze in is right by the stage. Aside from the 1966 theme, we didn't call the party my fiftieth, though it's quickly obvious that word has gone round, as many of those performing have written songs, sketches and poems in my honour. I'm touched by the sentiments but quietly horrified too, paranoid that people will think I've deliberately positioned myself centre stage to lap it up, like a syphilitic medieval monarch receiving the hosannas of his court. Some of the contributions are predictably queer or smutty; nerves prickle through me as I scan the faces of my family, some of our older neighbours and parents of youngsters present, but all I see is joy and kindness and faces stretched red by drink and laughter.

With the night, all gets blurry. Preds lights the fire in the beacon at the far end of the pool, its flames raised towards the peak of Fron Goch, now a comforting silhouette against the gloaming northern sky. Moths to the flame, a few partygoers drift down. One couple, still in the hot rut of their early courtship, strip off for a swim and then some. We leave them to it, their only instruction not to get any bodily fluids in the water, thank you very much. They're not the only ones; the night spawns a few unanticipated blazes of passion, just as it should. Back in the big barn, I spend a few hazy hours on the decks, and keep dozens dancing. By the time the music stops, it is milky dawn; survivors huddle around the fire, talking trash, drinking tea and fighting sleep. At seven, I am the last man standing. From sponge cake and Scrabble *yn Gymraeg* to starlit narcotic seduction, it has been the day of a hundred and more bespoke parties, Rhiw Goch's infinitely elastic knack.

Before my fiftieth and Preds' fortieth, the last big birthdays celebrated here were Reg's eightieth, in 2007, and George's ninetieth, late the previous year. Although very different occasions from this – a dozen or so for afternoon tea – almost all of the guests from then are enthusiastic regulars at our bashes too. The ease with which we have absorbed

their friends and neighbours is seamless, but slightly odd too. Are we so much their sequel that affection has just seeped effortlessly from their regime to ours? To some of the local ladies of a certain age, the ones who squeeze your thigh after a large gin and tell you how much they '*love* the gays!', I wonder whether we are distinguishable individually at all. Perhaps it is like *Dr Who*: the regenerating queens of Rhiw Goch, that lavender Tardis on the hill.

The only friend of George and Reg's to vanish completely from our radar is a woman who blew into their lives in the mid nineties, when she and her husband moved into a nearby cottage. She quickly became indispensable, running errands and showering them with gifts. Her life was perpetually full of drama, shared as liberally as everything else: sudden diagnoses of life-threatening conditions (which then mysteriously fizzled out), a collapsing marriage, money worries, regular house moves and career changes, even a dead cat who, it transpired, was very much alive. With his bicycle days ending, and his mind starting to slip free of its moorings, George dejectedly chewed over her troubles in his diary, while basking in the floodlights of her attention and changing their wills in her favour.

Reg was never so taken with their *soi-disant* new best friend. Though deeply grateful for the help, he didn't want her to have his beloved house. Penny's arrival in his life, swiftly followed by ours, presented him with the perfect solution. In passing the baton to another couple, especially one that reminded him so much of themselves, he could in some small way heal his own fractured identity with a bequest, a leg-up for the next generation of gay men, and an inheritance far beyond bricks and mortar. He set to making sure it was all official. Though the spell would be just as deeply cast, there was to be no *Howards End* deathbed scribble, all too readily ignored: 'Why, it's only in pencil! I said so. Pencil never counts.'

As with any elderly people of property with no obvious heirs, Reg and George had around them a circle of friends of all intents, from blameless to venal. Most of us, in truth, were a bit of both. There are very few places left as unspoiled as Rhiw Goch, even in mid Wales, and those that are almost never come on the market. The prospect of an original sash window or fireplace can play havoc with those of us so inclined.

To win this unspoken lottery, and without the option of a no publicity box, was overwhelming. I soon learned that I was allowed no reservations about it at all, for people could not bear to hear them. My doubts and fears – of change, of being uprooted from the place I'd *chosen*, of the two of us being forced into intense and isolated codependence – became dark shards of ingratitude that I had no way of processing. If I tried, I was sometimes stopped dead by friends suddenly snapping, 'But for God's sake, it's all right for you: you've inherited *a bloody house*.' It was always the trump card, played not as a flourish but thrown down with brute exasperation.

This was a shock, though it shouldn't have been. Of our many contemporary anxieties, property is by far the most incandescent. We are all consumed by its white heat, however loftily we pretend otherwise. For so many, the housing ladder has vanished from view, and shows little prospect of reappearing. Anything other than an insane and constant acceleration in property prices is presented as the gloomiest of economic news. And for those who do manage to scramble over the line of home ownership, their houses are no longer mere homes; they must be good investments, a pension, a statement, a lifestyle, security, status, the ultimate selfie. Anyone getting an easy ride must learn to deal with the suspicion and envy.

In our first year at Rhiw Goch, the book *Deep Country* by Neil Ansell was published. An account of five years in a cottage in the Welsh mountains, off-grid due to dilapidation rather than eco-design, it is a beguiling tale, particularly of the bird life around him. Some reviewers, though, fastened hawklike on the fact that Ansell paid an annual peppercorn rent of just £100 for the cottage. It's mentioned only once in the book, and is wholly incidental to its content and tone, but to journalists in London, pissing away thousands on a cupboard in Clapham, this was the wildest fantasy of the lot. They probably weren't misjudging their audience's tastes, either.

Though I knew how lucky we'd struck, my darkest dread was being subsumed by a lava flow of Forsteresque fate, as it swept me along and razed my carefully constructed life to the ground. It wasn't friends I needed to talk it through with, but Preds, though I could bear to broach the subject directly with him only once. 'What if I *hate* it?' I finally asked him. He of course assured me that we would therefore find somewhere else; both absolutely meaning it and absolutely not.

*

On the night before Reg and George first saw Rhiw Goch, their then home, the disastrous Penhempen, went up in flames. A clothes horse packed with linen fell on to the fire in the library, igniting immediately. Books, furniture and walls were badly singed before they managed to put the fire out. It was not the only conflagration to occur that week. Three days earlier, George had had 'an explosive showdown' with their problem neighbour, who was trying to barricade their driveway. It was April 1980, and definitely time to go.

Once again, George's dream had turned to smoke. Just before they'd moved into Penhempen, little more than three years earlier, he had chirruped excitedly to his diary, 'Each visit we like the house more. We are to take over the 4 kittens in the barn (they love milk!) A lovely setting and so peaceful!' It wasn't, of course.

The only vehicular access was along a track belonging to the neighbour, whose bungalow was a couple of hundred yards above them on the lane. At first, all had seemed well. It was the winter of 1976–7, and a harsh one, especially after the milder semi-coastal winters at Cefn. On their second day in the new house it started snowing. George records that 'we were snow and icebound the next few days' and that their neighbour often had to 'get me up [the track] with a tow rope with his jeep'. The camaraderie was short-lived.

By the summer, problems with their water supply had become apparent. Water pressure fell from late June, and within a fortnight the supply 'has ceased *completely*'. Having been too busy and too content to write his diary, George took to it again, and in a fiery scrawl detailed the daily problems, and his obsessive checking of tanks, pipes, stopcocks, levels and outflows. Neither could the issue be glossed over to paying guests: toilets blocked, taps barely trickled. On moving to this purportedly grander property, George had decided it was time to upgrade their clientele too. He had been convinced that an old farm would lure in a better class of punter than an old pub, and that they'd also be prepared to pay more. To that end, and after much anguish over the expense, he had taken out six weeks of advertisements in *The Lady* magazine. Subscribers to *The Lady* most certainly expected a flushing lav.

The neighbour soon became the chief culprit in the water saga. The systems were integrated but antiquated, and George grew increasingly certain that they'd sabotaged Penhempen's supply to ensure their own. Despite new pipes and stopcocks, there were further problems the following summer.

Things escalated, and way beyond water. Slanging matches erupted in the lane, cattle and dogs were let loose, solicitors were consulted. The neighbours erected signs ('STRICTLY PRIVATE PROPERTY'; 'KEEP OUT UNLESS AUTHORISED') and demanded that anyone wanting access to Penhempen must first clear it with them. One evening, B&B guests were blockaded in by cars parked deliberately across the track, and the police were called. It was the winter of 1978–9, the coldest for decades. Their central heating system had packed up too and the main fireplace belched smoke into the living room whenever a north wind blew. Three years at Cefn, now three years at Penhempen, and George was house-hunting once again. Reg despaired of them ever finding peace.

The following winter, their friend Pam, in the ancient cruck house that George had so admired back in Darowen, rode to the rescue. She had heard that nearby Rhiw Goch was coming on the market, and although she too was having neighbour problems and was desperate to move, decided that Reg and George's need was greater. She was also keen to have them back in the vicinity.

They were thrilled with their first viewing, and started negotiating on it immediately. George called a smallholding estate agent, to put Penhempen on the market, though he was deeply pessimistic that they would be able to sell. As Daniel, Pam's son, put it to me, 'I remember them saying, "I don't know how we're going to get anyone to buy this place, it's just going to be impossible not to find out about [the neighbour problems]." It was just terrible, ugly.'

All the same, they sold up almost immediately. The buyer, a military man from Surrey, had been searching for a smallholding for months, and seemed unfazed by the belligerent signs and twitching curtains. Throughout the sale process, George fretted daily to his diary that their buyer might bump into the neighbour and, with that, the deal would surely collapse: 'Phoned solicitor – the Colonel can't back out once contracts exchanged (re him meeting D—!)' The neighbour and the Colonel did meet, however. To George's surprise, nothing was said and it made no difference to the sale.

This suggests that while the neighbours' behaviour had been difficult and undeniably provocative, George had also fanned the flames. His obsession became personal and frequently puerile. At times he was spoiling for a fight, even goading the neighbours' teenage daughter into a pointless row. He had delighted too in setting little traps for them, sometimes over the most inconsequential of matters: 'Altercation with D— over plum tree by stream! Got him to tell a lie – he says it is his – he's wrong!'

A key ingredient in the problem was that Penhempen had belonged to the neighbours only a few years earlier. Indeed, it had been in their family for generations, before they had sold up to the people from whom Reg and George had bought it. Often on farms there are two or more houses; in the 1960s, with hill farm incomes perilously low, it had proved irresistible to sell one to some English visitors searching for a holiday home. Disputes had been common, especially when the reality of strangers in the farmyard had become apparent, or the incomers had wanted to live there full-time, or, in Reg and George's case, live there full-time *and* run it as a business.

Penny believes that the core problem was simply homophobia. Reg alluded to that too, and there are a couple of diary entries that point in the same direction. Just before their final Christmas there, George wrote, "Appy 'Arry asked me not to encourage "certain types" to Penhempen! Apart from being a fool he is obviously mad – In a word I told him he was preaching to the converted.' Nothing more explicit than that, though, so if homophobia had been part of the trouble, as would be entirely likely in the late 1970s, it had either washed over George's head or he'd chosen to ignore it.

Most likely, it was the latter, because that was his lifelong strategy in relation to his sexuality. He refused to allow it to bother him, and blanked it out if it was bothering others. One of his regular cycling pals recalled George brazening out numerous awkward situations. 'He just stared these people down,' he said, since he was 'a tough old thing' who was always '"take me as I am" – he didn't care'. 'He couldn't give a shit,' echoes Daniel.

This solid stance, feet planted squarely on the ground, is greatly admirable, and helps to assuage the occasions when it slides into pomposity or petulance. So many gay men learn to become habitual shape-shifters, moulding themselves in an instant to fit any given situation, to not give themselves away. Constantly calibrating the risk of awkwardness or conflict means that their essential flame can become weak, forever flickering in the crosswinds or being blown out altogether. With George, it burned steady and bright, if occasionally a little too hot.

A strong flame sparks other pyrotechnics: not just arguments and tantrums, but volcanic sexual attention and hot-blooded politics. George was prone to the lot; so am I, even if I work hard to suppress it. Perhaps I shouldn't. His flare-ups made for spotlit blazes of passion; when they passed, there might be debris but it was reparable. Those of us more inclined to damp down the flames end up pushing them far underground, where they can do a great deal more damage. Fires in coal seams and peat deposits often smoulder for decades. Far worse than any fleeting conflagration, it is they that render a landscape uninhabitable.

*

Politically, we appear far apart. Reg always loved to mock what he called my 'champagne socialism', and even in his last years, with such truncated powers of speech, he could still get furiously eloquent in defence of Churchill, Thatcher or any member of the royal family. George's politics were equally conservative, with both small and capital 'C'. At Cefn, some B&B regulars came to stay on the way back from an anti-abortion march in London, of which he heartily approved. During the 1978–9 'Winter of Discontent' – their unhappiest at Penhempen – he raged at the trades unions and Labour government. When it finally collapsed, and Margaret Thatcher was elected, he was thrilled: 'Sat up till 5am. Good old Maggie. The country is TORY again, thank the Lord!'

Forty-five miles east of Penhempen, I was also agog at the 1979 election, the first I'd noticed. I was only twelve years old, but watching Mrs Thatcher on the teatime news as she swept into Downing Street, I already didn't believe a word. As she recited St Francis of Assisi's famous prayer, I noticed that she snuck a look down at her notes to make sure that she was not about to mix truth with despair, nor substitute error for hope. (That was all to come.) She had been in power for just a couple of hours, but she clearly represented everything I was growing to loathe about suburban Middle England: its hypocrisy and conformity, its penny-pinching mindset and purse-lipped world view.

I was thrilled that she and I were already sworn enemies, for I had also just been blooded in the fire of democracy. To coincide with the election, a teacher at school had organised a mock version. In the wake of the Jeremy Thorpe trial and its salacious tales of dead dogs and gay sex, no one had wanted to be the Liberal candidate, so I'd volunteered. Even at twelve, I was regularly smacked around as a poof; my reputation could sink no lower. Although I was beaten by two different Conservatives and the National Puss Party, swotting up on my adopted party's manifesto had convinced me that I was indeed a Liberal, and before long I had joined the party.

In 2015, eight general elections later, I was one of only eight principal challengers across Britain who couldn't beat an incumbent Liberal. After five years as junior members of the coalition government, the LibDems were annihilated, losing 49 out of 57 seats. Not Ceredigion, though, the coastal seat centred on nearby Aberystwyth. Inheriting Rhiw Goch gave me enough of a financial cushion to spend two unpaid years as the Plaid Cymru candidate there, in a seat the party had held only a decade earlier. In the 2017 election, two years after I failed by a margin of three thousand votes, Plaid did indeed regain it, wiping the Liberals from the Welsh political map for the first time since 1859.

That their generosity enabled my brief political career as a Welsh republican would have tickled Reg, but horrified George. At Penhempen, he proudly recorded voting against devolution for Wales in the 1979 referendum, and celebrated the result: 'A massive No!' Neither was there room for any nuance about Meibion Glyndŵr, whose holiday cottage arson campaign he kept a fanatical eye on. The neighbour feud only intensified his suspicions towards the Welsh, and when, before dawn on a Sunday morning in late March 1980, forty people were arrested in a sweep of raids, house arrests and roadblocks across Wales, George was jubilant: 'Arson thugs rounded up at last! They must be guilty judging by the number of complaints about police tactics!!'

They weren't though – not one. The head of CID later said that 'the intelligence wasn't correct', because 'from the absolute beginning there was no evidence against any person I questioned – they were absolutely innocent'.

Only one person was ever successfully prosecuted for the fires, and that was thirteen years later. Over two hundred cottages went up in flames during that time, although some transpired to be insurance fraud by opportunist owners, and some put-up jobs by the security services themselves, to discredit the cause of Welsh nationalism. The nearest blaze to Rhiw Goch, three miles away, fell neatly into both categories. There were huge local headlines at the time that sinister Meibion Glyndŵr had slunk into the area, but soon the truth emerged that the petrol was poured and the match struck by the holiday home's owner, a serving policeman.

Rhiw Goch passed from two loyalists of the Conservative and Unionist Party to two members of Plaid Cymru, a party with Welsh self-determination and 'community socialism' as its constitutional aims. On paper, we couldn't be further apart, yet to my amazement, George recorded voting LibDem in 2001 and then at the next general election four years later, he voted Labour. Reg sometimes voted LibDem too and, much to my surprise (and discomfort), so did I in 2017, as part of a tactical vote swap. Politically, having clung to opposite edges of the bed, the springs went and we all rolled into the sagging middle.

George's political mellowing was considerable. His high Toryism in the 1970s, though invariably expressed with consummate politeness, was rigid, and anyone who failed to live up to the exacting standards of a self-made man was quickly dismissed. In November 1976, just before they left Cefn for Penhempen, he wrote, 'Last Sat. took in [X] & the 2 children evicted from "Jim" drug pusher's wife's cottage. Grave mistake – got them out on ~~Tues~~ Wednesday. He is a <u>BUM</u> using the children as a <u>FRONT</u>. Living on US!' He never recorded what became of them.

Such stringent ethics were not universally applied, since George was quite content to swing the lead if it suited. Shortly after moving, he had a small hernia operation, and was delighted to realise that he was eligible for sickness benefit. He thought nothing of accepting this while still continuing to work, or of pushing Reg into claiming unemployment benefit when the B&B was quiet. A year into life at Rhiw Goch, he was appalled to receive notification from British Telecom that they would soon have to share their phone line with a nearby farm, 'because there are no spare wires in the locality and you were the most recently connected subscriber in the district'. George bombarded them with letters and phone calls of protest, insisting that he had an ailment that could cause serious problems at any moment: 'I live in an isolated spot. I have no neighbours. I have no-one to drive me to hospital in case of emergency,' he wrote, describing their phone line as 'my one source of comfort in my situation'. He finished plaintively: 'over the years, my doctors have told me that I must avoid worry or stress'. BT backed down.

Another diary entry leaps out for its uncharacteristically savage language: 'Monday 12 December 1977: Reg reading about Duchess of Warwick (socialist whore).' In the first few years of the twentieth century, this compromised and complicated woman had been a pioneer of the Social Democratic Foundation, one of the forerunners of the Labour Party. In that capacity she had worked alongside Edward Carpenter (1844–1929), the great queer rural hero and pioneer for us all. For a quarter of a century, he and George Merrill (1866–1928) had lived as a couple in the village of Millthorpe, near Sheffield, running a market garden. Their home had been a magnet for Carpenter's devotees, especially the succession of men inspired by his visionary writing about human sexuality, society, socialism and paganism. It always struck me that Carpenter, a passionate advocate of nudity, fresh air, outdoor pursuits, healthy eating and the worship of athletic young men, had much in common with George, despite their apparently antithetical politics.

Carpenter's cast-iron strictures became generously elastic when faced with a handsome flirt, and so did George's. Twenty years after booting out the '<u>BUM</u> using the children as a <u>FRONT</u>', he gave sanctuary to another young man, and allowed him to use their address to sign on. On a few occasions, when the lad was travelling, George even signed the fortnightly benefit claim on his behalf, so that he could pretend that he was there and available for work. In return, there was massage ('Aromatherapy! with Ylang Ylang! – super!'), and when the young man's girlfriend was back down south, there was sex. A symbol for this peppers his diary entries through the 1990s, appearing with impressive regularity, and an assortment of accomplices.

'Oh, George and his massages – it was always the same. And he'd come to me afterwards and say, "How could I not? They are *so* pretty."' With that, Reg rolled his eyes at me, and laughed. In truth, he was far more bothered about the benefit fraud than the slippery bunk-ups. George's excuse could be mine too, because when it comes to inveigling handsome young men back home for a massage and whatever follows, I'm an old hand. It was my regular booty trap in all-nighters and squat parties of the nineties. Some bulging-eyed beauty, a little strung-out as a narcotic comedown threatened, could invariably be tempted back by the promise of tea, a smoke, gentle tunes and an oily rub-down.

George was no less methodical in luring his prey, even without the stimulants and poor lighting that I depended on.

When he and Reg died, I commemorated them in the *Guardian*'s 'Other Lives' obituary section. It's a sweet feature, for everyday life stories are often more remarkable than those of the cosseted or famous. Had the *Daily Telegraph* – their paper of choice, as much for its superior fire-lighting qualities as its politics – run something comparable, I would have tried them first, but it wasn't an option.

Both of them, and George in particular, would have loved having an obituary in a national newspaper, and been astounded by how far the online version travelled across blogs and social media accounts. I can't deny, though, that I adore the irony of Reg and George, who had buckled at the knee for Margaret Thatcher and never got up again, being commemorated in the *Guardian*, a paper they had almost certainly never bought.

SUMMER

Taking a cue from his favourite Victorian novels, George would often summarise a page of his diary under a capitalised headline at the top of the page. Instead of 'HA! A SURPRISE INTRUDER' and the like, we have the more prosaic concerns of 'WEIGHTLIFTING BEGINS' and 'EASTER – SNOW, SLEET & SUNBATHING!' In August 1983, there is a surprise heading: 'FIRST SEABATHE IN 10 YEARS'.

I assumed that George would share my passion for open-water swimming, if not in rivers and lakes then certainly on the long, sandy beaches only half an hour away from both Cefn and Rhiw Goch. Yet there is no mention of ever visiting them in the first decade of life in Wales. In their previous life on the sunny south coast, beaches had loomed large, those on Purbeck in particular. It was there that George had taken Reg on their first Bournemouth date in 1952, and it's easy to see why. Beaches are liminal and liberated spaces, open to all yet apart from reality, where both layers and inhibition are readily shed.

It was a routine he returned to intermittently over the next fifty years, particularly after moving to Rhiw Goch. Although the oldest of the four of us on arrival here (sixty-three, to Reg's fifty-three, my forty-four and Preds' thirty-six), he was by far its most libidinous recent resident. When we first moved in, I spent days with his photo albums and diaries, marvelling at the succession of lads cluttering George's second spring, his deferred adolescence. It was a spring that melted into a long summer, one he fought like a tiger to prevent ever ending.

On Tywyn beach that broiling August Sunday were Reg and George, their friend Pam and her son Daniel. 'Beautiful hot day, cloudless blue sky. We all had a marvellous time. Four times in the sea!' wrote George. Daniel, tall and handsome and about to turn sixteen, was back from boarding at the Royal Ballet School. It was thanks to him

that George had rediscovered cycling earlier that year. Over the Easter holidays, the two of them had been out on rides every single day; within six weeks of getting back into the saddle, George wrote, 'Feel very fit and my legs very muscular & strong.'

The summer of 1983 was a proverbial scorcher: 'horseflies like dragons! Wonderful tan!' The week before the first trip to the beach, Daniel had offered to teach George some weightlifting techniques. No persuasion was needed; George whisked him off to Newtown and without hesitation blew twenty quid on a pair of dumbbells. They returned to Rhiw Goch for the first lesson, splayed out on the parched back lawn, George in just the tiniest of pants. There were more beach sessions and daily weights and cycle rides, all lovingly captured on camera.

For a couple of years, George's diary is full only of bikes and the boy, and when they coincide, he is in heaven. It was far beyond just physical attraction. George's complete focus on Daniel sprang from an adolescent desire for exclusivity, to be the very best of wrestling/weightlifting/sunbathing/cycling pals, and it was mutual. 'He was made of steel,' says Daniel now, 'his constitution – and his mind – were just incredible. On our bikes, he was always leading the way and I was trying to keep up. And I was seventeen, and the dancer!' This Spartan physicality – 'an understanding that it is not just about being fit, but taking it to another dimension of artistry' – was an ideal that united them both, even when one was building a body on the cusp of adulthood, the other fighting a furious rearguard action against its depreciation.

The bicycle was George's time machine:

> Riding to Abergwydol this morning ... I was, for a fraction of a second, 18 years old and slogging against a headwind on the Moor of Rannoch in Scotland (or was it Dartmoor?). The wonderful feeling of freedom was just like old times.

As a later bike buddy had it, 'That's the thing about cycling: it does appeal to something from your childhood, it really does. Some cyclists push themselves, become mile-eaters, have set goals and become totally obsessed. Others love it for the sheer joy of doing it, and the fact that it brings you closer to your child nature. George was on both sides of the camp.'

Delayed adolescence is a common theme in many gay stories. Throughout his long life, George had a few goes at it. None was as powerful as that which erupted from the intoxicating freedom he felt on their move to Rhiw Goch, combined with Daniel's puppyish attention. Like many of his generation, his youth had been curtailed by war, and beyond that by an onerous sense of responsibility to make his way in the new world rising from the ruins. He had always been the mature one, the responsible one, the one to check the paperwork and do the sums. On retiring, he could let rip.

Another sign of a second (or perhaps third) youth is that this is the era most faithfully chronicled in his diaries, that most teenage of hobbies. Once Daniel left to work abroad, the entries become increasingly sporadic, until they dry up completely for a couple of years. He returned for a brief visit at the end of 1984, and in a Christmas Eve entry that says as much between the lines as within them, George wrote:

> Daniel looks very well and relaxed – he is a lovely boy – Oh! to be 17 again – ! Anyhow, God has given me health and happiness in life and a good and constant partner in dearest Reg. No man could ask for more than I have received in this life or been happier – The bicycle has been a great little vehicle (in both senses!) in my life since I began again on 18th March last year and I bless it.

Those two heady summers of beach trips with Daniel created a blueprint for George. Over the next fifteen years, the spirit of their generous comradeship and genuine mutual admiration was pared by sheer repetition into a hard-boiled formula for seduction. Should you be the young man plucked from his cycling groups, you received the lavish attention, the personal tour of showpiece bike routes, the food, the wine, the Mahler, the massage and – if the Lycra shorts stayed stubbornly on – the beach trip. If all went to plan, George got out his red pen and drew the magic symbol in his diary.

Again, my hauteur is filtered through the scarlet gauze of intimate recognition. At dawn on the very same summer days that saw George herding men into his honeypot in the sand dunes, I was leading some ragged beauty from the dance floor towards my sunrise pulling bench, overlooking the lake in a Birmingham park. It too was a well-grooved route, precisely chosen for its seclusion yet optimum view, its weeping willows and musky flowers, the burble of a nearby brook and the bats that swooped their finale as the sun inched upwards directly ahead. There, I'd reel him in with well-worn patter of urban wilderness and pagan wildness. Had I been able, I'd have wheeled down some speakers and a mix-tape to seal the deal; a static Brummie version of David Hockney's choreographed musical car odysseys through the California deserts, an art form that surely began life as a seduction technique.

The same, perhaps, but with one overwhelming differ-ence: in those suddenly far-off pre-millennium days, I was passing thirty, *and George eighty*. He took raging against the dying of the light to new heights; his focus and effort were immense. For a while, the lupine behaviour became his habitual setting. Among the many testimonies of George as an erudite and courtly neighbour, one stood out, from a man of my age, remembering when he first lived here in his twenties: 'I used to go up to Rhiw Goch, mainly to see Reg. I loved chatting with Reg. I never really got on with George; he was always friendly, but a little . . . *lewd* in a way. I always felt more uncomfortable around him.'

There are patterns that so many men of his generation fell foul of. Already into middle age just as the 1960s started swinging, they were eager for their fair share, but unsure how to obtain it. The only available way, and the only way they'd been schooled in, was to misuse status or power. All too often, misuse led to abuse.

There was a lot of it about, and a great many blind eyes being turned. On that same 'Beautiful hot day' on the beach in August 1983, while George and Daniel posed and grinned and dived like dolphins, I too was sixteen and by the River Avon in Evesham, God-bothering sunbathers. I was at an evangelical Christian summer camp nearby, and we'd been sent on an outreach session amongst the sinners basking in the meadows. 'After a bad start, the Lord really guided me around some lovely, receptive people,' my diary blithely records, which I think translates as 'not quite as many told me to piss off as I'd been expecting (and some of the men were *gorgeous*)'.

At the camp, I was one of half a dozen teenage boys sleeping in a barn dormitory, overseen by a forty-year-old bachelor who'd been mustard keen to volunteer as our warden. He was the shiniest of them all, with a huge, leather-bound Bible by his bed, full of colour-coded sticky notes and passages neatly highlighted in different fluorescent pens. As we were baked awake every sweltering morning, he'd catch each of us hobbling off to the toilet, tousle-haired and trying to hide a hard-on, in order to 'start the day with a hug for Jesus!' It always went on a few seconds too long, and invariably involved a little light frottage for Jesus too.

*

In the middle of another fierce heatwave over thirty years later, I decide to beat the bounds of Rhiw Goch, as they appear on an 1845 tithe map. The farm was just shy of a hundred acres at the time, its lowest point at three hundred feet above sea level, its highest nearly a thousand.

At quarter to six on an already muggy morning, Taff and I slide out under a sky the colour of apricots and down to the stream in the field below. I've waited for a dry spell, as two-thirds of the bounds to be beaten are streambeds. Though the water is low, it is still a challenge: rocks are slippery and fallen timber ubiquitous. Fences too: new pine posts and taut wires are just the latest addition. Ghost borders, long obliterated, live on in twists of old wire. Rusted cables sprout from tree trunks, thick coils of surplus fencing curl in forgotten corners. Sagging across streams is the party bunting of the Welsh uplands: old barbed wire with tufts of fleece snagged in its teeth.

We struggle up from the stream and into the farm's old corner field, one that I've never been in before. On the tithe map, this is Cae Clippiau, the 'Field of Slopes', now a Christmas-tree plantation. The rising sun backlights the willowherb, pink and profuse on neglect, and a sandy soil teeming with rabbits. We cross the lane and climb the flank of Bryn-y-Brain towards Y Ffridd, an eight-acre semicircle of rough pasture enclosed from the common. I've never been here either, and it takes my breath away: literally, as it is a five-hundred-foot climb and the heat is rising, but figuratively too, for the sudden encounter with our bygone perimeter wall is strangely moving.

In Snowdonia or the Brecon Beacons, this drystone wall would be impeccable: a jigsaw of boulders painstakingly restored to fuel the illusion of timelessness. Here, far from national park sensibilities, the stones are smashed, the wall in a state of collapse and long usurped by barbed-wire fences. At over nine hundred feet, the top of Y Ffridd was the summit of the farm. Looking far down the thistly slopes to the stream where I first began my walk, I am hit by the realisation of what a tough old crust this was to tease a living from. The soil is thin, acidic and prone to mud, and of the twenty fields, only one could be described as level.

In 1845, when the map was drawn, the landowners of Rhiw Goch were a Shropshire squirearchy, and their tenants a pair of bachelor brothers, Evan and David Anwyl. Relatives of theirs farmed nearby, and Anwyl is still one of the surnames of the area today. Evan and David were here for the rest of the nineteenth century, farming their slopes in the customary small-scale mixed pattern of the day: the most sheltered fields near the house for growing arable crops and vegetables, the livestock in the higher pastures beyond in the summer, and down at the bottom of the farm in the winter. Their mother lived with them until her death in the 1860s, together with a succession of maids and young servant-farmhands, never more than one of each at a time. Compared with many of the nearby farms, Rhiw Goch was never a large household.

The farm's freehold was sold from one estate to another in 1911, having grown thanks to the enclosure of a further twenty acres of wiry pasture from common land towards the top of Bryn-y-Brain. The 116-acre holding remained intact until its sale after the Second World War. Between then and Reg and George's arrival thirty years later, fields were parcelled off and sold in chunks. Most ended up as part of larger holdings owned by a branch of the Bebb family – another big local name, and a famous one too in Wales. One of their many prolific cousins, Ambrose Bebb, best captured this place. In 1941, he published a double diary that describes it in detail: one half his own account of the previous year, the other[4] a creative imagining of 1841 as extrapolated from the correspondence and notes of his great-great-uncle William Bebb, a near neighbour of Rhiw Goch.

In 1841, just before the tithe map was drawn, times were bleak: the Hungry Forties. On top of rural depopulation and economic stagnation, there was widespread political, cultural and religious upheaval. Reform of the Poor Laws meant that the spectre of the workhouse hung over the countryside. Many people, especially from this corner of mid Wales, were choosing to cut their losses and start again in America; in this account, William Bebb was agonising over the possibility himself. Letters exhorted him to join the exodus, and in 1847, he did.

During another hot July, as recorded in his own 1940 diary, Ambrose Bebb visited the area for a few days. He stayed at his cousin's farm – latterly Penny and David's – and was enchanted by it all:

> This is a perfectly peaceful place, awash with the burble and chatter of flowing streams. All about me are verdant seas of fern, wooded glens, small random hamlets, shepherds climbing and farm girls calling after their dogs and sheep. Just as it has always been! O, how agreeable it all is!

To Bebb, an incurably romantic nationalist, this patch was the very essence of 'dearest Wales', that 'restored in me a lost vitality'. Out on a walk one day, the sight of the tenant

[4] The two diaries have been translated into English and published under the title of *A Welsh Hundred* (trans. Marc K. Stengel, Authorhouse, 2011).

farmer and his adult son at Rhiw Goch gathering the hay only inflamed his rhapsody:

> such a charming scene! Here, my fellow countrymen, is your genuine birthright in all its glory . . . your throne and your consolation with which to endure the interminable perfidy arrayed against you. My Wales, my own people . . . I love you beyond the power of words to say.

Hindsight can be horrible. Not long after the war, that same farmer's son at Rhiw Goch hanged himself in the ash tree opposite, aged thirty-five. His father went mad with grief and left the area. The estate decided to sell up, precipitating the farm's ultimate break-up and decline. And as I beat the bounds down from the top of Y Ffridd, throughout the huge panorama before me there is no one to be seen. There rarely is. No shepherds climbing, nor farm girls calling; just me and a chorus of ghosts.

From the bottom of the slope, it is streambeds all the way back to the start. The dog and I follow the water downhill as it gathers momentum across Y Rhos, 'the Heath', the field I would most like to have back, for its springs would make a wonderful pool. I am desperate for a dip, and that is coming, down at the bottom of the beech wood, where the stream joins the river. The corn mill just downstream is now a holiday home, lived in for one week a year, if that, and by the head of the old mill race is a pool deep enough for a wallow in the trout-brown cold. Lying with my head in a rocky spout, I daydream to the river gurgling around me and the sun-flicker on the canopy above. As ever, the water has brought me back.

Over the lane, and the last stretch along the bottom of Cae Dan y Tŷ, the 'Field below the House', as lovely as ever. At the foot of the waterfall gully, I quit the stream and pull up through the wood where my kites once nested, and home. Beating the bounds of 1845, even at a lethargic pace, has taken just over three hours. On today's boundaries, to walk around the edge of our field and garden, the spring and the nant, it would take a leisurely ten minutes.

Cae Dan y Tŷ was the last field to go. The decline was steady and swift from the 1951 sale of Rhiw Goch: house, barns and 116 acres to a local businessman for £1,000. The fifties and sixties were lean times for upland Wales, when many smaller farms died, their land sold off to wealthier neighbours, the houses either abandoned, sold or rented out at a pittance, often to those from England. Many became holiday cottages, though a growing trickle of urban émigrés were making it a full-time move. Amongst them was the tenant farmer installed at Rhiw Goch by the new owners, an eccentric Midlander named Len who'd arrived in the area with just a cart and donkey to his name. To pay his way, he kept chickens and a few cows, taking the eggs up to a communal collection point a couple of miles away, while the milk was whisked away by a tanker from the Milk Marketing Board.

By the time the house was next on the market, in 1972, the accompanying farmland had shrivelled to twenty-three acres. The new owner, a London metal trader, paid £5,200 for it, but never lived there. He rented it out for a while to a Buddhist monk, and then used it as an occasional holiday home, and as a place to plunder. In his eight years, he flogged off most of the remaining fields, remortgaged what was left and won planning permission to convert the house into holiday flats – something that fortunately never came to fruition. He applied to build an adjacent bungalow too, though that was refused, twice.

Selling up to Reg and George in 1980, he made a handsome profit, as they paid £35,000 for the dilapidated house and one remaining field. He tried to sell them Cae Dan y Tŷ separately, for another £5,000, which they initially accepted. Completion was conditional on the farmer with grazing rights quitting it by the end of the following April; he didn't, much to George's relief. Although he loved 'our waterfall', and showed it off to every visitor, by the time the next spring came round, George was far happier to get his £500 deposit back; 'we are off the hook', he was happy to note.

Ironically, three decades of post-war decline saved the house. Had it continued as a farm, and perhaps even expanded, it is almost certain that the outhouses, including the original longhouse dwelling, would have been demolished. Instead of the old barn, with its medieval timbers and thick stone walls, there would be metal pens and aluminium sheds. In place of gardens and greenery, there would be tarmac and concrete.

When Reg and George moved in, the rot seemed terminal. The house was a mess, render was falling off the front, and inside was filthy and damp. The outside was even worse. Apart from the small walled enclosure at the front, there was no garden. So as the farm borders contracted, the garden pushed back, out into the paddock and field. Brambles and nettles needed clearing, fences sorting and flowerbeds digging, but their joy at being there made the work seem easy. Reg was thrilled to be back amongst the old crowd, and George ecstatic to have escaped Penhempen. They'd left there in July 1980, but could not complete on Rhiw Goch until September, so took a rented cottage in the middle of Darowen to tide them over. The hiatus there proved to be one of their happiest times of all.

It was a summer in sweet limbo: no real responsibility, no guests to cater for, just freedom and excited anticipation of what would come next. They'd often leave Darowen and walk over to Rhiw Goch with the dogs and, if it was empty, do a bit of gardening or clearing. One day, they tried the door and found it unlocked, so started to clear inside as well. They moved in officially on the second Monday of September, with the help of neighbours. The following day, they took delivery of three stray kittens, and rounded it off – if I'm interpreting George's diary correctly – naked in the garden: 'Gardened & pottered & had a pink Bath (in the Grotty!).' Eight years and three houses since first moving to Wales, Reg and George were finally home.

The gardens at Rhiw Goch had to be created from scratch. Reg put in hours of digging and landscaping; George planted a rose bush and joined the Gardeners' Book Club. Roses were always his favourites; he'd read up on the latest greenfly or blackspot treatment and loved the job of spraying. When they went visiting, he would take a single rose to be presented with a flourish to the lady of the house. In 2002, George mentioned to his new best friend, the lady of perpetual drama, that he and Reg had been together fifty years. She seized on it as a project, and persuaded George to plant a rose bed in celebration, starting with the dusky pink floribunda known as Happy Anniversary.

The flower best associated with Reg is the pelargonium, the potted red bloom often called a geranium. Every year, the old Welsh system of transhumance – moving livestock between the winter hendre and the summer hafod – was replayed at Rhiw Goch, but in scarlet flowers. At the end of May, when the possibility of frosts had finally passed, the great switch took place. A dozen or so vintage pots, having overwintered in bedrooms, were hauled out and lined up along the front wall, as if Cath Kidston had designed a shooting gallery.

So many people told Reg how much they loved to see the display as they drove past that it became a crucial focus for him, a semaphore signal to the world that all was well, even when it really wasn't. Inevitably, gardening as demonstration sport, keeping up appearances, became increasingly important as he and George grew frailer, so while the out-of-sight gardens at the back went quietly to seed, all was kept tidy out front for the benefit of the passing world.

Preds kept the pots going for our first few years, though gradually wilder planting took over. The top of the wall is now a fiesta of Mexican fleabane and sedum succulents, above a pile-up of ox-eye daisies, acid-green spurge, fiery montbretia and valerian, white foxgloves, and bushes of rosemary and thyme. Best is the crabapple tree that he planted by the front path. I love that it's dullest in summer, and dazzling elsewise: pouting pink and cream in spring, tigerish in autumn, and at its very best on a cold winter morning when frost glitters on the coral baubles of fruit.

His cycle of wonder keeps coming all year. Colour too, though his signature flowers are almost all monochrome: the avenue of creams and whites between the house and big barn, and the purple-black velvet of irises and opium poppies that bookend it. For Preds, the definitive bloom is not even a flower, but his beloved blowsy green mats of mind-your-own-business. The day we moved in, he tucked a few sprigs into the paths around the back door; it has spread to plug cracks and cloak stones as if it's been here for ever. A native of Corsica and Sardinia, mind-your-own-business is wholly at home on the slate and stone of Wales: a gift of grey-and-green camo fatigues from the freedom fighters of another place elbowed to the margins.

My summer flower, one I barely knew before moving here, is the ephemeral harebell. The five-petalled corolla, a pentagram in papery denim, appears deceptively delicate; it thrives in brutalised hedgerows and neglected banks. Its sudden appearance in mid July represents the apex of high summer, even though – and this has always slightly spooked me – the Welsh for July is Gorffennaf, from *gorffen haf*, 'the end of summer'. A perfect hit comes when the surrounding countryside has been bleached flaxen by a heatwave, for the golden grasses and 'harebell's hazure sky' (John Clare) are made for each other.

For most gardeners, and Preds is one, the challenge is to sustain pleasure in all four quarters of the year. For some – Vita Sackville-West at Sissinghurst the most celebrated example – there is a clear zenith to the calendar, as brief as a couple of days, towards which everything is aimed and all else subordinate. This annual orgasm is worth every shred of restraint for the other three hundred and sixty-odd days; indeed, the denial becomes an integral part of the pleasure. Were I a gardener, this would be my way too – just as had I lived under rationing, I'd have soon forsaken marge and jam scraped transparently thin through the week, preferring dry crusts or even an empty belly so that for one weekly splurge, I could gorge on fresh bread slathered in generous slabs of butter, jam and cheese. In all earthly pleasures, whether food, flowers or fornication, this is the way of the glutton and the slattern.

On the lane above the house is a hedgebank that plays this game, peaking vividly and so very briefly just after the summer solstice. Five foot high, around seventy yards long, it is inaccessible to even the springiest lamb, and so escapes uneaten. Watching it flower in sequence is like waiting for the stars to align: the fleshy spring peas, honking trumpets of foxglove and Wimbledon-white stitchwort all caught

just before they fade, as the sunshine glare of hawkweed, candy-pink herb Robert and electric-blue pompoms of Devil's-bit scabious scamper up to join them. Cushioned by ferns and daisies, sorrel and yarrow, the rainbow hedge-bank is as transient as summer lightning.

Or a shooting star, perhaps: seen best on August nights, lying in the field under the Perseid meteor showers. Most of my summer pleasures come from the day's margins. There are the full-moon swims, slicing black ink into ripples of silver, five-o'clock dog walks through rose-pink morning mists, and, at the other end of the long day, heady scents of flowers and food on the evening air, or a sudden kiss of vestigial warmth from the stones of the old barn an hour or more after sunset. For a week or so in July, there's a spectacular near-death simulation available. Time it right and a post-dinner stroll up the drovers' track is rewarded by the rays of the setting sun flooding down a hundred-yard tunnel of hazels, rendering us light-blind and groping through a golden fug. A few weeks later, and the twilight stroll takes us along the lane to a deserted outbuilding where the barn owls nest. With luck, we're rewarded by the sight of the fledglings' flight school around the adjacent field, swoops of snow in the gathering shadows.

In preferring to dabble in the edges of summer, I am clearly no George, basting himself bronze under a hot day's high noon. I envy him his sun worship, coddled in the heat of war and simmered on the beaches of Dorset, and envy too his and Reg's focus on making hay while the sun shone. In its 1980s heyday, the Rhiw Goch B&B thrummed like a machine through the summer holidays: Reg cleaning, cooking and washing, George front of house and keeping his ribald opinions of guests to his diary.

The enthusiasm in their visitors' book is heartfelt and far beyond the usual platitudes that we've all scribbled under the watchful eye of mine host at checking-out time: 'Out of this world' (British), 'Best food since I've been in GB' (American), 'Stayed the second time and will come again and again' (Swiss), 'In Paradiso Sumus' (British), 'The loveliest B'n'B ever!' (USA), 'And a so delicious cooking!' (French), 'How can we thank you – a real privilege to be here' (British), 'An island of peace and kindness!' (German), 'Tutto veramente eccellente' (Italia), 'By far the best in every way' (Irish), 'Never been so reluctant to go!' (NZ), 'Cartrefol dros ben!' (Cymraes).

Rhiw Goch perfectly honed the skills they'd developed in the two previous B&Bs. Penhempen was grander, but that wasn't what their visitors were after. George scaled down his pretensions too: there was no more advertising in *The Lady*. Neither was there ever any in *Gay Times*, which in the eighties had the holiday market to itself, and lucratively so. Every month, dozens of its pages comprised adverts for gay-run or gay-friendly B&Bs and hotels throughout Britain and beyond. Such a directory was essential, for there was no guarantee of acceptance within mainstream options. It was nothing unusual to be turned abruptly away from places with 'Vacancies' signs in the front window, even to have the door slammed in our faces.

Many of the adverts in *GT* were for rural getaways, often run by hearty lesbians. Rhiw Goch would have fitted perfectly, but, for whatever reason, the idea of courting the gay market was never explored – indeed, from the visitors' book, it appears that they had very few same-sex couples as guests. They far preferred to pitch themselves as 'The Old Welsh Farmhouse in the Hills', as their promotional leaflet put it. It was produced in 1981, ready for their first summer season at Rhiw Goch. Printed on mustard-coloured paper, a sepia photo of the house fills the front cover. The old-fashioned feel seeps inside to the text:

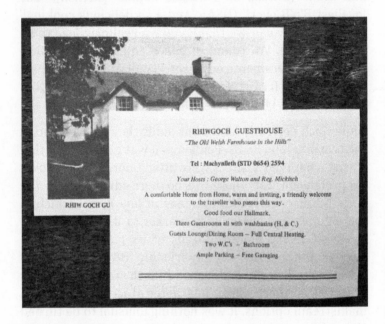

It looks and sounds more 1961 than 1981, and therein lay their market: nostalgics and traditionalists, albeit with a socially contemporary edge. Their guests' style bible may have been that winsome sensation of the day, Edith Holden's *The Country Diary of an Edwardian Lady*, but amongst their most loyal regulars it was the women wearing the trousers, at least metaphorically. Many were dressed in the frills and flounces of Laura Ashley, *The Country Diary* brought to life – and aptly so, for Rhiw Goch lies midway between Ashley's first shop in Machynlleth and her factory at Carno. If zeitgeist is place as well as moment, Reg and George hit both.

For those so inclined, the B&B was a perfect fit. They didn't mind the smallish bedrooms, the paper-thin partition between the toilets, nor the notices telling them not to flush at night. They excused the all-in-it-together atmosphere, and even found that it enhanced the experience. Lasting friendships were forged around the shared dining table and in the armchairs by the fire.

Inevitably, August is our busiest month for visitors too. The house buzzes with life, though as we once again run the hoover round and change the beds, we have been known to mutter icy thoughts that the main difference between now and thirty years ago is that Reg and George earned good money from the annual onslaught. They even made old friends pay to stay, and would perhaps have tried the same had any family members ever visited. They never did, though, not once, in all the forty years that Reg and George lived in Wales, and in that one fact is perhaps an indication of the single-mindedness with which they pursued their new life. Preds and I could never be so ruthless, I'm glad to say, though that is at least partly thanks to their legacy.

For all the outdoor dinners and moonlit swims, the easy days and hazy nights, I sometimes find the weight of expectation on summer overwhelming, especially once the schools break up and a quick trip into town becomes a study of family tensions in matching cagoules. An area that relies so heavily on tourism can kid itself for much of the year that it is economically and culturally sustainable, but the illusion is left for dead by the thundering juggernaut of the summer holidays.

I'm starting to see that the Welsh are right: for me too, July is *gorffen haf*, the end of summer. August has long been one of my least favourite months, plagued often with illness, both of body and spirit. In three of the last five Augusts, I've lost the hearing in my one good ear and been plunged into a dark and lonely tunnel, even worse when we are full with guests. Trees look tired, and the landscape listless, particularly along the lanes, where towering walls of bramble and bracken begin to collapse beneath their own sodden weight. I wait for the golden sound to cut through my deafness, and then it comes. Clarity and September are calling.

SOUTH

Within two months of visiting George in Bournemouth in the summer of 1952, Reg had joined him. For the first time in his life, he was leaving London, and that made him very nervous indeed, but the war-torn capital was hard work. Early that winter, the city was choked by a smog that killed thousands, and Reg knew he had made the right decision, joining the man he loved in the pine-scented sea breezes of the resort that liked to style itself the 'queen of the south coast'.

Since its foundation in the early nineteenth century, Bournemouth has always fancied itself as a cut above. The town's commissioners fought hard to prevent the railway coming, and when it finally did arrive – decades late – in 1870, they unsuccessfully demanded that the railway companies stop selling cheap day return tickets, as this was bringing entirely the wrong class of people to town. Whelk stalls were banned on the front until the Second World War, and slot machines from the pier until well into the

1960s. A letter to the *Bournemouth Times*, from just before the war, captures the town's eternal harrumph: 'Yes, Bournemouth has certainly changed and if August Bank Holiday 1938 was anything to go by a good many residents must have emphatically decided that change has not been for the better.' In Bournemouth, it never is.

George had arrived at the beginning of 1949. Stanley helped him find a base, a grimy but spacious brick hut above a builder's yard, reached via a steep flight of steps. The two of them swabbed it clean, painted it inside and out and brought in a few sticks of Utility furniture. On the gable end of the building, facing St Swithun's Road, Stanley care-

fully painted the name 'GARRET' in the centre of the whitewashed wall, and the words 'Photographic Studio' repeated in a sloping modernist font either side of the door. The business, the planning of which had been so abruptly halted by the war, was finally born.

As would be seen a quarter of a century later with the B&Bs in Wales, George was punctilious in his marketing of the venture, and for the minimum outlay. The Garret's bright white frontage and clean black lettering stood out from the post-war clutter and were visible from the approach to Bournemouth Central station. At street level, he built a wooden noticeboard, headed with 'GARRET STUDIO' and enclosed by glass doors, to showcase the studio's best work, including a rotating 'Picture of the Week'. It was a nod to Hollywood – or at the very least Pinewood – in a drab, ration-book streetscape.

Inside, the theme of classy modernity continued, garnished with just the right amount of bohemianism – enough to create an ambience of wonder and slight dislocation from the world beyond, but not so much as to alarm potential customers. Using curtains to screen off his living quarters, George created a large studio space, which doubled up as a venue for afternoon tea and cocktail parties.

A couple of doors down the street was the famous Francis Redvers puppet theatre, whose colourful entourage of players soon became friends. In those early years, George fell happily into Bournemouth's thriving theatrical scene, the ideal place to find a steady supply of photographic models and boyfriends, often simultaneously. To play the part, he even took up smoking for a while, a habit he loathed. Pictures from the turn of the 1950s show George at his most camp and carefree: film starlet sunglasses and sandals, a white shirt, short sleeves rolled tight to the biceps, tucked into high-waisted and belted skimpy white shorts – and with the legs to do them justice. This latest costume was a very long way from the regimental khaki of the war, or indeed the scratchy britches and argyle socks of the youth hostel years before it.

One expense, his telephone line at the studio, proved its worth when Reg called out of the blue in the summer of 1952. Before long, he too was in Bournemouth, and working in one of the town's chichi department stores. They bought a house in the Winton district, north of the centre, and became one of many established gay couples about town. A hundred yards from the Garret, the Lancaster Hotel was overseen by their friends Noel and Harry, who hosted regular parties attended by men drawn to twinkling Bournemouth from all over benighted Britain. There were other hotel bars and dance floors, beaches too, and pick-up spots in the manicured gardens running down the town's famous chines, wooded ravines that cut down to the beaches. In 1891, Thomas Hardy had described the town, thinly disguised as Sandbourne, as 'a fairy place suddenly created by the stroke of a wand, and allowed to get a little dusty'. It was still true sixty years later, and is recognisable enough today.

Not everyone was enchanted by the glitter of the seaside city. Naturalist Gerald Durrell, whom George photographed and counted as a friend, left town in a huff when the local authority turned down his offer to build them a zoo – change, as ever, was deemed not for the better. Durrell slammed the 'constipated mentality' of the townspeople and headed to Jersey instead; his older brother Laurence caustically described Bournemouth as a 'living death'. I'm with him on that; for a place that makes so much of its fresh air, I find it suffocating. Hardy's 'city of detached mansions' has become the city of electronic gates and surveillance systems, none more elaborate than on the promontory of Sandbanks, regularly – inexplicably – feted as one of the most expensive patches of real estate in the world. Even at the high-water marks of Attlee and

Blair, and through the many Liberal incursions into the West Country, no Bournemouth seat has ever elected anything other than a Conservative MP; the party currently holds 52 of the 54 seats on the borough council.

Haughty resistance to change often means missing out as the mood moves on, and so it proved for Bournemouth during Reg and George's time there. The 1950s were boom years, but they soon evaporated in far stronger Continental sunshine. You could only get away with repeatedly stating that the English Channel is up there with the Med if punters knew no better for themselves. Bournemouth's traditional holidaymakers, aspirational self-made men and their good lady wives, the pushy and the brassy, were first on the plane for the new package holidays to Spain, and they never came back. Amongst them were my other grandparents, the not-at-all-bookish pair, whose annual pilgrimage from Tudorbethan Solihull to Bournemouth was unceremoniously abandoned on discovering the real deal in Majorca. Guest houses and hotels became flats and old folks' homes; by 1970, a third of the population were retired and the death rate was more than twice the birth rate. Like a leathery pensioner sat too still for too long, the place was threatening to seize up.

George's work was beginning to ossify too. In the Garret's early days, a boho optimism shone through his photography; the compositions were playful and witty, the subject matter varied, and his use of light and shade always dramatic. There wasn't much of a market in Bournemouth for arty monochrome photography, however; his bestseller – by several miles – was a cute study of his collie cradling the telephone receiver. As with his more experimental work, the avant-garde Garret parties dried up too, and he wasn't much concerned when, in the mid 1960s, he lost the premises to a road-widening scheme. Bringing the business into the spare bedroom at home clipped his ambition even further; the priority now was just to grind out a living. That meant an endless round of photographing Freemasons and Rotarians stuffed  into their best bib and tucker in the chintzy, smoke-choked function rooms of Bournemouth's many Fawlty Towers. He hated it, and started to plan their escape.

Reg wasn't so sure. He'd settled well in Bournemouth, and adored his job dressing the windows and sorting out the displays at the three Robert Old menswear stores in the area. After work, there were concerts at the Winter Gardens, theatre shows at the Pavilion and the Palace Court and half a dozen cinemas to choose from. At weekends, they'd drive out into the countryside for picnics and sightseeing, or – the old favourite – take the ferry over to Studland and its nudist beach. It was a good life, and, most importantly for Reg, it felt like a safe life. For gay couples in post-war Britain, there was no guarantee of that.

After the informal liberalisation of the war years, the author-ities had clamped down on homosexuality with renewed viciousness. Politicians, the police and the press combined to hound gay men like never before; Home Secretary David Maxwell Fyfe promised 'a new drive against male vice' that would 'rid England of this plague'. In 1952, the year Reg joined George on the south coast, the *Sunday Pictorial*, sister paper to the *Daily Mirror*, ran a three-part series under the heading of 'EVIL MEN', promising 'an end to the conspiracy of silence' about homosexuality in Britain: 'Most people know there are such things – "pansies" – mincing, effeminate, young men who call themselves queers . . . but simple decent folk regard them as freaks.' They described homosexuality as a 'spreading fungus' that had contaminated 'generals, admirals, fighter pilots, engine drivers and boxers'.

Through the columns of local papers traipsed a sad succession of men caught in compromising positions, often lured there by agents provocateurs; many killed themselves. In the spring of 1953, Reg's first boyfriend, Norman, was imprisoned after pleading guilty to three charges of gross indecency. Though the sex was consensual, one of his partners had stolen a gold ring and more from another forestry worker living in the same house as Norman. The theft charges were dropped when the young man turned the tables by claiming to have been the victim of an indecent assault; the police were far more interested in that. According to the *West Sussex Gazette*, the judge declared that 'It is no pleasure to pass sentence on a man who has borne a good record, but such offences cannot be lightly dealt with' as he sentenced Norman to seven years.

The national press salivated over celebrities snared in the same remorseless net. In that year alone, the year of the Coronation, there were some meaty scalps: Sir John Gielgud, whose arrest for cottaging in a Chelsea lavatory was smeared over all the front pages; Labour MP William Field, forced to resign his seat; and actor Rupert Croft-Cooke, imprisoned in Wormwood Scrubs on the most corrupted of charges. None were so breathlessly and so exhaustively reported – and none so near to Reg and George – as the Montagu trial that ignited in 1953 and came to Winchester Assizes the following year. It was the most British scandal imaginable, a salacious collision of sex and snobbery.

The beach hut party that was pored over and picked apart by the newspapers took place just along the coast, on the edge of Lord Montagu's Beaulieu estate. Many of Bournemouth's gay men knew some of those on trial, His Lordship included. For Reg and George, Beaulieu was a favourite day out; in their 1952 guidebook, Lord Montagu's introduction declared that 'Beaulieu is essentially a place at peace'. It wasn't to last. Although George tried to discourage his interest, Reg was fascinated by the lurid coverage. Terrified too: conclusive evidence in this and other trials, Norman's included, was culled from address books, letters, diaries, even scribbled notes found crumpled or torn in pockets and bins. And as with Norman's case, the airmen who'd been at Montagu's beach hut were given immunity from prosecution in return for their incriminating testimony.

The witch-hunts turned good, quiet men like Reg, so instinctively conservative and conformist, into outlaws. He became more paranoid, and would never use a public lavatory – a phobia that lasted for the rest of his life. Even receiving a welcome postcard from George when he was away was fraught with fear. There on the back of the unsealed cards, open for all to read, were dynamite sentiments of love and longing, signed 'George' or 'Geo.', never just 'G', as was the usual gay code. Plenty of men were arrested for less.

Despite the chilling atmosphere, the brutality of the law fuelled an inevitable counter-attack, a head of steam building towards reform that was nudged steadily along by some brave – if often inadvertent – heroes. In a case that echoed the circumstances of Reg's Norman, wartime codebreaker Alan Turing was arrested for indecency after reporting being robbed by a pick-up; his suicide in the summer of 1954 can be seen in hindsight as a turning point. Politicians and the press relied on lisping predatory stereotypes as their go-to hoodoo gays; the diffident mathematical genius who had helped turn the war around in Britain's favour did not fit the caricature.

Inevitably, much of the quiet resistance came from within tightly locked circles in the arts, the classically educated, confident and well-connected men that George was so bedazzled by. They included Terence Rattigan, London's most successful post-war playwright, whose mannered dramas often included subtle or buried gay themes. Composer Benjamin Britten lived openly in Suffolk with his lover and muse Peter Pears; his opera *Billy Budd* (1951) had Pears in the role of Captain Vere, doomed to love – and forced to condemn to death – the handsome eponymous hero. E. M. Forster wrote the libretto, and was a friend of novelist Christopher Isherwood and poets Siegfried Sassoon and W. H. Auden. Sassoon and Forster had both stayed at Clouds Hill with T. E. Lawrence, who in turn was a long-time fascination of Terence Rattigan and subject of his play *Ross* that toyed with questions of Lawrence's sexuality.

Reading one of George's books, P. N. Furbank's 1977 biography of E. M. Forster, alerted me to a lesser-known lynchpin of this incestuous milieu. Although J. R. (Joe) Ackerley was Forster's closest lifelong friend, the two writers differed fundamentally in how they dealt with their homosexuality. For Morgan Forster, his literary and political timidity in only posthumously publishing gay-themed work was mirrored in his frugal private life. For Ackerley, the equal, and opposite: he was brazen, promiscuous and scaldingly honest in both life and books.

Ackerley died a month before the 1967 Sexual Offences Act became law, partially decriminalising homosexuality. Being legal would have made no difference to how he conducted himself, nor to what he wrote. There are gay themes in every one of his works, from the twenties to the sixties, and handled without flinching; he is a meticulous chronicler of these censored decades. His only novel, *We Think the World of You* (1960), is a grimy tale of thwarted longing, blackmail and the intricate codes that governed life at the intersection of class, money and sexual taboos. Like all his work, it was based on his own experiences, here of a (mostly) unrequited passion for a (mostly) heterosexual young chancer. At once hilarious and horrific, its layers of clipped, repressed Englishness cling to the reader like soot.

This coterie of mid-century gay men shared trajectories of wealth and class that George always envied. Sexual awakenings at boarding school and Oxbridge were part of a parallel life he could only dream of in the cramped Hackney terrace where he grew up. His drive to better himself, by reading the classics and attending galleries, concerts and lectures, was ammunition against his humble origins; an intellectual charge, but an erotic one too. In Reg, he had found the perfect foil. Though they both hailed from London's lower-middle shopkeeper class, George's assumed superiority was a central tenet of their relationship. Reg's lack of confidence, his dyslexia and disrupted education, even his foreign background and religion, placed him in the role of the subservient, the perpetual pupil. It was a white lie to which they both willingly subscribed.

*

George was most in schoolmaster mode on their trips abroad. As it was for many British gay men of the age, the lure of a south even more exotic than Bournemouth was irresistible, countries where two or more men travelling together was far less likely to cause an incident. Their first trip was in the spring of 1954: five days in Paris, flying from the new Heathrow Airport to Le Bourget aboard BEA's epochal 'Elizabethan' service. They walked miles, along the Seine, through Montmartre and up the Champs-Élysées, climbed the Eiffel Tower and the Arc de Triomphe, visited Versailles and the Louvre, George reading aloud the relevant sections of the *Blue Guide* and interrogating assistants in passable schoolboy French. It was Reg's first time overseas, and he took to it like a snail to butter. He was intoxicated – and only mildly intimidated – by it all: 'Have just had a lovely Dinner of VEAL!' he wrote in one of his daily postcards to his dad, before adding 'Very under done'. George also sent a postcard to Gus, addressing him as 'Pop' and reassuring him that his boy was well and happy.

Three years later, to celebrate George's fortieth and Reg's thirtieth birthdays, they sailed aboard the RMS *Andes* from Southampton to Lisbon for a grand tour of Spain. After a couple of days in the Portuguese capital, they took the train to Seville and then down to the coast of Andalusia and the Costa del Sol. Before long it would be swamped by high-rise hotels, but their photographs are of deserted beaches alongside dusty fishing villages. From there, they toured widely by bus and train: to Granada and Cordoba, and then up to Toledo, Ávila, Segovia and Madrid.

George's stark monochrome photographs of Spain are the best he ever took. The landscapes are epic and sculptural, unpeopled except for an occasional, distant Reg, often shirtless, placed like a tiny Cupid in a Renaissance fresco. Streets and squares boil with life, from children and donkeys to old women, top to toe in black, balancing baskets on their heads. Around every corner is a market, wedding or fiesta, the girls in flamenco pleats, the boys slick-haired and pouting. Although entirely black and white, the scenes overflow with colour that not even the sour stare of Francoist guards in the background can staunch.

Fascist Spain was not the obvious holiday option for a gay couple in 1957. For men in the fifties, the most common boltholes were Amsterdam, Paris or West Berlin, Tangier and Marrakech too, or the old favourites of Italy and Greece. In Spain, homosexuality was no more legal or acceptable than in Britain, and practitioners were punished even more harshly. Gay men were routinely imprisoned in mental institutions, internment camps and dedicated *galerías de invertidos*, 'deviant galleries'. Yet Reg and George were not alone: at their *pensión* in Granada, they became friends with another couple, two men who had driven there from their home in Germany. The four teamed up, and explored the snow-capped mountains of the Sierra Nevada in the Germans' car.

This awoke in George the idea of motoring on the Continent, although when he returned to Spain the following April in a tiny Standard Eight, it was not with Reg, but his old wartime flame and Bournemouth friend Stanley. Whether Reg was unable to spare the time off work, or George was pointedly

proving that he remained a free spirit, or it was a long-standing promise to Stanley, or all or none of these, is a mystery.

A fractious mood was set before they'd even left Southampton on the overnight ferry. Arriving early, they went to a cinema for tea and caught the latest Dean Martin and Jerry Lewis film, *Hollywood or Bust*, a limp comedy road movie following the pair as they drive across America. All grins and gurning on camera, while behind the scenes their relationship was dying acrimoniously, it was Martin and Lewis's final film – and not a good portent. Once on the ferry, Stanley drank himself into a stupor, spent much of the night keeping George awake by being sick in their cabin and then had an early-morning panic attack. After docking, they were forced to wait for two hours for access to the car, and on finally escaping the ship, got thoroughly lost in the backstreets of

Le Havre in pouring rain. Eighty miles and some watery sunshine later, they stopped for food, recorded by George in his notebook: 'lunched al fresco on Stanley's bloody sausages (took Milk of Maggi!) had 160fr [about 2/- or 10p] bottle of Bordeaux from the Co-op, but had to eat Cheddar cheese'.

It took them only two days to drive the length of France, crossing into Spain at the Col du Somport, over five thousand feet up in the Pyrenees. A far cry from the warm beaches of Andalusia twelve months earlier, there was a snowstorm in the pass, and as they descended to the old Aragonese capital of Jaca, it didn't much cheer up: 'Intensely cold wind. Cold hotel. Bought bottle of Coñac to save life, 38 pesetas. Saw Cathedral (only warm spot in Jaca)', whimpered George. The breakneck pace continued: most days they covered two hundred miles or more, ticking off stops in Burgos, Barcelona, Valencia, Segovia, Toledo and Peniscola, before hurtling back through France to the Normandy coast and home.

For George, the contrast was stark between travelling with Reg, hanging on his every word and obeying instructions to the letter, and Stanley, boozing heavily and frequently getting them lost when he misread the map. It inspired some of his slushiest postcards home, brimful of tender endearments: 'Dearest Reggie . . . I do hope you are keeping well and not feeling too lonely. I think about you all the time', and signed 'Love Geo'. They sent Reg into a tailspin of conflicting emotion: giddy affection coupled with very real terror that they might provoke an officious knock on the door at dawn. The odd postcard from Stanley didn't help: from the Sierra de Gredos, 'We had a delightful picnic lunch beside a mountain stream with two young goatherds hovering near!' Certainly, there are many more comely young men in the photos from this trip than from any of the others.

There never was another holiday with Stanley, though it proved to be the prototype for many others with Reg, always in April and May, over the following decade. Crowds were thinner than in high season, flowers at their most ebullient, and the sun strong enough for George to kick-start his tan for a Bournemouth summer. In a hotel on the shore of Lake Garda:

> Whole afternoon on Lake Terrace, gorgeous, very warm sunny day. Sunbathing in swim trunks. Lots of 'personal' photos. Soaked up sun until last minute. At 6pm sun sinking behind trees. Italian money down to 4,000 lire, must change 1st of (£40) Travellers' Cheques.

Often given a double room with no fuss, they felt free, in ways that were still unimaginable at home.

In 1961, George replicated the Spanish road trip with Stanley for Reg, albeit at a more leisurely pace through France. (Reg on their hotel in Nemours: 'OK, Very French, but cleane'.) The following spring, in just over a fortnight, they drove to Rome and back. Despite three punctures and a leaking axle, their little ten-horse-power car chugged through the Alps and down to the French Riviera, through Nice and Monaco ('parked opposite Palace') and into Italy. Again, the pace never slackened. On their first full Italian day, they left their overnight stop at Noli at nine ('dreadful traffic again on this coast road'), picked up – for the first time in George's driving career – the motorway to Genoa, had a quick picnic lunch in a mountain pass, stopped for an hour early evening in Pisa, just long enough to see the cathedral and the leaning tower, and then continued for two further hours to their overnight stop in the Tuscan hill town of San Gimignano.

Italy was where they most frequently returned over the next few years and, decades later, in fond reminiscence. It was an *amore profondo*, one so evocative of my grandparents – the ones with the same books and maps, not the Brummie ones basting themselves in the Balearics. Even the names – Siena, Orvieto, Domodessola, Assisi and Arezzo, Lakes Como and Garda, and, above all, *Venezia!* – were exactly the same as those incanted to me as a child like a call to prayer.

Similar too were the hundreds of slides, technicolour tableaux of statues, squares and churches, with glamorous passers-by frozen in a *dolce vita* moment. If I examine George's slides closely enough, I half expect to spot my grandparents in the background, flicking through a Michelin guide at a pavement cafe, or passing by in their Ford Corsair. Its yellow clip-on headlights – French law at the time – were always left on long after getting home, an ace in the game of suburban one-upmanship.

Were he to be caught in someone else's photos, chances are my grandfather would be pointing a camera himself. Like George, the main point for him of a Continental tour was to photograph it. Film it too for a few years in the mid sixties: both of them fell for the cine craze, which only ratcheted up the heft of necessary kit. In his notebook for their 1964 holiday is George's 'to pack' list, starting, 'Cine camera, Cine films, Exposure meter, Cable release automatic device, Still camera, Colour films, Lens hood, Camera case, Tripod and tilt head'. My grandfather was even worse, routinely taking three stills cameras with him on holiday and capturing exactly the same shot with every one of them, a joyless grind of a habit that put me off photography for years. George was more spontaneous, especially in capturing people. The camera adored Reg, and George would place him artfully in settings best suited to his colour slide film: lying abashed in carpets of Alpine flowers, smiling sweetly on a lush green riverbank, or posing like a movie star at cafes in sunny medieval squares.

George and Reg had four spring road trips to Italy, via France and Switzerland, a succession interrupted by a package holiday to Yugoslavia in 1963 and, three years later, flying to Greece to admire the men, both flesh and statuary. Reg wasn't much impressed ('Athens Goodish', he sighed to his diary), but things took an even worse turn when George was hospitalised with an inflamed appendix; after three days, 'Much more Cheerfull, Moaning about things so he is Getting Better.'

Reg contributed only rarely to the notebooks, but when he did, the difference in outlook is fascinating. Their 1962 road trip to France and Italy was one where they kept separate diaries. On the day that they left Bournemouth, George noted only the 'Commencing mileage on clock 22689, 180 miles B'mth to Dover, Arrived Dover 10.20 (Left B'mth 5.20)'. Reg, meanwhile, was otherwise preoccupied: 'Starting Holiday's to Rome. Must clip back aubretia when I get back. Also get terlass [trellis?] for Sweet Pea's', and then later, a querulous 'Feeling funny inside.'

The passage to Dunkirk was rough, not helped by the fact that they had to try and sleep on the car deck in their tiny Standard Ten. George: 'What a crossing over the channel! My teeth went too! Very ill but it passed and easy motoring in France although I could hardly keep my eyes open most of the time.' Reg, meanwhile, I can hear as if he is sitting with me:

the Boat was full of scream[ing] French Boys and Girls and the noise was 'terridable' and then there was four English army men whith gitars + Bandjobs [banjos] and made a racket they only new one tune it was hell. Then poor George started to fell sick as the Boat rockt so but was alright so I acted like N Flour Nightengale and I was most tender . . . Feeling like Death. Also feeling a wee bit sad as 'Dunkirk' has some sad memores for the 'English' anyway it was very Dark.

While George was preoccupied with car problems and the schedule, Reg was absorbing it all with gusto: 'went to church lit a candle feel at home in foren churchs . . . our room lookt out too the Valley also Mountains very near & a very good meal most enjoyable. Lovely Boys & Mother very sweet.' In San Gimignano, famous for its medieval towers, Reg wrote that 'it is very old just what George and I like. I seem to like "Italie" also the food (It was Good "Spagtete" with fish soup veg).'

George, meanwhile, used his notebook to tot up the costs of every plate and reassure himself that they were getting a good deal out of the hotel's all-inclusive rate. In Rome (Reg: 'just one bed in room!!!'), George liked the first night's restaurant so much that he decided they'd go there every evening, where he had the same food – lasagne and Pollo alla Romana – each time.

In April 1967, to mark George's fiftieth and Reg's fortieth birthdays, they returned to Italy in the most romantic way possible: by taking the overnight train to Venice. They adored it, though Reg had his worries: 'Haveing coffe near holt hotel. Oh Dear. Small water road near is at low tide and it dos smell. Box's of Veg's near by Don't fancie eating them. Local's don't seem to worry.' He was underwhelmed too by the glassware of Murano: 'it is all very Dear also its not all lovely, real old Mums & Blackpool looking' (Preds said much the same when we visited four decades later).

The following year's holiday, a return to Rome, was their final trip abroad. They never crossed the Channel again, but took instead to exploring their own country. After all, as of 27 July 1967, their relationship – their very *existence* – was no longer illegal. There was no need to stay put in the gay playpen of Bournemouth.

By heading to the West Country, the Lakes, to Scotland and Wales, George was reprising his tours from either side of the war. For Reg, now in his forties, it was the first time he'd ever travelled around Britain beyond the upholstered south of England. There was another impetus: the holidays soon became a reconnaissance for a new life. George's passion for photography had dwindled, the Garret was long gone and

Bournemouth was boring him. There were only so many Sunday picnics to be had at T. E. Lawrence's Clouds Hill, the solitary cottage on a Dorset heath that he so loved. He wanted his own version: a manly pied-à-terre, remote and self-sufficient, smelling of leather and books, lit by candles and warmed by open fires. To persuade Reg, he packaged it as their own Howards End, a bower of flowers with a 'sense of space, which is the basis of all earthly beauty'.

Was there a light-bulb moment of conversion or was it a more gradual dawning? I picture bara brith on doilies in a Marches tea shop; a surreptitiously squeezed arm at the view down a teeming gorge; raised glasses by a pub fire as an improbable dream solidified into a tentative plan. In 1969, Reg's dad died, leaving him a small lump sum. Later that year, they holidayed in mid Wales, and loved it. Almost overnight, their focus switched from the shifting sands of the south to the old rocks of the west.

To record their new life, George started a diary, and opened it with a proverbial mission statement: 'Memories are given us so that we may have roses in December.'

GEORGE

Look closely at the faces of those tidy British men travelling on the Continent in the 1960s and you might have caught a distant, distracted air. They were struggling to recognise old haunts, for the last time they'd met had been in the flames of war. Although George was little prone to nostalgia, en route back to Le Havre at the end of their 1965 tour he decided to have a night at Vernon, a pretty Normandy town fifty miles up the River Seine from Paris. He'd last been there twenty-one years earlier, as a private in the 4th Battalion of the Somerset Light Infantry, as they swept in from the D-Day landings on the coast to liberate Nazi-occupied France.

'How strange,' George wrote in his holiday journal. 'Gasny could have been any simple little French village but Vernonette and the green hills I remembered well!' Both lie on the far side of the wide river from Vernon, and were the scenes of some of the fiercest fighting. Local Resistance forces had cleared the Germans from the town a week earlier and blown up the bridge, but the enemy had taken refuge in the steep wooded hills on the other bank, from where they fired into the town. Many residents hid in caves.

After booking into a town centre hotel ('Madame speaks good English and remembers the first assault of the Seine by Monty's army (and me!)'), George took Reg down to the river embankment to see and photograph the scene. The memories came roaring back:

> Can remember the crossing so vividly at this moment, with smoke bombs falling and the little speed boat assault craft skimming the broad river in minutes – though it seemed years. Saw the green heights of Vernonette in actuality, and saw another me in this same spot spanning the past, and heard the voice of Harry Jesty as he screamed his well-known war cry 'How I hate the —— army!'

I too see 'another me in this same spot spanning the past'. When George writes about the war, I am closest of all to him; his words resonate with a clarity and honesty that feels most peculiarly familiar. Aspects of his later life sometimes read like signposts of potential dangers in landscapes that I know intimately. Yet it is in the unfamiliar places and times, those to which I can never go, that my empathy for him flowers most freely. I spent the summertime of my twenties partying; George spent his fighting fascism and his own fear. To get to know him better, we need to follow him into battle.

For the first four years, he quite enjoyed the war. There was little difference to his old life, in that he worked as a company clerk and took every shred of leave to explore the hidden contours of the country – and, where possible, his comrades-in-arms too. On both counts, army life suited him well. Conscripted in June 1940 into the Royal Fusiliers, he worked at barracks and camps in Liverpool, Northern Ireland, Tyneside, Kent and the Isle of Wight.

Of the men, the most significant find was Stanley. Tall, slender and confident, with slicked-back hair, clipped moustache and a signet ring on his little finger, he looked like a classic wartime spiv, despite being a vicar's son from Bournemouth. He was very different from the diffident young men that were George's habitual conquests; too different, in truth. Although Stanley was  keen to continue what they had both gladly started, George inched away, protesting that they could of course stay friends. For once, the age-old get-out clause proved true: they remained lifelong mates, even beyond their fateful Spanish holiday. Every gay man has close friendships that started in bed – though for years afterwards, Stanley continued to hope for more. In September 1944, after they had both participated in the bloody liberation of France and were warily anticipating the continued assault into Germany, he sent George a poem reminiscing about a night they'd shared more than two years earlier:

> There is magic in the night –
> this night that dreams into the darkening sky.
> Tenderly, the breeze caresses the trees,
> whilst I, within these sheltering walls
> lie trembling too beside you.

... and in your fond embrace, I cling –
feel your breath so soft upon my face.

Moment of ecstasy –
this moment that is now, the future years.
The years I've known – have lived,
my panting heart sweeps back –
past life behind me.
Let timeless eons flee in your embrace.
Let this midsummer night be always –
my today.

Poetry was the currency of all George's wartime love affairs, though rarely quite as forthright as Stanley's. Not surprisingly for lads schooled in the twenties and thirties on a starchy diet of Kipling and Tennyson, their amateur verse leant towards the distinctly overwrought – or *o'erwrought*, as they would doubtless have had it. That they were also writing while contemplating the very real potential of imminent death only sent its blood pressure soaring even higher.

There was a lot to pack in: death and disfigurement, lacerating terror, quavering surges of lust and love, *Boys' Own* adventure, homesickness scratched to bloody stumps – and all conflated with the God-given certainty of fighting for this sceptr'd isle. Snobbery was inevitable. One of George's most devout correspondents railed against those at home who failed to appreciate their efforts, addressing 'You, who never look upon the sky at night / But snore disgustingly in a box of bricks'. When he and George had met in 1940, they shared their love of the wild places. On the Western Front four years later,

George received a poem reminding him of that love, for the Welsh–English borderland especially and 'the streaming sunset rays that / Light Sabrina's hair on 'Limmon's lofty top'.[5]

George also harboured hopes of being A. E. Housman. *A Shropshire Lad*, with its hearty evocation of bucolic youth and pheromone whiff of homoeroticism, had been the sleeper success of the First World War, the slim volume stuffed into many breast pockets in the trenches. At the beginning of his war, George was writing in stiff appreciation of nature (the Giant's Causeway: 'Here Nature doth exceed Her bounds / Here Mankind's wonders pale / Here sea and spray hold lordly sway / And speak their age old tale'), but as hostilities ground on, and he came closer to putting his infantry training into practice on the battlefield, the layers of conceit peeled away and the tone rapidly darkened. Inevitably, the muse awoke especially at times of loss, of either a location or a lover; it is no surprise that the two become so entwined.

In the months leading up to D-Day, George was on training manoeuvres in Lancashire, before being moved south to the Hursley marshalling camp, near Southampton. Living in bell tents in the trees – the better for avoiding aerial

---

[5] Sabrina is the Roman name for the River Severn, which rises on Pumlumon ("Limmon').

reconnaissance – for an entire month, he and his five thousand fellow troops were given plenty to occupy their time, but still it dragged. He'd left behind a boyfriend in Lancaster by the name of Hugh, and was pining ('Must I have you wish "Good luck" / And shake me by the hand?'). On 5 June 1944, the night before they were due to sail to France and unknown horror, he was writing him love poetry:

> What of Beauty did I see
> Before your soul found mine? . . .
> It was dark then,
> I walked a dim corridor of Life,
> But ever on I stumbled
> Drawn by a strange inner force
> Toward a pin-point of light,
> A distant, far-off light that was you.
>
> Lying here, sleepless and despairing
> I long to feel ~~your~~ tender touch
> That bringeth sweet oblivion.

Did he send the poem? I suspect so, for George was convinced that he was about to die, and wanted an epitaph, one that mixed aching eroticism with a final line straight from *The English Hymnal*. And if he did, was it 'your tender touch' or the more generic version that made it into Hugh's hands? Either way, it is a heartbreaking image: George spending what he truly believed might be his last night curled up in a corner of a tent, agonising over it.

Landing on Arromanches beach, the battalion surged through Normandy, and the sticky overlap of death and terror, comradeship and carnality, oozed on. After the fierce battle to take Mont Pinçon, seeing 'serried ranks of Death', mixed lines of German, British and American corpses, elicited a wistful 'You who faced each other, tensed to kill / Lie peacefully together'.

Into the volatile mix went existential doubt and a crisis of faith: the 'well-ordered course' of his childhood teachings proved woefully insufficient in the heat of battle ('The tumults of unbelief / Unseen, unknown, unfelt – / Yet soon they come'). Things improved once the battalion had successfully crossed the Seine at Vernon. Luck played its part when over three-quarters of the shells aimed at their camps failed to detonate: 'we silently blessed some underground worker in a German arms factory', wrote the battalion's historian, Lieutenant Colonel C. G. Lipscomb. After that, progress was relatively straightforward, and fast. News arrived that Paris had been liberated, and as they pushed on towards the Belgian border, the welcome became increasingly fervent, as Lipscomb records: 'Every variety of fruit, wine and carefully hoarded bonbons was lavished upon our column. From daybreak to dusk each succeeding village and town seemed to abandon all other pursuits in order to cheer the "Tommies".' They crossed into Belgium on 15 September, and into the Netherlands six days later.

For the next seven weeks, fierce fighting alternated with extended periods of rest as they consolidated positions. George had yet to shoot anyone dead, and he was far from sure that he would be able to:

Soon I shall go forth to kill,
What if it is against my will?
We're told, 'he's just the beastly Hun
When we attack you'll see him run!'

What of his father, mother, wife?
Will they weigh as lightly
The balance of his life?
Do I not think nightly?

Does he not see as I the sunset
Flashing strange fire in the west?
Does he not curse the rain and wet
clothes, nor long for sleep, for rest?

This is my rifle, see it spit Death
unto yon Ridge, seeking a place
for lead to maim or kill
What if it is against my will?

His mood darkened further on receiving an unexpected brush-off in a long-awaited letter from Hugh, perhaps provoked or panicked by George's poem. In a pattern that repeated itself throughout George's war, what were to him spiritually charged acts of love were only comfort fumbles for others, fumbles they furthermore had absolutely no wish to be reminded of. As winter closed in with a near month of solid rain, he was exhausted and afraid, and now heartbroken too:

I have read your words today
the sun is tarnished with decay –
my heart lies torn and trampled
and at bay.

My heart was proud, it cried aloud
the love I bore for you.

How do I live, now your love is spent?
I loved, I trusted, my faith was strong,
I lived to love, perhaps I loved too long?

The company were rested over Christmas, and George was allowed forty-eight hours' leave – his first since March – to meet with Stanley in Brussels. He was heading to the Eastern Front in Asia, while George's battalion was to push on into Germany. Despite the obvious progress of the Allies, either prospect must have looked deeply foreboding as they and others gathered for Christmas lunch. Thanks to grateful Belgians and smooth-talking Stanley, it was as lavish a spread as anyone had eaten all year, helped by free-flowing beer and wine.

In February 1945, Operation Veritable, the concerted advance into Germany, began. General Eisenhower later described it as 'some of the fiercest fighting of the whole war . . . a bitter slugging match in which the enemy had to be forced back yard by yard'. Pathé newsreels of the battles are horrific: endless indiscriminate battering by tank and machine gun of places already blown to bits. In the Reichswald forest, they and other battalions co-ordinated a surprise night attack, which netted almost a thousand prisoners of war. From there, the battalion marched south towards the hamlet of Halverboom, and the worst day of George's life.

A couple of weeks later, he typed up his memories. Of all the diaries, letters, notebooks and poems that I've read, stretching from the 1920s to the 2000s, the hundreds of thousands of his words, these six thin, yellowing sheets contain the most potent. For once, he is looking me straight in the eye, and not blinking.

He records the night before the slaughter. As the company were marching from the forest, orders came to stop and bed down for the night, much to his relief. They took over the cellar of a burnt-out house, as they had done countless times before, and swung into the routine of clearing and cleaning it, while upstairs the stretcher-bearers, doubling up as company cooks, brewed some tea and began preparing dinner. 'Our supper that night was a grand affair,' writes George, 'for we had real potatoes with our M&V [tinned stew] – and a fruit salad from the jars in the cellar.' The warm fug was soon broken, when 'a squeaky, tinny voice from far away sounded in our comfortable cellar', ordering an attack the next morning. Although a commonplace occurrence,

> I was never able to stop the sinking of my heart . . . that swept me into an abysmal gloom . . . Plenty of shit dropping – Dull thoughts throbbing, throbbing their incessant clashing harmony inside, hopeless, hopeless, hopeless existence that was ours – hopeless, hopeless war that dragged on and on with no end in sight – attacks – attacks – attacks – God give me the power to scream – to scream until it hurt – Slowly the throbbing would go as numb as my brain and it didn't matter – the throbbing is dull now – it was quiet – no gunfire near enough to let the nerve get raw again – what did it matter? This time I would be killed – It wasn't right anyway that I had cheated Death so many times before – Yes, I had cheated Death – it

wasn't right – I'd give in this time. I would die this time
and it would be all over for me – this daily terror of waiting for terror.

On guard duty that night, lit by the glow of fires still smoul-
dering from the bombs, George heard an argument in
another of the cellars of the house:

I popped my head into the yellow light to see. There was
a woman there, a Polish girl who had worked for the German owner of the farm. One of the stretcher-bearers
wanted her to go and sleep upstairs, the other two
wanted her to stay – They all had the same thought I
knew but neither would admit it.

To settle who wins the right to rape, they fetch a company
lieutenant, an Argentine, remembered in Lipscomb's history as 'a born leader and fighter', but by George that
'no-one had much respect for him'. He insisted that the girl
stayed in a room near his. 'I heard the next morning',
George continued, 'that one of the stretcher-bearers had
caught Pedro in the act and had thrown a bucket of water
over him!'

That morning, armoured personnel carriers known as
Kangaroos were waiting to take them to the front line.
George had never travelled in one before, and was spooked
by how they muffled the sounds of war, and intimidated by
their crews, 'detached and superior in their overalls . . .
taller and big-boned – talked differently from the infantry'.
Their commanding officer, Major Mallalieu, had assured
them the previous evening that the Kangaroos were loved
by all who'd used them, and that was enough for George. 'A

good old stick, old Mallalieu,' he wrote, 'he had a way of making us believe things he never believed in himself – and how we laughed at danger when he belittled it for the benefit of our morale.' Although two years George's junior, Mallalieu was exactly the kind of man that he admired, adored and envied: tall, debonair, and with an impeccable pedigree of colonial army family, childhood in India, boarding school and a small stately home in Somerset.

They were driven straight into the thick of battle:

> The noise was gathering momentum – mortars, spandaus, our rifles, LMGs[6] and 2" mortars and our own artillery. News seeped through that several had already become casualties – hit whilst getting out of the Kangaroos – two dead . . . so soon.

A mortar exploded nearby and sniper fire strafed all around.

> I was terribly afraid that our attack was doomed to failure. Rarely had we met such opposition as this. I felt sick at heart – furious that these bloody bastard jerries should resist. Why didn't they retreat now – they'd have to sooner or later.

The major and the rest of the party advanced into the fire, leaving George and three others hiding in a dugout, waiting for the call. Their radio was broken, having been blown from its perch by a mortar, and just as they were contemplating following their comrades, one of them returned.

[6] Light machine guns.

Breathless, his face flushed with exertion and excitement, his eyes streaming tears, came Hawkins. He reached us and sank exhausted to the ground. I saw that his face was wet from crying and some expression of dread calamity was written unmistakeably in his eyes, in his very manner ...

I was suddenly terribly afraid – it was not a personal fear – I had never experienced this fear before. It went deep down in my soul ... Slowly, stumbling from lips that were loath to obey, we heard ... 'The Major ... dead ... Pedro has taken over ... yes, the boys ... are alright ... you're to go to Company HQ' – his shoulders shook with great sobs ... His grief struck like sharp arrows at our hearts.

A sniper had picked off Mallalieu as he climbed down from a tank, having just given the order to fire. One of those with George in the dugout was Mallalieu's batman, who 'broke down completely'. In the grief and the terror, George cried too, as unashamed as the others. 'We were very tender to one another and spoke softly, as lovers whose mutual emotion had drawn them together ... words came haltingly with broken inflection in the voice, impossible to hide even if we'd tried.'

Death and sex; *le petit mort*.

Twenty-five other men from 'C' Company also died in the chaotic first attack on Halverboom. It was, according to Lieutenant Colonel Lipscomb's account, 'a very sticky half hour'.

*

In Brussels that last Christmas of the war, Stanley gave George a tantalising glimpse of the new world coming. He was taken to bars and parties and introduced to people the like of which he'd never met before: unashamed homosexuals, eccentric Continentals, pacifists, bohemians and artists displaced from all over Europe. After VE Day, George remained on the Continent for another year, and frequently headed back to Belgium to see these new friends.

The excitement was palpable; everything seemed possible. His pre-war hopes of making a living from his creativity were rekindled, though now he wasn't sure which talent to concentrate on. He reworked much of his wartime poetry, though it never quite sparked into life. He tried painting, but his sombre landscapes were even flatter. As an artist's subject, though, he was brilliant: a Dutch portraitist found the dark young Englishman a worthy muse, and painted him several times, perfectly capturing his quiet, intense brio.

He loved being painted, just as he loved being on both sides of the camera. Photography was his real craft, and even if it wasn't accorded the status that he craved of classical arts like poetry and painting, he was old enough – nearly thirty – and wise enough to know it was his best bet. As the demob testimonial from his company captain put it, the 'exemplary' George had 'a great deal of common sense which he puts to very good effect'. It would be just as necessary, possibly more so, in peacetime and austerity as it had been in conflict. Bournemouth and the Garret would soon beckon.

Despite travelling so extensively on the Continent, their 1965 stopover in Vernon was the only time George returned to his wartime battlegrounds. Some veterans made regular pilgrimages, in respect for their dead comrades or in searching for their own lost selves, but George was not one for either kind of nostalgia. He had no wish to reacquaint himself with the terrified young infantryman pouring his angst and loneliness into poetry. Life was minted new, and needed seizing. Doubt would not be entertained again.

And why should it? He was still young, in excellent health, with good friends, a roster of lovers and decent prospects. Victory in the war had only confirmed to him that to be English was to be blessed, even under post-war rubble and a hated socialist government. It is notable that when writing up his experiences of the decisive Rhineland conflict, George describes the area as 'obscure' and 'inaccessible', a portent of his descriptions thirty years later of mid Wales. While it is perhaps understandable to see depopulated Powys, out on the Continent's western edge, in such terms, the territory between the Dutch city of Eindhoven and the German megalopolis of the Rühr could only possibly look that way through the most avowedly Anglocentric – *London*-centric, even – of gazes. ('FOG IN CHANNEL – CONTINENT CUT OFF', as the perhaps apocryphal newspaper headline had it.)

Reg and I always sparred happily about politics, but I'm not sure how well George and I would have managed the same conversations, had they ever occurred. We both would have found each other's assumptions and attitudes infuriating, I'm sure. From his Continental holiday diaries, I smirk at his affectation, such as the joy with which he spots on the Costa Brava 'two delightful English ladies at the hotel, one is (I'm sure) *Lady* Tufnell' (his

193

emphasis), and wince at his enthusiasm for visiting places in Italy associated with Mussolini, and in Spain, to hear, read and even 'dream all night!' about Franco. On their 1964 trip to France, Switzerland and Italy, they shared a diary, contributing alternate entries. It brings something new out for them both: Reg dutifully scribed the mileages, prices and petrol stops, while George loosened his stays and even took the mickey out of himself. They seem blissfully united, and George resisted any temptation to correct Reg's wayward handwriting, spelling and punctuation. To a man so meticulous, that cannot have been easy.

By now, well over a decade into their life together, George was well aware that his apparent superiority in their relationship was something of a masquerade for outsiders. He rarely admitted as much, even to his diary; to do so would perhaps unpick too much of the bravura persona that he had so painstakingly constructed. That character was the man who can, the man in the know – those were the qualities that made him authoritative, respected and useful. No one was to see the vulnerable, confused youth ever again. Sending a postcard to 'Pop', Reg's father Gus, from Granada in 1957, he explained – in careful capitals, the sort you'd write to a child – how to address the envelope if he wished to send Reg a letter:

> SR. R. MICKISCH (i.e. no Christian name or ESQ)
> LISTA DE CORREOS,
> MADRID.

He was never as familiar with his own father. The pictures of Gus in Bournemouth, larking around on the beach with the two of them, are in keen contrast to the family photos on George's side, of anxious faces in austere rooms. They were a mysterious household. When on wartime training in the north-east, George took to wandering around Newcastle upon Tyne – where he had been born and lived before his father's shop had failed and they'd moved to London – in the hope that the city would nudge some memories or recognition. It didn't, not at all – much to his intense dismay.

Around the end of the war, George's sister had a baby boy, and although she went by a new surname and the prefix of 'Mrs', there is no mention of a father. Perhaps she had married but he died in the war; perhaps the tale is of illegitimacy and shame. Perhaps too there is some connection between whatever happened and the family's transience. The Hackney terrace in which George grew up was demolished for slum clearance in 1937; the family were moved into a brand-new council block of flats on Homerton High Street. Though it was never bombed or evacuated, by 1944 they were no longer there, and were all – mother, father, sister, baby, George too when he returned – living in a dingy basement flat in a nearby Edwardian terrace. Within a few years, both of his parents were dead.

While her son was still young, George's sister met and married someone else, taking her third surname. Her husband adopted the child as his own, though they never had any more. George did his best to be a good uncle to the boy, but when he reached young adulthood, there was some grim scandal and contact was severed. By then, George's sister was depressed and on medication for her nerves. The two of

them, as the only siblings, always shared an ardent relationship, with much thrumming between the lines of their
postcards and letters, but it too withered away. She was
even initially unaware that George and Reg had moved to
Wales, and shocked to find out. 'I do miss seeing you George
as you must know,' she wrote in the letter expressing surprise at the news, and although there was the odd letter and
a Christmas card every year, he never saw any of them again.

This forensic ability to focus on what he wanted, and
excise entirely from his mind and life anything that he
didn't, became George's defining trait, for better and
worse. It gave him phenomenal drive and focus, but also a
fiery stubbornness and a stomach ulcer. On moving to

Rhiw Goch, he finally achieved an inner truce. Ambition was sated; there were no further peaks to scale. It was only then that he could admit even in the privacy of his diary that 'Reg is right – as always!' Through sometimes gritted teeth, I say the same of Preds.

One area of life at Rhiw Goch absorbed almost all of George's attention. 'I suppose I must bore people with my cycling, but I don't care, I love it so!' he wrote soon after getting back into the saddle in 1983, and it was no exaggeration; he really didn't care. The same single-mindedness kept him cycling until just shy of his eighty-sixth birthday in 2002, the final ride written up in his log book with characteristic grit:

> Cycled (and walked!) to Melin (less 200yds!) Mild, o'cast. Shorts. Knees better walking & cycling, but pain in gullet cycling. *!Last cycle ride 21 APRIL (Abercegir)!* 3 months!!! Must keep it up!

When he could no longer cycle, his bike lived in the hall as both a statement of intent that he would one day return to it, and an altarpiece, as revered as saints' relics. It drove Reg potty, and the day George left the house for good, so did the bike.

His obsessive pursuit of the body beautiful was another double-edged sword. It gave him untold motivation, but also made him self-obsessed and a terrible hypochondriac. Many gay men have dysmorphic relationships with their own bodies, an inability to see their physical selves as they really are. Although it manifested in quite different ways, George and I are as one on this as well. So too in its origins, in frosty childhoods where affection came only in the strangest of flavours, and on the strictest of rations.

Coming here, George's sole task, one in which he was supremely successful, was to fan the embers of later life back into flame, to push far into the autumn his *haf bach Mihangel*, 'Michael's little summer', the Welsh phrase for an uncharacteristically hot late spell, an Indian summer. And in arriving, in reaching that sunlit plateau, he could lose all excess baggage, trim every ounce of fat and become the streamlined man-machine of his dreams.

To that end, he steadily ditched old responsibilities, initially on to Reg and then, when she stepped in, on to Penny. The bike aside, even those that seemed integral to his sense of self were shed with surprising ease. We were all terrified of the day when he'd need to be told to surrender his driving licence, but then he was needing to ask directions to get into town, a journey he'd done thousands of times, and just wasn't safe any more. Penny framed it to him as a huge financial saving, which cut straight through the fog, and he took it without a murmur of protest.

Dropped with equanimity were people too: not just his family, but old friends and flames, various neighbours, workmen and even – after an inexplicable bust-up that flared out of nowhere – the postman. He edited the photo albums, ejecting entire relationships from their pages, and destroying all the racy ones. His diaries were similarly filleted of anything too incriminating or embarrassing: there are missing sections, pages and even half-pages sliced carefully out.

This rigorous editing exercise is intriguing. Was it all for himself, or did George have half an eye on what people

HERO-CYCLIST OF
WILD WALES
REPELS INVADERS!!

3 MAY 1983

might make of him after he had gone? Was he thinking – hoping, even – that someone would pore over his huge archive of images and words, perhaps do something with them? There's a puzzling aside in his diary of January 2004: 'Philip Bennett rang (Eddy's brother). Eddy has been taken to a Care Home. Eddy was husband to my late sister.' For whom is that explanation? It is possibly an aide memoire to himself, that he was already aware of his mind slipping, before dementia was diagnosed? Perhaps, though, he was trying to make his editor's job easier by adding his own footnotes.

All that remained after his careful editing was itself soon wiped by the indiscriminate exorcism of dementia. As one of his closest cycling friends put it, when George had had to give up the bike, 'Part of him, the light, went out then. He lost his sparkle, bless him, and retreated inwards. The last time we saw him, he said, "You will forgive me, but I've forgotten your names", and I realised, oh gosh, he's gone.' And although frustration at his diminishing horizons sometimes reignited old sparks of temper, at Reg or one of the carers trying to get him to shower or change his clothes, he was a most serene patient. Dementia sufferers (and I have known a few) retreat into their essential selves, often distressingly so. Although increasingly silent, the essence of George remained unfailingly polite and calm.

His love for Reg was one of the most ineradicable aspects of George's identity, and amongst the last to go. Near the end, when Reg was once taken to the local rehab hospital, George – already there – saw him across the foyer and burst out, 'There's Reg! I *love* Reg!' Even the nursing staff, inured to daily doses of heartbreak, looked momentarily teary.

'How are you, George?' I asked him on a sultry July day three weeks before he died. In that stale space, the lounge of his nursing home, he gazed calmly back at me, the morphine pinpricks of his pupils almost lost in a sea of cornflower blue. He had no idea at all who I was, but weighed up my question with care: 'I'm very well, thank you. Very well. We've had a little bit of trouble with the neighbours, but that's all finished now. Yes, it's all finished now. It's all turned out rather well.' He fixed his blue eyes on me and smiled in satisfaction. It was the clearest statement I had heard him say in more than a year.

The 'little bit of trouble with the neighbours', the inferno that had threatened to engulf him more than three decades earlier, was the last ember to be extinguished. And although the subsequent owners of Penhempen had their run-ins with them too, they dealt with the neighbour problem in far more practical ways and soon established a working ceasefire. They remained there for the rest of their lives, becoming much-loved members of the community. The house is still cherished and used regularly by their children and grandchildren. It is an ideal fit, as Rhiw Goch was for George and Reg, and for Preds and me. George was right, more so than he could possibly know. It really had 'all turned out rather well'.

THIRD QUARTER

The Element of
WATER

❖

The Season of
AUTUMN

❖

The Direction of
WEST

❖

MICHAEL

WATER

In our first year at Rhiw Goch I sought (and so found) much to confirm my suspicions that we had made a terrible mistake. A month after moving, I wrote in my journal: 'I'm seriously concerned about the lack – and difference in quality – of water here.' It was a clear contrast between my previous home, the tall terrace where I'd been for ten years, and our new one. Below my old house runs a river that I loved with a passion. I would walk by its slate-blue depths daily and swim in its pools whenever possible. On returning home from a trip away, if I was having trouble landing, I'd head to the riverbank to inhale the crisp scent of the water as it tumbled down from the mountains with the exuberance of someone breaking the juiciest gossip. When a swim wasn't on the cards, I would dab river water on my temples and neck like cologne, willing its notes to linger.

'The water here seems dead by comparison,' I wrote, having given it all of four weeks to decide. Sniffing the streams suspiciously, there was no discernible chemical tang, though I was coldly certain that there should be. At least I was able to diagnose the problem: 'farmerphobia', an ignorance, bordering on suspicion, of those working the land. My old place is in a small village only a handful of miles away, but in a very different countryside: pock-marked and post-industrial, where most old farms have become either holiday homes or roofless ruins. Through-out the last century, agriculture had been elbowed to the margins by everyone from the Forestry Commission to the leisure industry.

Water was the conduit for darker fears, one being an ambivalence about belonging. I could slot easily enough into the bustle of a quarry village that had always been the home of people from near and away, but here was a community of far greater settled depth. I might never fit in. Somehow scarier was the possibility that I'd slide in too neatly, that this soft, plump landscape would swal-low me with a satisfied *plop!* and I'd disappear from view. I had long depended on my outsider status, burnished it to a shine and worn it like a war medal. Could I cope with no sharp edges to cling to, no fold in the map in which to hide?

There were more urgent, specific concerns too. Living for ten years in a countryside denuded of farmers, I had felt able to roam freely, for there is no one to shout at you for straying from the path. It might be a dead landscape, but it is at least an ostensibly open one. Access – or the lack of it – obsessed me, and I was afraid that we had moved to an area where every walk might end peering down the barrel of a shotgun. I once discussed it with Reg, always a great walker, and that hadn't helped. On visits to Rhiw Goch, I'd sampled the local paths on the OS map, and had occasionally been flustered to a halt by impenetrable lines of barbed wire. Are many rights of way blocked round here? Who blocks them? I asked him. 'No names, no pack drill!' he replied with a conspiratorial wink. He meant it light-heartedly, I know, but it only made me more nervous.

The first time I met the man who farms all around us, he told me plain: walk anywhere you like. As his family own nearly all of what used to be Rhiw Goch land, that was a blessed relief to hear. I often bump into him up in the fields, our dogs hurtling around together as we chat and laugh, sometimes for the best part of an hour. I'm an extra pair of eyes for him, too, untangling daft lambs from fences and reporting sickly ewes or ailing calves. And as my intimacy with the new landscape grew, so did my confidence and sense of freedom. Even those earlier walks, truncated by fences and hot indignation, proved to have been nothing more than me misreading the map.

The 'dead' water soon began to show signs of life as well, if more subtly than I was used to. Here, the flows are sinuous, viscous even, when compared with the acrobatics of the mountain torrents. Their names spell it out: below my old house is the Afon Dulas, the 'River Black-Blue', from the keen and piercing end of the colour spectrum; beneath Rhiw Goch is Nant y Gwinau, the 'Stream of Rusty-Browns', from the muddy shades at the other end. Even when Nant y Gwinau sidles forty feet down 'our waterfall' (as George liked to think of it), there remains something curiously languid about it.

Thanks to neighbours, Ordnance Survey and some well-honed instincts, I truffled out new swimming spots in nearby rivers and lakes. The river below us yielded some fine dunking pools, while in a rocky chasm just off the lane into town I found a deep, fast flume that is always exhilarating. When Penny told me that they used to take their daughters swimming in the mawn pools on top of a nearby hill, I headed up there and into ponds the colour of old-fashioned porter. Peaty water always makes for a distinctive swim, especially in its silky afterglow. My most

regular dip was a twenty-minute walk away, in a stream-fed pool that friends had dug from the far end of their meadow. Even in a heatwave, it is piercingly cold, as conifers shield it from the afternoon sun. Floating among the lilies and dragonflies, I soon got ideas, and began to plan a pool at Rhiw Goch.

Outdoor swimming is to me what cycling was to George: not just a form of physical exercise, but a metaphysical necessity. Cold wild water restores me, the act of submersion an unbeatable, thrilling synthesis of the flesh and the spirit. The effects are instant, and lingering. As a small child, I was terrified of the water, and would insist on sitting primly in the gallery when my dad took us all to the swimming baths. One day, for some reason, I deigned to give it a go, and went from being traumatised by the water to being bewitched by it in the space of a minute. A lifelong obsession was born, one that has only grown with age.

Over nearly twenty years of living in Wales, my taste in wild water has radically shifted. Like most Midlanders, I grew up mesmerised by the distant sea, and on first uprooting followed the centrifugal power that propels us straight to the island's edge; for me, into that tiny granny flat by the coast. After a year of daily beach walks and swims, the counter-pull inland kicked in. It was a straight swap, and no contest – the sandblast gales of the shore for the shrouded permadrizzle of the hills. Wind enervates me, makes me jumpy. Mist and rain hunker me in.

Though the western ocean is only half an hour away and clearly visible from the top of our hills, it can seem like a mirage. I'll sea-swim a few times a year, and always be glad of it, but my real love now is fresh water, in pools and rivers and excitable chutes. Bobbing along, dappled in a cocoon of oak and ash, fern and moss, the spray of an upstream waterfall casting rainbows above me, I am reborn. Unlike the sometimes scratchy residue of a sea swim, my skin shines soft and scented. Senses are sharper; light and colour explode with depth and texture.

My best swim of all is also half an hour away, in a spring-fed lake in the gold belt mountains of southern Snowdonia. Even on the hottest bank holiday, and in stark contrast to the beaches, I'll likely have it to myself. September and October are loveliest – the surface water still mellow from the summer, the depths biting, the light softer and one entire shore a pointillist canvas of scarlet rowan berries. Glowing and sipping tea from a Thermos, I idly imagine the ice breakers coming, for I am of course Thoreau, and this is my Walden.

Each of the springs around Rhiw Goch sings a different tune. Y Rhos, the heathland above the beech wood, is a sump of watercourses breaking for freedom, their febrile chatter the only competition to the birdsong. The most mysterious well hides in a steep oak copse planted for the navy two hundred years ago. Like a hearth in the hillside, or a doorway into the underworld, its five-foot stone walls and massive lintel boulder enclose a dark, mossy chamber that drips a constant icy whisper. The water is velvety and evaporates on the tongue to leave just a hint of sweet earth. Few even know that it is there, and no one has any hard facts about its provenance. It appears on no map and is near no house, yet its construction shows great care and precision.

After the fights at Penhempen, which had all kicked off over the failing water supply, it was a relief for Reg and George that Rhiw Goch had recently been connected to the mains. Into the 1970s, the house relied on its own spring, up by the drovers' track. The waters emerge from the roots of a massive oak and tumble down a couple of hundred yards to join Nant y Gwinau just above the waterfall. The old gathering tank of brick and broken concrete is still there, though now there's a more haphazard construction – plastic half-pipe, metal tank and saggy netting that is often home to at least one frog – to collect and pipe the water down to our swimming pond. Preds has hacked down tree branches to give me a view of the pool from my desk, so that even when I'm not in it, I can see and feel it.

To bathe in thirty thousand gallons of our own spring water is the sweetest luxury imaginable, even in winter when the low sun can't quite melt all the surface ice. The pool has changed my take on our landscape, too, for instead of skimming its surface I am immersed within it, just one of millions of fellow creatures spending today as every day, hoping to stave off death. And how close they come: dragonflies in lurid bodysuits zip over for a better look; swallows and martins shriek down to speed-skim the water only inches from my face; wagtails shake their tushes from the fence; cuckoos and woodpeckers strike up a tune in nearby trees.

On early-morning dips, I'll sometimes startle a heron and feel blessed as it flaps away like a pterodactyl. When there are cows in the field, they crowd the fence to chew and stare at me, this strange man-fish puffing up and down. In the pool's first year, we didn't build a robust enough fence; the cows trampled it and got in. Considering one bank is a narrow ridge above a sharp drop to the lane, it is a miracle that we didn't wake up to eighty stone of bullock floating stiff in the lilies.

The responsibility of a swimming pond rests predictably heavy on me. As did George at Penhempen, I obsessively monitor the output from the spring and feel a rising panic when a dry spell sees it dwindle by the day. If that combines with sunshine and high temperatures, the water warms up and can become murky. I lose hours searching for miracle natural boosters and algae-busters, or watching online videos by tattooed survivalists in the woods. Like them, I take the flow and clarity of my water all too personally.

*

My childhood volte-face from aquaphobe to water sprite had many ingredients; one, long before I recognised it, was erotic. Municipal chlorine was an olfactory aphrodisiac years before honeysuckle, cinnamon or George's ylang-ylang ('Super!'). Of the public pools of my childhood, I preferred the older ones with communal changing rooms, where forbidden flesh could more easily be scanned. Better still was the outdoor pool at a hotel a few miles out of town. My dad had done some work for the owners, who in return had invited us to use the pool – a moment of casual generosity that we milked for years. At eleven or twelve, I was cycling up there with schoolfriends and, after a swim, encouraging them to strip off with me in a rhododendron clearing. Deep neural pathways were gouged.

Through my teenage and college years, there came a welter of art that married water with gay sexuality, and I lapped it up. Alan Hollinghurst's debut novel, *The Swimming Pool Library*, dripped with promise in the swimming clubs and changing rooms of gilded, cocksure lives; peering through their steamed-up windows, I plotted my way in. Edmund White's *A Boy's Own Story* proved that the same libidinous ripples from 1950s Michigan pulsed all the way to 1980s Worcestershire. Although the book's opening on a Midwestern lakeside holiday was impossibly distant, the ache for skinny-dipping and sleepover fun with the sons of family friends made me throb with recognition; jealousy too, for Edmund White was far better at it than me.

In my first term at university, I went to a party where in one room Derek Jarman's *Sebastiane* was showing on Channel 4. Sneaking in to watch – I was still pretending to be straight – my eyes popped and synapses exploded on seeing the loving shots of writhing men drenched by sun and sea. I stayed as long as I dared, and fooled no one but myself. Days later, the party's host approached me in the union bar and whispered, 'If you need to talk, I'm always here.'

Although Jarman's juxtaposition of water, light and glistening flesh was an unquestionable turn-on, it blazed a little too strong for my more puckish tastes. I felt the same, and still do, about David Hockney's Californian pool paintings, in which his naked beefcake baked under blank cerulean skies. I was, it transpired, far more of a costume drama queen. Also in the first term at university the Merchant Ivory film of E. M. Forster's *A Room with a View* came out – and helped me to do the same, thanks to the scene where Simon Callow and the lissom twosome of Rupert Graves and Julian Sands take a naked dip in a woodland pool. The bosky setting was every bit as steamy as the carefree nudity, and the scene replayed endlessly in my head, albeit with a very different ending.

The success of *A Room with a View* led Merchant Ivory to film another Forster: *Maurice*, the gay romance only published after the author's death, more than half a century after he'd written it. As gamekeeper Alec Scudder, Rupert Graves was again naked and glorious, his and Maurice's place of secret assignation a boathouse on another seductively rustic creek. Though I was twenty, inching out of the closet and furious at Thatcher, I secretly ached for a country house weekend of skinny-dipping larks, spied on from behind a tree by a handsome gardener, who later that night would climb into my chamber and have me on crisp white linen. Like the guests at Rhiw Goch, I too was hiding from the brittle 1980s in *The Country Diary of an Edwardian Lady*, though my refuge was in the pages that would have been ripped out and burned.

Reading *Maurice* only made the itch keener: 'He was an outlaw in disguise. Perhaps among those who took to the greenwood in old time there had been two men like himself – two.' The greenwood! I literally pined. 'Two men can defy the world.' I slunk through the shadows behind Maurice and Alec, down to the boathouse, the evening sun reflected in ripples that washed the walls and there, stock-still in the dancing light, the outline shape of *him*, waiting.

Wales is a perfect fit for an aquaphile. Water is its foremost element, and never far away, whether squelching beneath your feet, trickling lustily somewhere nearby or falling in prodigious quantities from the sky above. Its ubiquity stokes a fundamental identity beneath everything, rather than just the crescendo kinetics of male sexuality. Where once, only minutes ago, paucity of opportunity and the thunder of youth combined to steer every al fresco swim into a lecherous quagmire, now, finally, the many other dopamine hits get their turn in the swell. Unlike George, I view the silting up of libido mostly with pleasure and relief, and when I plough up and down my pond now, the thrill is aesthetic, cerebral and spiritual. Its curative properties are physical, boosting a sluggish circulation and cooling arthritis and gout, and psychological, recentring me in the elemental landscape and dousing the ferment that threatens daily to inundate me.

Not that Welsh rain merely falls – it is far too cunning for that. Often it sweeps sideways across the hills in billowing great curtains, or hangs almost static in the air so that the first inkling of its presence comes when you suddenly realise that you are wet, and cannot immediately tell why. And thanks to the meteorological wizard-gods of the west, it's not especially unusual for it to rain out of a clear blue sky. I live, it seems, in an infinitely prolific metaphor.

Days when the weather closes in and the world is curtained off are some of the best. Familiar shapes mutate into eerie spectres, views vanish and sound is damped down as surely as if a grey blanket has been laid gently over the land. We are alone, and can breathe easy.

With the possible exception of a summer heatwave, blanching the fields gold and making sapphires of the harebells, extended dry spells never feel quite right. Even the landscape looks amiss. Welsh peaks need sun-shafts, wraiths of cloud and distant dark squalls to ramp up the drama; under blank skies they can appear terribly humdrum and (whisper it) *small*. If the mosses on tree trunks and rocks have become parched and listless, even on their shaded northern flanks, the unease is palpable. Worst is that *gwynt traed y meirw* in early spring, the icy east wind that has scythed over the feet of the dead, cracking open the dusty soil and leaching colour and contrast from the scene. This is a soft, spongy landscape that urgently needs – and usually gets – a regular soaking.

Prolonged spells of wet weather drove George mad. 'RAIN!!!' he thundered into his diary, 'rained all night, rained all day! Gah!' In the first couple of years at Rhiw Goch, before the cycling began, such days sent him into his library and the far-off worlds of cheap fantasy novels. On the bike, he fashioned a rain cape to help, but even with that, there were sometimes days on end with no let-up, and he would be forced to prowl the house like a caged animal. He worried about losing fitness if a few days slid by with no cycling, so took to the library again, but for weight training, stretches, sit-ups and press-ups, his new science fiction.

Days like those were no fun for Reg. In the 1990s, when the B&B operation had subsided and George was out conquering the hills, Reg loved the quiet time alone at home, drawing, painting and cooking, walking the dogs and receiving neighbours for coffee and a catch-up. A housebound George meant that Reg could never quite relax. The scrapes, bumps and occasional outbursts from upstairs were bad enough, but worse was silence, which he knew would eventually be broken by a fusillade of worry about work on the house that George had just noticed needed doing, who they could trust to do it – and how much it might cost.

I know my sarcasm about George's penny-pinching verges on the catty. Though Oscar Wilde's aphorism about knowing the price of everything and the value of nothing echoes regularly on reading his diaries, he knew both, and prized them equally fiercely. His upbringing was cramped by bankruptcy and poverty, his young adulthood by the austerity of the post-war years. Entirely understandably, he never lost his terror of the money flow dribbling to a standstill.

Consequently, though he pursued his dreams with great determination, it was always in the most sober and responsible of ways. In Bournemouth, that meant acting the highly professional photographer, being reliable, reasonably priced, on time, tidy and unobtrusive. There was often no guarantee of work; he just turned up on spec at dinners and dances and hoped that the occasion was sufficiently glittering, or the attendees sufficiently tipsy, to make it worth his while. No client, not even the most port-addled Freemason belching cigar smoke into his face, would have had the slightest inkling that George probably despised him.

Even when the next dream, moving to Wales, was well under way and Reg had already relocated, George still had the self-discipline to get out there and wring a few extra quid from the career that had long ago lost its appeal. Writing to Reg from Bournemouth in early 1974, he told him that he had 'just been to the Heathlands to a Hoteliers' Supper Dance – didn't expect to do any business and took £8!' He picked up some useful inside information too: 'A Mrs Owen there says the "Birmingham Mercury", a Sunday paper, is good for holiday business, better than the "Birmingham Post" and she speaks from experience.' Mrs Owen was absolutely right.

To make the new life happen in Wales, George had to direct proceedings from afar. Although Reg was coping brilliantly, far better than either of them had expected, George kept a very tight hold of the purse strings, negotiating from Bournemouth with workmen and suppliers, and spending his free time scouring antique shops and the small ads for furniture and carpets. Cefn, the first house, was in a very poor state, needing not just renovation but substantial rebuilding too. George totted up all the figures, and found that they had 'nearly a thousand in hand'. It was tight.

Decades later, Reg talked of how difficult those early years had been, and how his faith – in God and in George – had kept him going. He was right to be so sure. George might count every penny, and pounce on anyone who he felt was trying to rip them off, but he was rigorously thorough and never cut corners. His attention to detail was such that, nearly fifty years later, Cefn remains much as they left it, as does Rhiw Goch. There have been no nasty surprises, no lurking horrors and no need to do any substantial renovation of either place.

In this regard, I really do wish that I were more like George. There's a stubborn pragmatism to his budgeting that has always eluded me. Once upon a time I wore my financial ineptitude as a badge of pride, but now I see that it is a truly perverse quality to be proud of. By paying as little attention as possible to money, I liked to believe that it proved me to be some sort of freer, higher spirit; although, by making just as much of an emotional issue of it, only from the opposite stance, I was no better than the tightest skinflint or flightiest squanderer.

Like all of the things that enhance life – love, beauty, art – money needs to flow, and in both directions. Place emotional or logistical blockages in the stream and you risk creating stagnant pools and barren wadis, as well as flash floods of panic. It is not even a question of quantity. At times the stream is full and fast, at others sluggish and tortuously slow, but either way, it must flow. I fear that mine is an essentially childish approach, one that hasn't much changed since Christmases of forty years ago, when I'd gleefully amass the cash and tokens I'd received, before hitting the shops at opening time the day after Boxing Day and triggering the agony of seeing my stockpile gradually dwindle to zero. The moment of contentment was so brief, the rest a slow torture.

*

In our first year at Rhiw Goch, some visitors came to stay, people we haven't seen since. Here's why: on leaving, one of them took me aside and said, 'Yes, it's a great house, but you *really* need to get rid of the two old men now.' Reg's paintings still filled a wall in the living room, a hangover from his funeral; their photos and knick-knacks were scattered everywhere. I recognised my friend's train of thought, and know that he meant well, but he had badly misunderstood us, the house, and our relationship with Reg and George in both life and death. Even were it possible, we could not 'get rid of the two old men', put them out with the bins on a Thursday morning. Though their presence at Rhiw Goch has ebbed, as ours has deepened, not a day passes without them continuing to teach us something new. *They* are here because *we* are here, and that is a sacrosanct principle of their gift. Even if it makes us old before our time, that's fine. Preds and I were both born middle-aged.

The imperative to keep things flowing is one of Reg and George's most urgent legacies, and it is not easy terrain for us. We are both chronic hoarders, and now have an awful lot of corners to fill. My abiding fear, that swamps me when my brain starts to crack, is that if we leave this tendency unchecked, we might drown in our own detritus. I keep picturing Reg's final bedroom in the front parlour, his bed entombed by towers of books. That came at the end of a largely tidy life; we're almost there already.

Hoarding touches another liquid yardstick, that of the half-full or half-empty glass. A close relative of both 'the grass is greener' syndrome and overweening nostalgia, they are all inculcated not just in particular families or cultures, but across whole generations too. To those that had fought in the war, and who had seen close up the glass shattered altogether, its rebuilding and refilling was a massive collective effort that manifested itself not just politically, but in art and architecture, philosophy and literature, religion and sex.

Writ large across an entire age group was a determination to improve the world, and gratitude to have the chance to do so. There are so few of them left, the generation that experienced the war as young adults. Those that saw fascism full in the face have acted as an anchor on us all, but as the last of them slip away and the anchor is pulled, it is no surprise that we are once again drifting into those same shark-infested waters. That alone is reason enough to honour Reg, George and all our grandparents, and to keep their voices singing.

To the generation below – our parents – the war was only a hazy memory: distant danger manifested as childish excitement, and hardship that steadily and measurably eased throughout their adult lives. Some coped with the gradual liberation better than others. Improving opportunity and security were readily enough shared, at least in the good times, though many have been quick enough to pull up the drawbridge behind them as colder winds began to blow.

Even in the ample years, the emotional dividend often failed to keep up, and remained frozen in ancestral tundra. As is painfully clear now, Middle England, so used to seeing its own reflection in everything, is not coping well with a changing world. Over the course of my lifetime, the tenets of this inheritance have become ever more obviously threadbare, though the signs were always there. I spent much of my young adulthood trying to be a glass-half-full kind of man, because that is the illusion I was taught to spin, but it has never really been so. Had I asked as a child whether our glass was half full or half empty, the response of many around me would have been hot denial of its very existence: 'Glass? What glass?' Pause. 'Oh, *that* glass.' Another pause. 'Who's emptied it?'

For Preds, swaddled warm in his dowry blankets, the childhood beaker always brimmed full. It might seem ironic, since his upbringing in a threatened minority culture is in such contrast to mine in the bumptious exceptionalism of Britishness, but perhaps that dazzling ability to make the best of an outsider status is one of the keys that drew me to the *noddfa*, the sanctuary of Cymru. Sometimes I idly wonder what my life might have been had I been heterosexual, had all the doors opened smoothly in my direction. I would not be here, I'm sure of that.

For all the comfort of Preds' childhood, beyond the farm gate it was a different story. Welsh-speaking Wales has long been terrified that its glass is emptying at an alarming rate, and will soon be bone dry. Though the imminent apocalypse is routinely overstated, there was plenty in the 1970s and 1980s to be taken as evidence of its advent: an economy especially vulnerable to deindustrialisation, communities hollowed out by depopulation and holiday homes, a dependence on marginal land, the relentless anglicisation of tourism and television.

In *The Man Who Went into the West*, a biography of the poet R. S. Thomas, Byron Rogers describes the rural Montgomeryshire of the 1940s and early 1950s, when Thomas was rector of the remote parish of Manafon, in the hills twenty miles east of Rhiw Goch. Thomas continually searched for an idealised Welsh-speaking community, going progressively further west until he reached his final parish at Aberdaron, the last village at the end of the Llŷn peninsula, that deep-veined arm of land stretching out towards Ireland. He didn't find it at Manafon, at least not down in the villages and valleys: 'it is still there in the hills behind the hills', writes Rogers, 'where the Welsh language, like the view, begins at 1,000 feet'. The language as a contour is a canny fit: overlay a topographical map of Wales with one of the spread of Cymraeg, and there is remarkable congruence. And every ten years, out come the census results showing that the contours have yet again contracted, the outside waters have risen further and the language is retreating into ever fewer islands and isolated heartlands.

Maps are powerful icons, especially for places that feel existentially threatened. Thomas self-published his first poetry collection, *The Stones of the Field*, while vicar of Manafon; his wife, the artist Mildred Eldridge, known as

Elsi, drew the cover, a wind-bent tree in thin, rocky soil, over an outline map of Wales. The tone and topic of Thomas's stark verse are immediately established.

On my wall is the 1903 six-inch Ordnance Survey map of our parish. So many of the houses and farms marked are now piles of wet rubble, if that. Their ghostly names sigh on the evening breeze: Hen-dîr, Pen-rhôs, Anllwyd and Llain, Rhyd-yr-hosan and Dôl-y-bont, the double minors of Esgair-fach and Tal-y-wern-fach, the lyrical death rattle of Lluest-cethingrych ('at least the name will still live on the maps when even the walls have crumbled,' wrote George after they'd walked up there one gusty January day). Within a mile of Rhiw Goch, there are a further seven houses and a chapel that are now holiday homes, some occupied most weekends, some never at all. But it is the comparative maps charting change – of language, population, birthplace, employment, wealth – that provide the most poignant iconography of the Welsh condition, in the unshakeable fear that so much of the best of it is steadily draining away. No matter how others see it, or how much rainfall it catches, subjectively the glass is always almost empty.

In recent years, the 'size of Wales' has become a journalistic trope for measuring large areas. It is used particularly to illustrate stories of destruction or despoilment: felled rainforest or bulldozed jungle, a broken-off polar ice shelf or melting glacier, spreading desertification or an oil spill, the region affected by an earthquake or a tsunami. All too fittingly, a 'size of Wales' is not just a unit of area, but a unit of loss.

AUTUMN

In 2012, our second Calan Gaeaf – Halloween – at Rhiw Goch, death hung heavy in the air. The media was full of the arrival in Britain of the *Chalara* fungus, or ash dieback. Since first being identified in Poland in 1992, the disease has ripped across the European mainland, and arrived on our shores via infected saplings from a Dutch nursery. Reports suggested that it was spreading quickly from the initial bridgehead in south-east England. The prognosis was gloomy.

In response to the news, I ricocheted out for a day-long walk to visit and photograph the ash trees nearby, scared that it might be the last chance. Over the previous couple of years the ash had moved from the periphery of my vision, always there but little noticed, to being a tree that I went out of my way to spend time with. I've come to love its gangly outline and Gothic pallor, its grey geometric bark and gentle-giant solidity. On bright nights, I like to walk the lane beneath a monster ash, tripping out on its leaves strobing the moonlight.

Such pleasure could soon be a thing of the past, I worried as I hurried to check in with the ash trees that mark so many of our old field boundaries, as well as the loftier specimens up the drovers' track. They don't look well, I fretted, before realising, Well . . . *do they ever*? They're ash trees; looking pale and bedraggled is what they do best.

Loss of a tree species casts a long shadow. At Penhempen in November 1979, a page heading in George's diary reads 'FIRST ELM FELLED', after Dutch elm disease had arrived in their nearby wood. By the following April, every elm had died and been chopped down, though there was an upside: 'Gave a hand and had a few logs.' To me, the disease is only a dim childhood memory that has left my generation barely knowing one of its bedrock trees. The thought of today's youngsters having a comparable blank with ash is so sad, for although a new arboreal threat is trumpeted almost every week – apple canker, chestnut blight, sudden oak death, and the rest that climate change will surely bring – evidence still suggests that ash dieback is likely to be the most devastating, and that it is spreading. It arrived in mid Wales in 2016; we shall see.

Even without a deadly fungus, lanky ash trees are prone to internal rot that can make them crack in a gale. A year after Reg and George moved to Rhiw Goch, there was an almighty autumn storm: 'bits of the ash tree opposite now and again are blown on to the roof or the front windows – and we jump!' noted George. It was time to get rid of the tottering tree, which had in any case been spooking them slightly, ever since an old man had passed by in the first week of January and told them about the son of the house hanging himself from it shortly after the war. That winter, three other ash trees up the drovers' track popped and came down too. Photos show Reg splitting wood from one just below the spring. The twisted carcass of the trunk, so lithe and pale when it fell, is still there nearly four decades later, stained and spongy, pockmarked by bugs and covered in moss.

Though the fields, coppices and tracks are dibbed with hazels and hawthorn, sycamore and willow, larch, elder, rowan, cherry and lime, four trees dominate our greenwood: ash and oak, beech and birch, and in those two couplings. The monster ash with the strobing leaves is just a few yards from its mythic twin, a mighty oak with a girth of seventeen feet. Both heave with life. Bees zip in and out of an old nest in the trunk of the ash; badgers have dug a sett in the roots of the oak. Sheep snuggle up to both; birds and squirrels flit through their branches.

There are taller, beefier oaks in the fields and woods around, but this one is *primus inter pares*. To the west, away from the house, its outspread boughs command a deep grassy bowl below the drovers' track, a natural amphitheatre where we sledge in winter. From the houseward side of its trunk, our spring bubbles from the roots, once to slake thirst and grow vegetables, now to fill my swimming pond.

With its military associations and manspreading canopy, it is inevitable that we perceive the oak as the alpha male of the wood, feet planted heftily in the soil as it keeps watch over the countryside. Equally inevitable after centuries of chauvinism is that ash is presented as its female counterfoil. King Oak and Queen Ash are everywhere from fairy stories to Wiccan rituals, and it's hard not to slip into such reductive thinking. Oakish George and ashen Reg fit the bill, though remember the twist: for all its vulnerability, ash is whip-smart, the chosen staff of *Mabinogi* magicians, the world tree of Norse mythology, and with an unsung punk androgyny.

Even the most fervent ash devotee would struggle to claim that its autumn foliage is a highlight. The thin cluster of leaves is one of the last to arrive at the springtime party, and six months later is always first to go, slipping from view when no one is watching. The oak, meanwhile, hogs the hearth and ripples with pride, flexing its sunset colours for all to admire. There is oak in every direction: in woods and spinneys, along tracks, lanes and boundaries, standing sentinel in fields. Many of the larger plantations date from the eighteenth century, when the slow-growing Montgomeryshire oak was a prized component of navy warships; a swan with an oak sprig in its beak crowns the county's insignia in recognition. As munitions factories go, there are none lovelier than these rusting oak woods at Calan Gaeaf.

Discovering somewhere quite new is all the more thrilling when it has long been right under your nose. On moving house, we fill in our mental map of the area only piece-meal. Routes become favourites by sheer luck and habit; others, equally deserving, somehow fail to catch our eye. Below the house, there is an old cart track buried in the oaks above the river. George stumbled across it one wet Monday in their first November: 'found a lovely walk along the riverbank towards the big waterfall,' he wrote. 'Beautiful! and very visible under the leafless trees.' Not to us, it wasn't. We'd been here three years before Preds discovered it on a walk with his nephew.

There was an even more egregious example waiting to be noticed: an isolated oak grove at the far end of the same field. Although visible from my desk and only two hundred yards away, we were here five years before I went for a closer look. It was autumn that finally alerted me to it. In spring, summer and winter the dozen trees melt into the wider wooded tableau, but as October fades, their unusual colour stands out: a dusky salmon pink, against the prevailing backdrop of yesterday's mustard. The semicircular conclave of trees sits in a crook of the lane as it wheels downhill in a lazy hairpin. Out on a limb, it is a secretive and strangely dainty corner, a silent note in the symphony and a reminder that for all its virile associations, oak too has its softer side.

For the beech wood two fields away, its showstopper comes in early May when feathery leaves unfurl and in one day it catapults from gaunt austerity to elfin playground. It is a moment of exquisite transience, as the canopy quickly hardens into summer. The autumn show is slow: a month-long swell of basso profundo in which the tinkling chimes of gold and russet become imperceptibly clearer every day. On the ground, a beech wood is forever autumn: little else is allowed to grow beneath its outstretched arms, so that the carpet of fallen leaves is permanent and only refreshed by November's bright new crop.

Given a choice for my final walk, like a condemned man's last supper, it would be to this beech wood. In there, I dissolve. It is where I *dod yn ôl at fy nghoed* – literally 'return to my trees', figuratively 'come to my senses'. In autumn, the paramount sense is smell, that Proustian rush of nostalgia, whisking us to another place or time in a heartbeat. There are so many triggers: the first whiff of wood smoke on damp air, an umami wallop of fungi in the woods, the tang of fast water after the dribbles of summer. Sometimes the season's perfume is impossibly sweet, the sugar high of the katsura, the candy floss tree, as its leaves shimmer pink and dying near the back door, or the smoky nectar of autumn raspberry bushes that perk up breakfast from August to November. Sometimes the sweetness makes you gag, the cloying punch of death in the fields from old ewes that fell over and never got up again.

The smell of the beech wood, like the smell of the mountain river below my old house, is the one that brings me back home, and never more so than in autumn. I am instantly soothed by its brown and leathery bass notes that somehow hold a distant hint of rich tobacco smoke. In such fanciful moments, sat with my back square against one of the elephantine tree trunks, my hands idling on the mossy armrests of its roots, I am in a chesterfield by the fire at my gentlemen's club.

Dropping through the wood in a series of little skips is the stream that begins its life up on Bryn-y-Brain, and that once constituted Rhiw Goch's boundary. The bulk of the beech wood sits on the far side. On our bank of the stream, the grace of the wood soon disintegrates into a scrubby mix of trees dominated by birch in assorted states of collapse. The scent here is lighter and more astringent – still the gentlemen's club, but in the watery sunbeams of the morning after.

This half of the wood has none of the imperial swagger of the beeches. Its charms reveal themselves only slowly, as you bump your way down to the river over rotting stumps and trickling sumps of moss and leaf mould. The birch trees huddle in what appears to be funereal communion, though look harder and you'll see elegant solidarity. A quiet beauty too, in the papery bark striped like toy tigers, the harlequin leaf mottle of autumn and the purple lacery of winter. The young trees stretch athletically in the morning chill, flexing their smooth and sinewy limbs. Their older brethren, racked by arthritic twists and bulges, look on admiringly, and with no trace of regret.

*

In Machynlleth's calendar, the biggest event is the Calan Gaeaf lantern parade through the town's streets. Held at the end of October, it is one of the few occasions that brings out every section of the community: farmers, townies, hippies and holiday-homers alike. To us all, it is noise and fire, smoke and chatter. To the struggling pubs, it is a rare night of three-deep bars and ringing tills. To the kids, it is soaking up applause for their lantern creations and posing for proud aunties. To some, it is a solemn marking of the Celtic new year, the skipped heartbeat when the veil between the worlds is at its thinnest and the dead at their nearest. To a local church, it is – as they warned one year in leaflets distributed house-to-house – a dangerous return to witchcraft. The reaction to this – incredulous hilarity – was nigh on unanimous.

Although death is an ostensible aspect every year, the lantern parade of 2012 was different. It came at the end of the most traumatic month in Machynlleth's long existence. On the first of October, five-year-old April Jones had been kidnapped from outside her family home on a town estate. Within hours there were dozens and then hundreds of volunteers combing the surrounding fields, hills and riverbanks to look for her. The number of searchers swelled even further the following morning, and continued to grow. To their ranks were added hundreds of police and other emergency services, journalists, broadcasters and, inevitably, in their wake, gawpers. The hunt for April is still the largest missing person's operation in British history, and it was top of the news agenda for weeks. When it transpired that the hideous worst had happened, that she had been taken and murdered by someone she knew, the shockwaves rippled around the world.

On the day she disappeared, I was on the train up to Scotland for a lecture tour. Every day that week, I arrived in a new town, checked into my hotel and spent the afternoon glued in horror to the rolling news channels, watching from afar her poor family exhausted and distraught, digging into impossible reserves of dignity to face the hell that had consumed them. There on screen were my friends and neighbours searching and weeping, the familiar landmarks of my little town shrouded in a sombre grey downpour, my woods and rivers choked by police tape and turned from places of sanctuary into scenes of infernal darkness. Tears of impotent fury bubbled up, and I ached to be home with a hiraeth – that quintessentially Welsh notion of unattainable longing – stronger than I'd ever known before.

On finally returning, I found the area dazed and bruised, as if it had been brutally violated, and not just by the heinous crime itself. The insensitivity and sensationalism of the media had been one of the hardest things for people to cope with. It was shocking to see how they framed the story, the town, the area and us. There was endless sickly cant about the innocence of the place being rudely shattered, a soft-focus picture of simple Welsh country folk being visited by horrific forces entirely alien to them, that they had no hope of understanding.

Even the geography was tinkered with to fit that narrative: the killer's rented property, routinely described in the media as 'a remote farmhouse', was the most overlooked house in the centre of its village, less than a hundred yards from a busy trunk road. April's murderer had lived there only a month, and no one really knew him. But the journalists who swarmed all over for weeks, knocking repeatedly on every door and ambushing anyone they came across, even poking uninvited into sheds, garages, bins and gardens, just wouldn't accept this. Instead, the residents' reluctance to talk was used to fuel dark hints that the village was closing ranks around one of its own. It damaged people in ways they have struggled with ever since.

There was talk of cancelling that year's lantern parade, but thankfully April's family gave it their blessing. They needed it, and knew that everyone else did too: the coming together, the ceremonial lighting of candles and fires, the tears and hugs, the fierce pride in our battered town. It was a night of such power and grace, a reminder to us all of what a special community Machynlleth is, and never to take it for granted.

Reg had always known that. On his last birthday the previous February – his eighty-fourth – Preds and I went to see him in the Machynlleth care home. We'd brought him a card, presents and a cake, but the gift he most wanted was fresh air, something he'd not tasted in months. Through speech thickened by repeated strokes, he cajoled us into wheeling him in a chair to the shops. In a round trip of three hundred yards, we were stopped so often that it took the best part of an hour. On a quiet Friday morning, people appeared suddenly out of shops, offices and thin air to wish Reg well, one after another, clearly thrilled to see him. Although he could barely frame a coherent sentence, he smiled, clasped outstretched hands and proffered a cold pink cheek for kissing. They were saying goodbye, to one of their own.

Standing on that chilly pavement, it struck me that in Preds and Reg, I was with two of the most loved men in town: one a native, the other an adopted son. Machynlleth and Reg fitted each other so snugly, and always had. Once George had had to give up driving and Reg was free to take a taxi to town, he would spend half the day there, flitting from shop to cafe, accepting chairs, tea and cake, and paying for it with quicksilver chatter. Like George topping up his tan, he used those outings to replenish his levels of companionship, to give him enough to return to Rhiw Goch, where it would slowly ebb away.

After getting Reg back to the care home, we had a meeting at the solicitors' to sort out our house sale and the purchase of Rhiw Goch. The trusty machine of small-town country life had been ignited and was clanking into action. Cogs were turning, the right assistance arriving just when needed. I suddenly realised that the roots I'd been admiring beneath Reg and Preds were mine too, if only I could let myself accept them.

The treacle-brown solicitors' office has not changed in thirty years. Reg and George used the same firm, may well have sat in the same room poring over the same deeds, when they bought Rhiw Goch. By the reception desk is that moment frozen in time: a large framed photograph of Machynlleth in 1981, the town dolled up in its Sunday best as the host of that year's National Eisteddfod, and with its clock tower wearing a set of Prince of Wales feathers to mark Prince Charles's wedding to Lady Diana Spencer the previous week. Sporting the Prince's crest was no act of fealty. As the venue for the 1404 coronation of Owain Glyndŵr, the last native Prince of Wales,

Machynlleth was looking at London eyeball-to-eyeball, as an equal, daring it to disagree. The signs at the town's edge make it clear: 'Prifddinas Hynafol Cymru: Ancient Capital of Wales', they state, on the strength of this brief – and not entirely certain – episode six centuries ago. Few capital cities consist only of 'two streets and a pronunciation problem', as one German guidebook memorably had it, but chutzpah is an essential ingredient in any metropolitan psyche, and there is no shortage of that.

Although the early 1980s were turbulent times in what was rapidly becoming post-industrial Britain, Machynlleth was enjoying a purple patch all of its own. What industry the area had once sustained – slate quarrying to the north of town, lead and silver mining to the east and south – was long gone, in its place the great green slabs of Forestry

Commission plantation, and the many jobs and tied houses that went with it. After a few difficult decades, Welsh hill farming had steadied, especially since Britain had joined the Common Market in 1973, and farmers in marginal areas began receiving subsidies from the Common Agricultural Policy (CAP). At its peak in 1984, the CAP accounted for 71 per cent of the entire European Economic Community budget.

For many locally, farm income was further augmented by the plentiful piecework available from Laura Ashley. Between a hot summer's day in 1980 – when Lady Di posed in that famously backlit Ashley skirt – and the autumn of 1985 – when the eponymous founder died after tumbling downstairs on her sixtieth birthday – the Laura Ashley empire was unassailable in its mission to swathe the world in floral swirls. Lamps burned late in local farmhouses as wives gathered to cut patterns with sheep-shearing tools, or stitch hems and borders at the kitchen table.

Designer Antony Sheppard also chose Machynlleth as his base, opening three shops in its two streets. Other blow-ins opened art and gift emporia, with names like Fusspots and Joy; this has long been a town where you'll never run short of joss sticks or lovespoons. Alongside the ephemera, though, were the banks and bakers, butchers and grocers of a workaday Welsh town. Across the border, a small stone huddle of a couple of thousand people is a village, but in mid Wales, twenty miles along ropy roads from the next set of shops, it's an ancient capital with a weekly market over seven centuries old. Reg loved each of Machynlleth's Janus-like sides – the hard-bargaining old fella in a flat cap, as well as the hippy floating by in a waft of patchouli. He was neither, and both.

*

For a while after the strain of Penhempen, Machynlleth looked heavenly to George. 'Lovely to be back here again', he enthused to his diary in their first week at Rhiw Goch, after visiting the Wednesday market, which he found 'better than when we lived here before'. The glow soon faded. He found the town slightly claustrophobic and made little attempt to socialise there. Before long he was noting, 'Lovely day out at Shrewsbury. Really pleasant to be in an attractive city for a change, and to have such a rich choice of shops.'

He never doubted Rhiw Goch, though. 'We love this house more than all the others, even Cefn,' he wrote on 13 September 1980, within a week of moving in. 'It is so homely and so quiet and NO NEIGHBOURS!' Even things that would normally drive him to distraction seemed charming. The phone line went dead within days, though the bells – all four of them – 'tinkled all day long!' as the autumn wind rattled the line against overhanging branches. Pam and Daniel brought them three kittens from their barn; they were christened Mewsey, Tibs and Tabs and chronicled obsessively: 'Back 12.30 – Mewsey mewed!!! Cats all girls!' And the next day: 'Cats out for the first time. Twins came back, Mewsey didn't at first. All spent the night in kitchen and used soil tray!'

As the autumn nights drew in, the race was on to get the house fit for guests already booking for the coming spring.

In the house alone, there was an internal wall to be demolished, woodworm to be blitzed, damp-proofing and decorating to be done, central heating to be installed, a plumbing system to revamp, a new toilet to be put in as well as washbasins in every bedroom, and the whole place needed urgent rewiring. George's attention moved from the kittens to the workmen tramping in and out of the house. In both Cefn and Penhempen, he'd had to crack the whip on those he decided were either lazy or greedy. At Rhiw Goch, one in particular, recommended as the best locally for the installation of central heating and their new oil-fired range, caused progressively worsening palpitations:

Saturday 6 Sept: 2pm spoke to Pete at Talywern. He can do the central heating and plumbing too! Aren't we lucky?

Weds 10 Sept: 8pm Pete called till 11pm to talk about the work on the house.

Monday 29 Sept: Called on Pete. He called 5.15pm to survey the house (again!) re CH. Laid down the law – we want it *done!* and soon.

Wednesday 1st October: Saw Pete a.m.: he called on us with estimate for CH – £2,010.00 – I said 'go ahead'.

Wednesday 15 Oct: Pete came round about 12o'c & left at 3pm, but didn't do much except unwrap the radiators & work out his share of the discount.

Thurs 16 Oct: Pete arr & began fixing radiators to walls. Cold & wet. NE airstream. [Then added later:] Pete 10am–3.40pm.

Pete then had the effrontery to go away for a few days ('God knows when this CH will get done!'). On his return, George was watching like a hawk and clocking every minute. In George's diary, 'Pete' changes to 'F—' (his surname), a sure sign of growing displeasure.

Sat 25 Oct: F— supposed to come to concrete base of F/ Belge [the new oil stove for the kitchen] – no appearance no apology or explanation – no phone call no nothing. He is certainly not a man of his word – !!!

Monday 27 Oct: Dreadful day. Non-stop rain! Floods in N & W Wales, & Preston cut off! F— didn't arrive – so I rang him at 10am 'I want a few words with you'. He turned up with friend Ron at 10.30am, was very cold in fact rude. Went at 12.30 returned at 2.15!!! did an hour's 'work', I gave him the Riot Act before he went.

Thursday 30 Oct: F— walked out. 6.30pm Called on Gordon Edwards. He will come to look at the work done before he considers completing it.

Sunday 2nd November: Beautiful sunshine but *cold*. Reg phone F—. Wife answered.

By the end of November, after one of the wettest autumns on record, the house was sufficiently warm and watertight to start bringing in the boxes of belongings that had been in storage since they had left Penhempen. Most contained books, and they now had plenty of new companions, as George had been enthusiastically enrolling in various book clubs. These would often entice customers with introductory offers so irresistible that he'd sign Reg up too in order to qualify twice. Filling their new home with weighty hardbacks was George's statement of faith that this was for keeps. So too was his choice of books: dozens on gardening and plenty too from a more specialist club (*The Joy of Sex, More Joy of Sex, Playland, The New Massage*). He was hunkering in, stoking the fires to make the autumn of his life as warm and scented as it could be.

For all the rosy-cheeked wholesomeness of the Laura Ashley age, it was only thin topsoil. Transforming scrubby nettle beds into gardens, Reg and George cleared, dug and planted, but strictly in the ornamental fashion of the day. In their thirty years at Rhiw Goch, there was never a vegetable garden, nor even any fruit beyond the ubiquitous brambles, one gooseberry bush and a wizened old apple tree at the foot of the field. Reg was a dab hand with medicinal herbs, cooking up tisanes and poultices, but there was never any jam or chutney stewing away on the Franco Belge, nor homegrown veg to garnish the much-feted dinners of their customers. The only produce grown for their guests were the sweet peas and roses destined for tiny vases on bedside tables. They may have marketed themselves as 'The Old Welsh Farmhouse in the Hills', but it was with none of the muck still attached.

More than almost any other aspect of their life compared to ours, this makes me dizzy with vertigo as I look down the decades. So prescriptive is our narrative of moving to the country, all grow-your-own and seasonal smugness, so obsessive our nostalgia and comfort-eating and comfort-thinking-about-eating, that to spurn the opportunity to cultivate crops is almost beyond wit. My bookish grandparents had the same attitude: though happy to potter around the garden, they grew nothing edible beyond a few sprigs of mint and rosemary. Many of the generation that had had to Dig for Victory were swift to put aside their spades, and for ever; let others do the dirty work. Having endured rationing and shortages, they adored the supermarkets, the new out-of-town megastores especially: floodlit palaces of progress and

unimaginable promise. As the automatic doors – another revolution – parted to let them in, pensioners turned into wide-eyed children on Christmas morning.

Digging spuds and turnips was too reminiscent not just of war and backbreaking hardship, but of tediously monochrome food as well. Reg and George, my grandparents too, had their Elizabeth David cookbook, a glint of Mediterranean sunshine piercing the grey skies, but they were all proud veterans of the real thing too: motoring holidays on the Continent which were then relived for friends and relatives during interminably long slide-show evenings. My grandfather – and George too, I'll bet – always erred on the side of far too much detail in the commentary, and didn't take kindly to being hurried along to the next photograph, of the same church but from a slightly different angle.

The food was always a far better bet. In late April 1982, as the Falklands War raged, George had a 'most perfect day', having 'sunbathed nude all day', with 'a lovely deep tan beginning', and rounded off with one of his favourite dishes: 'lasagne al forno bolognese'. He accorded it the full title every time, investing it with the polish of a Puccini opera, and I hear my grandmother carefully enunciating the very same words, so proud of the Italian O level she gained in her sixties at an adult education class. I was besotted with her Continental cookery, and would contrast it sourly with the scraps on toast – beans, sardines, tinned tomatoes, egg – that were the staple at home. The grass was very much tastier on the other side.

Those of us brought up not just on the convenience stores, but the convenience food they stocked as well, all tinned, powdered, frozen or processed, have also fetishised

what we didn't have and did not know. We spurn the supermarkets and talk of sustainability and traceability, of authenticity and provenance. Even our culinary adjectives, double-barrelled at the very least, are as over-garnished as our tastebuds: locally-sourced, hand-cut, organically-reared, farm-fresh, home-baked, oven-fired, oak-smoked. It is, we want to believe, tuning into the heartier rhythms of our grandparents' attitude to food – even if our actual grandparents were at their happiest with a convenience meal from a vast shed off the bypass.

For Reg and George, a garden of heather, rockery and roses, now as dated as a Laura Ashley smock, was a state-ment of success; it represented leisure, not graft. That was the hard-won luxury most desired by their generation; for ours, it is authenticity. Preds plays with both, blurring these boundaries (and so many others) in his planting: food and flower, texture, taste and colour, the edible and the ornamental. My efforts go into foraging. From a young nettle and wild garlic pasta in March to breakfast mopping up the inky juices of November's final crop of field mush-rooms, the potential within a short walk is infinite, and every year, I add just a little more to my repertoire. Even if you return empty-handed, as I often do, the act of search-ing is so rewarding. Having to concentrate on liminal spaces – amongst the thorns, behind barbed wire, in tree scrub, hedgerows and edgelands – helps refocus the mind's eye and retune the antennae to the thousand tiny miracles erupting all around.

In my early days in Wales, when everything was still shrouded in Gothic romance, I once confessed to Preds my jealousy of his growing up in such a magical area. It must,

I said, have been the best place to be a child. 'Well, yes,' he replied, tactfully enough, 'but when you're a teenager, and you can't get a drink because everyone knows your mum and exactly how old you are, there's only so much fun you can have sat in a freezing-wet field, tripping your tits off on magic mushrooms.' I was so far gone that even this sounded wonderful, the prospect then of free drugs even more alluring than free food.

For decades, the only fungi I could confidently identify were the trippy ones, the tiny pixie hats of the psilocybin-packed liberty cap in particular. An MP once described them as 'the truffles of Wales', and it is certainly true that Welsh mushrooms are some of the most prized in Amsterdam head shops. For some people, doses of psilocybin are effective against depression. In a clinical trial at Imperial College London, one doctor said, 'Several of our patients described feeling "reset" after the treatment and often used computer analogies. For example, one said he felt like his brain had been "defragged" like a computer hard drive, and another said he felt "rebooted".' A friend nearby takes a few mush-rooms every day, and swears it helps him manage his mental health. I believe it, and although my foraged fungi these days are mainly ceps and chanterelles, para-sols and puffballs, I'm far from done with the tricksy little pixies.

For a season that creeps up on you so softly, autumn's ending comes as a wet slap. The starkness, and the dark-ness, arrive unannounced. One gusty day in the second half of November strips the trees of their remaining leaves. At the same time, out come the tractors to scythe down the hedges, lopping feet off the hazels and haw-thorns and leaving the tarmac as a nailbed of splinters and twigs – something that always infuriated cyclist George. Views stretch suddenly for miles. Corners that were hidden and secret only a fortnight ago are prised open for all to see. The countryside becomes a beauty stripped of make-up, every blemish caught in the low sunlight, looking the world square in the eye: take me as I am. There is nowhere to hide.

WEST

Up on the moors high above Rhiw Goch one Saturday afternoon in 1938, a couple of local men dug up the skull of a man hanged for murder two centuries earlier, still encased in its iron gibbet. The gruesome find was hung for a while in the barn of a nearby farm, that of yet another Mr Anwyl, before being taken down to Machynlleth for display in the bay window of Willie Evans' ironmonger's shop, right in the middle of the town's main street. Some older locals still remember being traumatised by the sight as children.

Sion Jones had murdered his wife and two children by throwing them down a mineshaft at Dylife. In its nineteenth-century heyday, Dylife was a lead-mining shantytown of fifteen hundred inhabitants; now it is only rust, ruins, a handful of houses and a struggling pub. Ten miles and a boggy mountain from either Machynlleth or Llanidloes, it was a hotbed of lawlessness far beyond official jurisdiction. Magistrates or police rarely made the difficult journey up there, except in circumstances as brutal as these. As the village blacksmith, Jones' final job was to forge the gibbet iron used to hang him.

Even aside from its grim associations, or an elevation that tilts it towards perpetual winter, Dylife has always been a place apart. Its liminality is innate, for this bleak moor, riddled with rot and poisoned by lead, is the primary watershed of mid Wales. Walk from the road's high point (1,680 feet) along the stony track to Glaslyn lake, and to your right rivulets tumble down a scarp and rush west to the River Dyfi and the Irish Sea. A hundred yards to your left, a faint gurgle in the reeds announces the infant River Clywedog, on its way east to join the mighty Severn. If I pee into that peaty trickle, traces of my DNA will soon be gliding through the Worcestershire towns of my childhood.

As more than four-fifths of Wales is upland, watersheds are its real boundaries. Architecture and customs change from one valley to the next, so too accents and even language. For all its soggy, otherworldly atmosphere, the Dylife watershed is a hard border linguistically. Eavesdrop on the rivers Crewi, Dulas or Fadian as they skitter past us and west to the sea, and you'll hear them chattering in the old tongue, Welsh. The Severn-bound streams, by contrast, soon broaden out into the smooth meanders and fertile vales of Saesneg – all-conquering English.

This is a principle evident elsewhere. Of Wales's thirteen traditional counties, the first to lose its Welsh was not Flintshire, staring across at the Wirral, nor Monmouthshire, not even officially part of Wales until 1974. It was our southern neighbour Radnorshire, where the language had more or less died by the time of the 1891 census. It is the only county of the thirteen where every river drains east into England. Words are water, and away they flow.

Exceptions prove the rule, too. Another Dylife river, the Twymyn, rises well to the east of the England-bound streams and initially follows them, before making a sudden break for it over a rock face and tumbling a couple of hundred feet in two breathtaking falls. After turning sharply, it rushes instead to join its westward brethren on their way to the sea, barrelling through tough little villages, including the one that is home to our doctor, vet, local pub and – in Preds' old primary school – polling station. Edgelands often wear their identity with exaggerated swagger, stockpile it high at the door like sandbags against a threatened flood, and so does the Twymyn valley with its bulwark Welshness.

From the field at Rhiw Goch, you can see a diagonal scar across the flank of the Pumlumon foothills a couple of miles away. It is the narrow mountain road through Dylife, one of Wales's highest routes, which I can so clearly remember first driving in the early 1990s when writing the initial *Rough Guide*. The tourist board had lent me a hire car and steered me towards the country's many spectacular mountain passes. None hit me with the force of this one. After stopping for a poke around the sullen stumps of Dylife, incredulous that this dark moonscape even existed, I followed the waters on their long descent into Machynlleth, eyes wide as unfathomably huge views crystallised into singular green valleys and woods, and huddled grey farms that appeared to have grown there.

Descending west, dizzy in the evening light that glanced off the river in the meadows below, the idea that my life could cross this watershed with the same alacrity still seemed impossibly distant. More of a priority was finding the man to do it with; only then perhaps could the dream solidify out of the haze. And he was a very long way off. This was my fourth *Rough Guide* research trip to Wales that year, and my first alone. In what were clearly auditions for the part of my husband-to-be in a Welsh fantasy life, I had taken three different men on the earlier trips. The first was a straight friend whom I adored unhealthily, and who continually – and oh so gently – had to douse my hopes in cold water. The second was a bisexual ex-boyfriend who'd broken my heart, and the third was the man I'd met on the rebound from him. He didn't even last the tour of Pembrokeshire: I drunkenly chucked him late one night as we bickered in a village churchyard, the owls hooting us to pipe down.

Although I met a few comrades forging confident queer lives in Wales, the presumption remained that if I was ever going to relocate here, it could only be as part of a couple, for the risk of eternal isolation was otherwise just too high. In London and Birmingham, I'd met many displaced gay Welshmen dark with hiraeth as they wrestled reconciling sexuality and home. Like tiny tributaries of the Wye, the Severn and the Dee, they too had trickled east into more fertile landscapes. To return west would be a tough push both upstream and uphill, requiring a strength they were not confident they yet possessed.

There is a saying in Welsh: *Gorau Cymro, Cymro oddi cartref,* or 'the best Welshman is a Welshman in exile'. It is not a compliment. The stereotype of the expat, lusty with patriotism after a few pints on match day, casts a long shadow down the decades of the twentieth century. Tucked in its penumbra are countless gay men, including many famous for an almost theatrically Welsh sensibility, but only from afar: impresarios Ivor Novello and Cliff Gordon, writer Rhys Davies, plantsman-artist Cedric Morris, actors Emlyn Williams and Victor Spinetti. The exodus continues even today.

Although nowhere was entirely safe in pre-1967 Britain, there were extra dimensions of difficulty in Wales. Unlike England, Scotland and Ireland, Wales has no real metropolis; it is an essentially rural culture, one furthermore where *mae pawb yn nabod pawb* ('everyone knows everyone'), as the first full sentence we were taught in Welsh class has it. Here, six degrees of separation is an impossibly distant dream, and the fear not of what people *have* said, but of what they *might* say, runs deep. Then there is the effect of chapel culture, which like all too many of the buildings from whence it sprang, stared grim and grey over communities, pursing its lips in perpetual disapproval.

For those who stayed, life was often bitterly cold. At the 1924 National Eisteddfod, one of the major prizes was won by young Ceredigion poet Edward Prosser Rhys for his work 'Atgof' (Memory). Within it there is the tiniest nod to same-sex affection, enough to ensure that it was never again published until well after his death twenty years later. In 1934, as a result of admitting his homosexuality, theologian Illtud Evans was expelled from the university college in Lampeter, just months before he was due to graduate. He never returned to Wales, and it took another Lampeter graduate and gay exile, Cliff Tucker, to campaign for Evans' posthumous graduation decades later.

Of the many mass arrests of gay men in the mid-twentieth century, none was as sordid as that which rocked Abergavenny in 1942. Twenty-four men were charged, some on the most trumped-up of evidence; fourteen were sentenced with up to ten years' penal servitude. One defendant killed himself; two others tried to but failed – and in one case had the suicide attempt added to his charge sheet. There was a spate of further suicides by other men in the area too. Even by the grimy standards of such cases, Abergavenny stood out and – thanks to an elegantly furious letter in the *Spectator* by Joe Ackerley – gained substantial national notoriety. The stench clung to Wales's reputation for decades.

Small-town morality and wildfire gossip are a toxic conflation, one that did not suddenly evaporate upon the law changing in July 1967. Even in the last decade of the twentieth century, when first getting to know Wales as a young gay man, I was dumbfounded by some of the twisted tales I heard out in the bars and clubs of Cardiff and Swansea: a claustrophobic mix of exploitation and breathtaking hypocrisy. Even those whose journey to self-acceptance had been relatively straightforward often showed symptoms of such conflicted anguish that it left me gasping for air. Yet the Wales that I was steadily falling for seemed so much more supple than these stories would have me believe. Glimmers of hope and possibility came fragmentarily, but with such dazzling acuity that they lit a path ahead. Away from the cities and the commercial gay scene – on walks up hills and by rivers, in cafes and country pubs, at parties and raves in quarries and forests – I found comrades, sensed others and heard whisper of many more.

Half wanting to test the water, to see whether this perception was just my desperation for it to be true so that I could move here, I went public with my enthusiasm, writing a piece for a Welsh periodical about the confluence of Wales and alternative sexualities. It piggybacked on the story of Ron Davies, who had just resigned as Welsh Secretary in Tony Blair's first government, after being caught cruising in a London park. To the British media, this was unfathomable, for Davies was the embodiment of macho south-Walian, rugby-playing, Labour-voting culture; how could blood so red be anything other than foursquare straight? In my piece, I pointed out that, as anyone who has witnessed drunken rugby celebrations can attest, boozy machismo and sublimated homoeroticism are clear bedfellows, and that there is a rich and wondrous vein of sexual wonkiness in Welsh culture and identity. One tabloid lined up a succession of people to condemn me: a Labour councillor from the Valleys said that I had committed 'a national slur' – 'if I met him, I'd hit him,' he continued.

Wheels turn. Councillors know now to button their lip before threatening homophobic violence, and queer history has become quite the growth area. Articles, books, blogs, exhibitions and stage shows have all combed Welsh stories for their contraband content, with much success. It is striking, though, how much criss-crossing of the watersheds this has required. Just as so many reclaimed heroes had to leave Wales to come out, many of the stories rooted here involve protagonists who came from beyond its borders.

The pattern was set by the most celebrated same-sex couple in Welsh history, the Ladies of Llangollen. An eccentric pair of Irish aristocrats, they had escaped to Wales in 1778 for a life of 'romantic friendship', though plenty suspected more. After the 1800 Acts of Union with Ireland, Llangollen was propelled from backwater status to overnight coach stop on the route between London and Dublin, and visiting the Ladies became a celebrated divertissement on the journey. Distinguished visitors would walk up to their home at Plas Newydd, taking a piece of carved oak as an offering. Wordsworth sent a poem of thanks to the 'Sisters in love, a love allowed to climb / Ev'n on this earth, above the reach of time', although he also referred to their beloved house as a 'low-roof'd cot', and was never asked to tea again.

Their fifty years in Llangollen both reflected and fuelled the first incarnation of Wales as a Romantic destination, the embodiment of the Picturesque. That was against the backdrop of Napoleonic conflicts and economic recession; since then, the Ladies have regularly swum back into focus during troubled times. They are temporal shape-shifters, a bespoke balm to every fractious age in turn: rustic escapees at the zenith of industrialisation in the 1870s; priestesses of the old ways as technology and terror barrelled through the 1930s; radical feminists to the newly liberated of the 1970s; a municipal logo for LGBT equality – and a highly marketable wedding venue – in the 2010s. Their appeal rolls on, and though always a pleasure, it tells us little about real queer lives in Wales.

For a culture to be at ease with itself, it must be as comfortable with its home-grown heretics as with its high-profile outsiders. Wales is not quite there: the pint-pot expat and the silver-tongued incomer still hold too much sway. It is perhaps coming, though. A recent television programme about homosexuality on the Welsh-language channel S4C was presented by a Unitarian chapel minister, a son of the parish that he and his husband now tend. It is the same rural patch where I was the Plaid Cymru candidate in the 2015 general election, and though I received a few horrible reactions, almost none were connected with my sexuality. Some metropolitan commentators were desperate to conflate the hostilities I faced with homophobia, which perhaps says more about them than it does the voters of Ceredigion.

Francis Lee, director of the beautiful 2017 queer rural Yorkshire film *God's Own Country*, noticed the same thing: how some urban audiences couldn't cope with the lack of queer-bashing in his tale and so accused him of being 'a bit rose-tinted'. His answer is mine too: 'I tell them: "What are you saying about people who live there? Are they intrinsically homophobic?" That isn't the case. They might not have a liberal middle-class attitude, where they sit around navel gazing about it. But that doesn't mean they're homophobic.'

Reg and George found the truth of that when they first arrived in the area almost half a century earlier. As debonair Londoners, they were already exotic outsiders; their status as a couple made them only marginally more so. Though so many had to leave to be themselves, rural Wales still had plenty enough of its own confirmed bachelors and spinsters, quietly living with or next door to their special friend, even if it was never acknowledged or afforded any status. Reg, always so uncomfortable in himself, was fascinated by gay people who could be at ease in the place of their upbringing, especially here, an area that conventional, metropolitan wisdom had as one of most difficult of all. It was a major ingredient in his profound admiration and love for Preds.

With his customary matter-of-factness, George never shied away from presenting himself and Reg as anything other than a couple. In 1989, a genteel publication by the name of *Country Quest* got in touch to see if they could run a feature on the fit-as-a-flea pensioner beating men half his age in gruelling bike races. George needed no persuasion, and the piece – headlined 'GEORGE'S STILL CYCLING AT 72!' – appeared soon after, and included a cameo appearance by 'his companion Reg'.

George had known immediately where he wanted the accompanying full-page portrait to be taken. The 1,300-foot climb up the mountain road through Dylife was part of his favourite bike ride, an eighteen-mile circuit that he did almost every day. It had taken him a year back in the saddle to manage it without having to get off and push at any point, and another couple of years to set his course record: one hour and thirty-four minutes on a 'cool but not cold (TOPLESS!!)' summer Friday in 1986.

The shot that he wanted was of him making mincemeat of the ascent, grinning broadly as he did so. It is a wonderful picture – one that we knew straight away to use on the front of his funeral service card. That it was pinned to the wall of his library also helped point us in its

direction. It was the chosen icon for the rest of his life, and perfect too for his despatch into the next one.

When I first crested the Dylife mountain road half a life-time ago, belting out of the hire car's stereo was the Pet Shop Boys' new album. One track, 'Go West', had become the anthem of my Welsh research trip. The original Village People version of the song, a 1979 disco thumper telling America's gay men to go boogie to the bathhouses of San

Francisco, had never much bothered me either way, but after a glacial rinse from Neil Tennant and Chris Lowe, the song shone hard as a diamond. Tennant, who turned 'Go West' into his personal coming-out statement, poignantly described their take on it as 'a memory of the dream of gay liberation', for in the gap between the Village People's version and theirs lay the AIDS crisis, and its vicious backlash against us. 'Go West,' it soared, 'life is peaceful there', and I soared back, bellowing each happy note to the hills as they danced across my windscreen. Perhaps I overtook George on his bike on the way down. More likely, he overtook me.

*

Although the American dream of the west, whether manifested by John Wayne or Armistead Maupin, is a far cry from ours, there are overlaps. West is best for elemental landscapes soaked in mystery and crossed by the songlines of the elders. It is the repository of ancient arcana and the dreams of seers. West travels at a different pace, its only immutable appointment the setting of sun on sea. In the States it is the Grand Canyon and Death Valley, Yosemite and the Navajo, Portlandia and Vegas, Beverly Hills and the Golden Gate. On this side of the Atlantic, it is Stonehenge and Avebury, tors and moors, Glastonbury and Caerleon, lost kings and drowned lands. It is Wales.

Through their first full autumn at Rhiw Goch, one of George's hobbies was house-hunting for friends. They'd had a supremely successful first summer in their third B&B; guests would often ask how it had all come about and, in the course of the conversation, let slip how much the idea of heading west appealed to them too. Some wanted to emulate Reg and George even more directly by also opening up a guest house. George was hugely flattered by this, and happy to be people's eyes and ears in mid Wales, sending on brochures, particulars and newspaper advertisements, and spending days driving around the countryside to visit houses and feed back his impressions ('it's modernised to hell and in sight and sound of the road! No go!'). Everyone wanted a place like theirs: authentic features, old and accessible, but with no neighbours or traffic noise. One of the thrills for George in seeing so many other houses was that it only confirmed how much they had struck gold with Rhiw Goch. There would be no more itchy feet.

No shortage of cold feet, though. For all the goodwill and excitement, there was almost no actual relocation. One exception was a couple, hotelier friends from Bournemouth, who were so enthused by George's report of a nearby place that they drove up in relentless November rain to take a look. The house was on the market for £35,000, and had been for some time; they offered £29,000, which was accepted 'without demur!' That the owners were prepared to lop nearly a fifth off the price with no questions should perhaps have sounded an alarm bell, but it didn't seem to. They stayed a further night at Rhiw Goch and 'left happy in the prospect of the new house. R— awoke early morning and thought "I've done the right thing" – such a good omen!' It wasn't. They never settled, and soon went back down south.

Another friend moved from the Marches to be nearer Reg and George, but that didn't work out either. A dreamy and restless soul who'd spent her childhood in a succession of country vicarages, she struggled to settle anywhere. In their address book, she has nine separate entries over just a handful of years, and they all whistle a certain folksy tune: The Thatch, Marigold Cottage (twice), Ash Cottage, Colophon Cottage and Vicarage Cottage, all in Clun; Tansy Cottage in Clunbury; the Wain House in Asterton; and Dell View Cottage, on Nook Lane in Kerry. Her brief plunge west, into an old farm on the drovers' road between Rhiw Goch and Machynlleth, lasted only five months.

With a poor success rate at house-hunting and his new hobby in cycling, George soon lost interest in sorting out other people's dreams. Perhaps just as well, since it is an occupation fraught with danger. My strategy has long been the opposite, in that I do far more to discourage people's relocation fantasies, though it usually makes little difference. So bewitched are they by the idea of a new life *Westward Ho!* that no amount of cold water can douse their excitement. They see and hear what they want to.

After a weekend visit one summer, a couple of friends, both prone to seasonal depression, decided to uproot to the area from hundreds of miles away. With grim inevitability, they bought a place that is as dark as pitch in winter, having decided that it was more important to trade less sunlight for more space. It has been a running sore ever since. I warned them – of course I did, because I knew all too intimately the effect of dark, damp winter houses – but they treated my alarm as the clucking of an old hen. After all, had plenty of people not said the same to me when I decided to up sticks to Wales? I'd told them about the doom-mongers predicting disaster for me; had I not proved them wrong? That my naysayers had been only beery acquaintances down the pub in Birmingham seemed not to matter.

My reticence to get involved in people's relocation comes after being badly burned in my first years in Wales. Some friends were so inspired by my move that they decided to do the same, and landed just down the road from me. I encouraged it, and looked forward to their company, but it soon became apparent that the move was an attempt to resuscitate their dying relationship, one last throw of the dice to make it right again. Unsurprisingly, it didn't work, and the whole edifice soon shattered. I have never known a more poisonous break-up, and can't help wondering if their sudden distance from family and friends only made it a whole lot worse.

Moving to an entirely new part of the world, willingly cutting yourselves adrift from the familiar and comfortable, is only marginally less obtuse than that other fabled relationship saver, having a baby. Yet still they come, hoping against reason, experience and even hope itself that the glimmer of cheer recalled from a weekend in Betws-y-Coed can somehow be sparked back into life, and fanned into sufficient warmth to last the remaining decades.

Sometimes, it is not even personal recall that we are attempting to rekindle, but something less specific, a cultural muscle memory. As Raymond Williams had it in *The Country and the City*, 'On the country has gathered the idea of a natural way of life: of peace, innocence and simple virtue.' Countless contemporary media squeeze the same mantra bone dry: daytime television's flagship show is called not *Move to the Country*, but *Escape to the Country*. But to which country are we being encouraged to escape? Our sense of it, as Williams makes clear, lies on a sliding scale, forever 'over the last hill', just out of focus and just out of reach.

Perhaps even E. M. Forster's greenwood is condemned to remain elusive. He certainly thought so. In 1913, he'd attempted an ending to *Maurice* – Alec and Maurice as happy woodcutters together in the forest – that was soon ditched after 'universal dissatisfaction' amongst the friends to whom he showed it. In a 1960 epilogue to the novel, still unpublished but by then two world wars and almost half a century old, he wrote that 'There is no forest or fell to escape to today, no cave in which to curl up, no deserted valley for those who wish neither to reform nor corrupt society but to be left alone.' In a final paragraph, under the heading 'Homosexuality', he gloomily concludes that Edward Carpenter's idyll is dead, and that 'the Wolfenden recommendations [for decriminalisation] will be indefinitely rejected, police prosecutions will continue and Clive on the bench will continue to sentence Alec in the dock. Maurice may get off.'

Forster's pessimism and nostalgia had got the better of him. Within a dozen years, the law long changed, Reg and George were building a new life deep in the countryside, and though they were unusual, they were far from unique. As a middle-aged couple of more than twenty years' standing, they represented the main exception to the rule that gay men belong in the city. A growing number have followed in their wake, comfortable couplings who have grown to look like each other, men who were always happier in a National Trust tearoom than a techno club darkroom. They devour the weekend supplements and property websites, bookmarking every cottage of their dreams, and, to keep at least some juices flowing, frantically cross-referencing them with their broadband speeds.

There is always a further west. Reg's old school buddy Little Reg, who dragged him out of the closet and into the underground gay scene of post-war London, left Britain with his partner Robert at the same time that Reg and George quit Bournemouth for Wales. Eternal sun-worshippers, they settled in a Florida beach resort, where they drank themselves to death. In a dismal letter of May 1986, when Reg and George still had more than twenty years of good living to come, Little Reg listed their health problems: he had cirrhosis of the liver and could not leave home because 'I get very nervous', while Robert had had cancer surgery and chemotherapy, and a couple of strokes.

> With all the sickness it has now left us broke, our medical insurance did not cover everything, in fact almost nothing

and I guess we shall be in debt for the rest of our lives, but
at least we are still alive. This is no country to be sick in.
All I can say at the moment is that the weather in Florida
is good.

There is always a further west, though often it's a mirage.

For William Bebb, Rhiw Goch's nearest neighbour in the
first half of the nineteenth century, correspondence
and notes published by his great-great-nephew Ambrose
show that the idea of heading to the new Welsh colonies
in America preoccupied him for years. This part of
western Montgomeryshire, wracked by poverty and
bubbling with political and religious discontent, had for
decades been one of the main areas of exodus to the
States. Bebb pored over letters from relatives and
friends who'd made the journey and wanted him to join
them. Life was good, they assured him, land was cheap
and fertile, and they were busily building a brave new
Wales thousands of miles from the rapidly emptying
glass of the original. Conversation at chapel and in the
markets concerned little else. In 1847, Bebb and his family, together with other near neighbours, set sail from
Liverpool to the promised land.

The earliest Welsh colonies had been in Pennsylvania,
Ohio and New York, in the north-east of the US. Their
success led to fatal over-optimism, and Bebb was persuaded by his charismatic cousin Samuel Roberts to help
establish a new Welsh Utopia in Tennessee, a Southern
slave state. Prospective settlers found that the land was
far less productive than promised, and perhaps not even
theirs, for title deeds were disputed from the outset.

Hunger, disease, lawsuits and then the Civil War finished off the dream. One investor, John Roberts Jones, wrote, 'I wish that I had never seen Mr Bebb ... and that I had never heard of Tennessee.'

It wasn't only pious chapel-goers that were exported to America. At the end of the nineteenth century, Brian Humphreys and his wife Ann gave up on their struggling farm near Dylife to move to the New World. Shortly after arriving in Chicago in 1899, their third child, Llewellyn Morris Humphreys, was born. He grew up to become Murray the Hump, Al Capone's right-hand man and one of the mob's most notorious gangsters. Humphreys was smooth, urbane and cold-blooded, living by his own maxim that 'If you ever have to cock a gun in a man's face, kill him. If you walk away without killing him after doing that, he'll kill you the next day.' His tentacles reached every corner of politics, the unions, the police and Hollywood: when in 1952 his daughter Llewella needed a date for her high school prom, he got Frank Sinatra to do the honours.

In 1963, two years before he died, Humphreys travelled to Wales on a false passport. Though he was a proud Welsh exile (naming your daughter Llewella is a surefire clue), this was the first time he'd ever set foot in the homeland, and he was determined to find roots. His third cousin Dafydd Wigley, later the leader of Plaid Cymru, recalls bumping into an American, quite possibly the Hump, that summer in the Montgomeryshire lanes: 'we [Wigley and his father] were told by the person accompanying him that we were related'.

He almost certainly visited the chapel cemetery beneath us, where a host of Humphreys are buried, including his grandmother Mary, the live-in maid for many years to the Anwyl brothers at Rhiw Goch. Perhaps he wandered across the lane to the tiny village shop and seed merchant's, to ask proprietor David Humphreys – another distant cousin – about the area and in particular the standing stone so prominent on the ridge above. From the cemetery, the stone commands the skyline and appears locked in a star-ing contest with the chapel, each willing the other to blink (the stone has been there four thousand years, the chapel closed after less than two hundred; it's clear who won). I hope that Mr Humphreys told him about the three stones of Y Noddfa, the Sanctuary, and the area as a historic ref-uge for outlaws. The old mobster would have liked that.

*

More than any other bearing on the compass wheel, west is the empty direction, the one to be filled with everything from our brightest dreams to our blackest fears. Or with people, for in these islands, weighted so heavily to their south-eastern corners, west has long been the quarter of depopulation. In the Great Famine in Ireland of the 1840s, it was the western province of Connaught that lost by far the greatest proportion of its people; to this day, County Mayo is home to only around one-third of its pre-Famine population. In Scotland, successive Highland Clearances disproportion-ately drained the western counties and islands. The collapse of mining and quarrying hit the rocky west – Cum-bria, Cornwall, Wales – and emptied them too, not just of people and livelihoods, but of their languages and lifeblood.

Follow the little River Crewi down from Dylife, past old mine adits and ruins, and it soon scampers through its first settlement. Unlike every other nearby village huddled around deep roots, Melinbyrhedyn is strewn across a common, its houses dropped slapdash into the bracken. Like Dylife, it owes its existence to the lead mines, but unlike its sibling high up on the watershed, or its cousins in the west of Ireland and Scotland, it hasn't crumbled to dust, though it came close. A 1969 newspaper report, written by another member of the local Wigley family and headed 'THE FORGOTTEN VILLAGE', shows how close:

> Ruined houses, deserted holiday homes, a few dwellings occupied by a scanty population – that is today's picture of the once thriving and industrious mining village of Melinbyrhedyn, west Montgomeryshire . . . The large

village chapel, traces of ruined houses, empty shops are eloquent of the depressing depopulation drift in Mid Wales, but they testify to the great activity of half a century ago.

'Once thriving and industrious . . . the great activity of half a century ago': as ever, and just as in Forster's greenwood, yesterday's glass was so much fuller than today's, and tomorrow's will be emptier still. Nostalgia paints a picture of a tight-knit and hearty community, its chapel full and its famous marching silver band oompahing round the lanes. There is no hint of poverty or claustrophobia, or that by then the decline was already well under way. The mines were gone, and needed no mourning, since they had crushed and poisoned their people with impunity. And the First World War changed everything: on one market day

in August 1916, a sale at Machynlleth disposed of fourteen local farms, including the one where Preds grew up, fifteen smallholdings, the inn at Dylife and numerous cottages, sheepwalks and hereditaments. Most of the cottages and smaller farms were derelict within twenty years, the land having been consolidated into bigger units.

Half a century in the other direction, and Melinbyrhedyn is unrecognisable from the picture of decay in 1969. The waters of the Crewi run far clearer, though they don't bubble with the same easy Welsh that they once did. Every single house is in good repair, and only a couple are not inhabited full-time. The one building that looks in need of love is the Beerseba chapel, closed finally this year. The population is slightly older than average, though a few children head out of the village to school every day. Gardens are well tended and productive; there are beehives and white cattle at the old mill, and a horse in the meadow downstream. The farmland is lush and feeds prize-winning sheep and beef cattle. A wind turbine licks the skies.

The village is an easy twenty-minute stroll along the lane from Rhiw Goch, but a far finer walk over the hills. It's my regular sundown route, especially in the dark half of the year between the autumn and spring equinoxes, when every drop of sunlight needs squeezing from above. An hour after the sun has left Rhiw Goch, it can still be found over the shoulder of Bryn-y-Brain, pouring gold through slits in dark clouds and flooding the fields and thorns with dying fire. Looking west, I'm dazzled by the sunset, and see what I want to.

MICHAEL

In my old village, the waters soon closed over my head. Returning a couple of months after the move, I found the fields I used to walk fenced off, and unabashed enthusiasm for the young family that had replaced me. In the pub, after they'd politely asked me again where I'd moved to, and what it was like, conversation hobbled to a halt. Already, I was 'away', like so many sons and daughters of the place, and everyone knew that they never returned, so there was no point being squeamish or sentimental about it. Limbo yawned: I was no longer there, but neither had I landed here.

All that spring and summer, we were squatting. Reg had died as we were on the point of buying Rhiw Goch, and with George's death a few weeks later we now had to wait until probate was sorted for it to become officially ours. We nervously waited to see if a long-lost relative of Reg or George might pop up to challenge our inheritance, especially after their obituary had appeared in the *Guardian*, and tried not to think about what people might be saying behind our backs.

It suited me to be hovering in administrative half-light, to float around the contours of the place but with nothing yet battening us down. Besides, it was summer, and easy enough to treat it like a strange camping holiday. With no landline and no Internet, the only way of contacting the outside world was to wander up the field and hope to snag a bar of mobile reception as it wafted by.

Everything conspired to make us go slow. We agreed to make no substantial changes to the house in the first year, that we should see the full turn of the seasons before undertaking anything major. I kept reminding myself of the advice that I doled out to others when they moved: to enjoy the newness of the place and never to wish it away, for it soon evaporates into familiarity, and we all know what that breeds, given the chance.

Conversations with new neighbours affirmed that this was a place that would unveil itself only gradually. A woman told me how much she still missed her native coastal Gwynedd, even after twenty years of living here ('It's the snows I've never got used to'), but that it had crept up on her and stolen her heart without her even noticing. One man, originally from Ceredigion, to the south of here, said almost exactly the same. These were tales not of instant infatuation, but of affection churned deeper by every turn of the year's wheel.

Headstrong map addicts project their mental blockages geographically, into a restless search for wherever we think might cure our literal dis-location. We fall for places as giddily as we do people, harbouring a fantasy of locative love at first sight, of turning a corner and there in a shower of stars and peal of bells is the place we are destined to spend a soft-hued forever. If such a place existed, I naturally assumed that it would be me that found it; to accept otherwise meant accepting that I do not know best, even in the one area of life in which I feel most fluent. Being at Rhiw Goch made me start to question this, for the first time in my life. A far larger truth began to dawn: that in the love of both men and milieux, the slow burn is what is required.

And suddenly, there was another disorienting factor to accommodate: money. Twenty years as a freelance writer had made cashflow problems a regular feature of my life, one that I assumed would be my lot for keeps. Preds' income, from bits of shop and farm work, was equally modest. On the very day that George died, so kick-starting the inheritance process and freeing us from the need to buy Rhiw Goch, the cheque from the sale of our house arrived. It soon dawned that Reg and George hadn't just given us a house, they had granted us a spell of freedom, the mental and physical space to create whatever we needed to.

There was one very specific purchase I was eager to bag while the money was there. I begged our new farmer neighbour to consider selling Y Rhos, the two-acre scrub riddled with springs that I dreamed of turning into a swimming pond. He found the idea hilarious. Farmers and swimming are rare companions; you'll almost never see a farming family heading to the beach on a warm summer's evening. Preds remembers only one such trip throughout his whole childhood, despite the sea being on their horizon. Our neighbour was having none of it, though when the

subsidy regime changed and started paying out for wetland, he promised me a choice of new pools. He dug two, each the size of a bathtub.

He was keen on buying our five-acre field by the house, and for the first few months mentioned it every time I saw him. After Rhiw Goch had come out of estate hands in 1951, it had been his family that bought chunks of the land as they came up for sale, and they have long rented our last field too. Once a year, George and Reg would motor over to his parents' farm for the evening, returning with a signed contract and a £50 cheque, which just about covered the solicitor's fee for drawing up the paperwork. Thirty years later, when we took over, the rent was still fifty quid; it's now a lamb every year for the freezer.

We soon stopped badgering each other for land, and have settled into a comfortable tempo, as with all our farming neighbours. It's a pleasure to bump into them in the lanes, fields or pub, and a quick chat often stretches into a long yarn over all sorts: politics, culture, sport, history, local life and gossip, sometimes in Welsh, sometimes English, mostly a tangle of the two. Occasionally it hits me like a brick just how profoundly different life is here from the world of my childhood, only a few dozen miles away to the east. A middle-class Middle Englander can, if he so chooses, bluster or bludgeon his way through almost anything. That is what we are trained to do, wherever we go. But it doesn't wash here. Of course, you can get away with it, in that no one will physically stop you, but you'll look like a swaggering idiot and it won't be forgotten.

It's not just a question of language or culture, or even money, but one of attitude and approach. You would be hard pressed to find two people more radiantly English than our nearest neighbours, Penny and David. Although they've had their old farmhouse for almost fifty years as a holiday home, real life has always lain in the leafy embonpoint of Sussex. Yet their sensitivity to this place, to the numen of Y Noddfa, its people and rhythm, is profound. Without them, Reg and George would have floundered terribly, probably sunk altogether. Without them, we would not have been eased so smoothly into our new life, for although it was Reg's decision to leave us Rhiw Goch, it was Penny's determination that made it happen.

She and David first landed here in 1967, when they bought the farm that had sent Ambrose Bebb into a whirligig of rhapsody on staying there during the war. They'd spotted

it semi-derelict and knocked on the nearest door – ours –
to find out who owned it. Len, the oddball Midlander who'd
arrived on a donkey and cart, was in Rhiw Goch at the
time. He told them that the farm's owner would be around
that evening; so he was, but he had no interest in selling.
When they returned home, Penny wrote to him to ask that
if he ever changed his mind, to please remember them.
Circumstances changed, and he did.

They caught the last throes of 'a Welsh countryside that the 20th century has barely touched', as the 1969 *Shell Guide* so effusively had us. It was a countryside that had substantially vanished even by the time Reg and George arrived at Rhiw Goch little more than a decade later. In the late sixties, almost no one had a television, and if they did, there was barely a signal. Few had cars; Penny recalls stopping to ask old people tottering along the lanes if they wanted a lift, and everyone having to mime their way through the conversation because they had so little English, and she no Welsh. Their other neighbours, in the now empty cottage where the barn owlets fly on a summer's evening, were a brother and sister who hand-scythed the corn in their one small field.

On Sundays, people in dark suits and hats processed along the lane to chapel, and Penny and David learned never to operate power tools or have the washing out. Down in the village was Mr Humphreys' shop, to which their four daughters would skip, clutching pre-decimal pennies in their hot little hands to spend on sweets. In 1970, a spark from a paraffin heater ignited a fire, and that was the end of the shop. Mr Humphreys died two years later, aged eighty-five, and is buried across the lane in the chapel graveyard, alongside Murray the Hump's grandmother and numerous other Humphreys, the Anwyls of Rhiw Goch, and a compendium of Davieses, Morrises, Pughes and Hugheses.

By the time Preds and I moved in, we knew that we didn't have long with Penny and David; they were by then in their seventies and would soon have to consolidate life into one location, which was always going to be nearer the facilities and family of southern England. We all made the most of it, with three years of regular feasts between the two houses, nights where past and future were kept at bay by the light and laughter of right now. In our first autumn at Rhiw Goch, they helped us plan a trip to Umbria, where they regularly travelled, and even secured us some accommodation there.

Neither of us had reckoned on the hiraeth that hit us like a thunderclap in Italy. We ended the holiday with a few days in Rome, and in the heat and chaos, shouting to hear ourselves above the incessant horns and traffic, we'd wonder how things were looking at home, whether the trees would be turning yet, where and how the light might be falling. *Home* . . . after six months of struggling to wear it, the word suddenly fitted. Umbria in late September had been bone dry, my only swim being in a soupy lake. I dreamed of Welsh water, tumbling and gurgling its way westwards, electrifying me with its clarity and cold. When we reached home – all the way by train from Rome – I scampered down to a river and plunged into its scrawny embrace.

On this stretch of river, the best swim is in a rocky channel running for fifty yards below a small waterfall. The current becomes stronger the nearer you get to the fall, so when you've had enough, you just let go and drift gently back downstream to the start, gliding through sculpted boulders under oak and thorn. Just below the fall is a smooth rock to hold on to as the current elbows past. When I first swam here, I would cling to that rock like a shipwreck survivor, flexing every sinew against the flow, fighting it. On this October dip, probably the last of the season, I tried instead to relax – and everything changed. With one hand on the anchor rock, I bobbed with the river's eddies, and as I was buffeted by its pulses, the lightest of giggles bubbled to the surface and burst into the spray.

Going with the flow was proving harder on dry land, but at last I was glimpsing the possibility. Almost three weeks away had sharpened my appreciation, and returning to abundant autumn helped no end. We toured the house, garden and fields, hooting at the harvest of nuts, fruits and fungi, the trees in their courtly robes, the musky aromas and sweeter light. For ten autumns at my old house, I'd watched with accelerating dread the hours of direct sunshine rapidly decrease, until the moment in mid November when they'd vanish altogether. At Rhiw Goch, I was having trouble trusting my senses, for as the days shortened, the light seemed brighter. There was no doubting it: the lower sun and thinning trees meant that the house was unquestionably lighter than at midsummer. Night skies were noticeably keener too. For the first time, I began to look forward to winter.

Although I share a name with the last blast of summer, a *haf bach Mihangel*, I am much more its parent season, autumn. My wardrobe makes that plain: a muddy whirl of browns, reds, ochres, greys and evergreens, much of it in tweed and wool. Autumn is the year's chill-out, its after-party, when it all gets a little bleary, but so much more relaxed too. Even in my dancing years, I often preferred the day after to the big night itself, as expectations are fewer and it's there that you enjoy the best connections and the heartiest laughs.

I have reached the autumn of my life, and am relieved to be there; that this has coincided with moving to a place of such ripeness is a synthesis to honour. Seven years in, and it is the season I most look forward to. The water in my pond is at its clearest, and so am I.

*

With its mutations and inner elasticity, Welsh is a wonderfully elliptical language, perfect for wordplay. None tickles me more than the name Rhiw Goch itself. It is not especially unusual: *rhiw* is one of the more common words for hill, and *goch* a mutation from *coch* (red), so the name is found near many a ruddy, bracken-coated slope. There's a Rhiw Goch pub in Snowdonia, a Rhiw Goch halt on the Ffestiniog steam railway, the remains of a Rhiw Goch quarry near Llangollen, Rhiw Goch farmhouses-turned-holiday homes at Aberaeron, Harlech and Dolwyddelan, and, until recently, even a Rhiw Goch bed and breakfast in Fort William, Scotland.

In place names, *coch* often hints not at bracken, but blood. Usually, it's the congealed memory of a battle or skirmish,

though in our case it's said by some to come from an uncor-
roborated age when executions happened here, and the
blood ran down the hill. And spelled slightly differently to
rhiw the hill, but pronounced almost identically, *rhyw*
means 'some' or 'sex'. (It's confused even further by *rhew*,
'ice'. One winter's morning, a pupil in my Welsh class
arrived late and flustered, explaining that it was because
she'd had sex on the car. We applauded both her grammar
and her sense of adventure.)

'Rhyw Goch' could therefore also mean 'Bloody Sex', and
the day I realised this, the house felt more mine. A place
called Bloody Sex – possibly with an exclamation mark
appended – seemed such an appropriate home for a middle-
aged grump and his long-standing partner. *Welcome to
Bloody Sex!* I liked its tone of tetchy resignation, which
entirely matched my own.

Even at the peak of my carnal career, when teenage swimming and sleepover spooning had hardened into dates,
boyfriends and affairs, there was always a mismatch,
breakage even, between brain and balls. If the ambience
was all sex – a sauna or cruising area, say – I'd be trying to
strike up a chat; when sex was not on the menu, I'd wheedle
it in, and with enough of a successful strike rate to cleave
a substantial habit. It is a recipe for plenty of casual
encounters, relationships that barely make it out of the
starting blocks, and a chronic emotional dyspepsia. That,
though, was my training, and it came from every direction, and at every turn.

The day after I was born, at the fag end of 1966, the Sexual
Offences Bill began its second reading in the House of
Commons. There was little of the anger and vitriol of

earlier debates around homosexuality, since most by then wearily accepted that the law must change, but neither was there any sense of celebration. Even the bill's sponsor, Pontypool MP Leo Abse, talked of the 'terrible fate' of the 'faulty males' who were 'prone to this failure'. Other supportive MPs called homosexuality an 'ailment', a 'disease' or – from Home Secretary Roy Jenkins, subsequently revealed as bisexual – 'a very real disability'. To prove that the country had not gone soft, prosecutions of men for gay sexual offences actually increased in the years following partial decriminalisation.

Shame scarified me close up too. I was four when my mum left; if I cried, the hopeless girl drafted in to look after my sister and me would scream in my face that I was the reason why. At bath-time, friends of hers would come round to poke and laugh at my tiny, terrified penis, though this alerted me to its potential, and I soon invented a game that steered other boys from our estate into my dad's garden shed and out of their pants. When we were caught, a squall of flush-faced parents shouted at us that we were disgusting, and that we must never, *ever* do it again. Nowhere was completely safe. One lunchtime, I was contentedly playing mummies and daddies in my primary school playground, the only boy in the gang; a teacher appeared and sighed, 'Oh Michael, why do you always play with the girls?' Without having the first idea what, I knew that I had done something terribly wrong. Worse, that I *was* something terribly wrong.

In the wider world, on TV or in overheard adult conversations, any mention of 'gays' dripped with venom and disgust, or was at best a sneering punchline. Each one would send a surge of electric recognition through me, and a hot blush of shame quickly damped down with icy self-hatred. By twelve, my voice had broken and I was shaving and discreetly mutilating myself. Sitting one day with the family Staffordshire bull terrier on over-grown railway allotments, I told him that I might be homosexual, swore him to secrecy and myself to never saying it out loud again. Instead, I became an expert in the instant calibration of every situation, and how to position myself within it side-on, invisible. Home was chaos, so it was easy enough to slip through unnoticed; at school too, because learning was sanctuary that I could process into good grades. Like water, I found the path of least resistance, and appeared to be flowing freely.

Shortly after turning fifteen, I stayed for a few days with a school friend. He introduced me to what the papers would now call a paedophile ring, operated by a sweaty creep out of his backstreet record shop. In my memory, he and his mates paid us teenagers to play with each other while they watched, giving me the two things I most craved: cock and cash. Reading my teen-age diary now, though, for the first time in decades, I see that I had completely blanked out the rest: that the shop owner, a married man with a son my age, had forced himself on me too, paying me off and pestering me for more. He was soon arrested, and committed to a psychiatric hospital.

I recoiled in the opposite direction: getting a girlfriend and getting God. Both phases ended as abruptly as they had begun, seen off by galloping hormones and widening horizons: sixth form, learning to drive, beer and boys. Music too: the charts of the early to mid eighties, from Frankie to Morrissey, were strangely gay, albeit mainly from the nod-and-a-wink end of the spectrum. When grilled about his sexuality, Boy George infamously declared that he'd rather have a cup of tea.

And then, through the euphemisms burst Bronski Beat. When they hit big in the summer of 1984 with 'Smalltown Boy', I was still a year away from escape, but I knew that their anthem – 'run away, turn away, run away' – was mine too. They wore pink triangle T-shirts on *Top of the Pops*, and the video was a tiny agitprop movie of queer-bashing, shame and escape to the big city. We all watched, and waited.

What liberated us three decades ago, though, may now be locking us in. 'Smalltown Boy' has become the default soundtrack to our relationship with 'out there', the not-city. Step on to any provincial railway station platform, especially in the dreich of an autumn twilight, and Jimmy Somerville's falsetto will haunt your brain until bedtime: 'run away, turn away, run away'. For too many, the city has become just another closet.

A year after 'Smalltown Boy', I finally got to re-enact it, leaving Kidderminster without a backward glance and heading to university in London. The family Staffie was dead, as was my promise to him. I gradually inched out of the closet and, like so many of my generation, had Margaret Thatcher to thank for finally making me go public, with the infamous Clause 28 of her 1988 Local Government Act. This banned the 'promotion of homosexuality' by local authorities and the teaching in schools and colleges of 'the acceptability of homosexuality as a pretended family relationship'. Spiteful but so legally baggy that it could never be specifically deployed, the clause worked instead as a kind of mustard gas designed to choke a generation. We were a platoon in Thatcher's 'enemy within', demonised even more viciously because of the ongoing AIDS crisis.

Being set in such clear opposition to the times galvanised us, and made so many of us stand up to be counted, but it took a heavy toll. On the battlefield, damage was everywhere, and horror an occupational hazard. In a remote field somewhere in County Kerry, I was once held for an hour at knifepoint in a locked caravan, when a man flipped out on me seconds after sex. But I was lucky. A distant relative of Preds was murdered by a hitchhiker, acquitted after claiming that he'd been on the receiving end of an unwelcome pass. A sweet, gentle friend in Birmingham, a man with the kindest eyes and a passion for art, had his skull smashed into twenty-two pieces and was then dismembered because in one moment of blurry sexual calculus at the end of a night out, he let hunger overcome judgement.

Nothing squared up: pride and shame, lust and love, anonymity and attention-seeking, our exterior and inner selves. I managed to be both promiscuous and prissy, a juxtaposition that sprang from a profound disjunction with my own flesh, something I now know to be body dysmorphia. It is not an eating disorder, though there was no shortage of those in my upbringing, but an inability to fully inhabit my physical body, or even to see it as it really is.

This dislocation goes back as far as I can remember, through the spring and summer of my life when – at least outwardly – I was all honey bees and flowers. Most of the time, I could not see this at all, and would automatically lose interest in anyone if they seemed to like me too much. Those that did pique my attention were, inevitably, the unavailable, the unreliable or the utterly unstable.

It's far easier to admit to this extreme self-deprecation as an effect of dysmorphia than to its flip side, the periods of blinding self-adoration. Most of the time, I'd hate what I saw in the mirror or in photos, but then suddenly it would switch, and I'd be dazzled by a beauty far brighter than reality, as I gazed, a young Narcissus, at my own reflection in the pool. I sometimes see George on the same shore, paddling his hand in the water as he admires himself from all angles. He fought to hold autumn at bay; I am diving into it, though which is the better strategy I cannot say. My fear is that if I could not integrate body and mind when they were both young and supple, how perilously wide might the fracture grow as I age and decay? My hope, though, is that I am growing into the physical manifestation of my self-image, and that the two might finally meet.

*

What would Edward do? It is always a question worth posing, to look and learn from that great queer rural hero Edward Carpenter, and his wildly unconventional household in Millthorpe, a village near Sheffield. Guests and pilgrims came in their droves, for enlightenment, comradeship and sex, a holy trinity best achieved simultaneously. When E. M. Forster visited in 1913, he recorded in his diary that Carpenter's younger companion, George Merrill,

> touched my backside – gently and just above the buttocks ... The sensation was unusual and I still remember it, as I remember the position of a long vanished tooth ... He made a profound impression on me and touched a creative spring.

On Forster's return home, the spring overflowed into *Maurice*. Though its 1988 film adaptation helped boost my fragile new identity as a young gay man, Forster was far too nervous of its impact on his reputation to publish it in his lifetime.

Like George in an equally difficult age, Carpenter refused to be bowed by others' unease. When a local right-wing agitator leafleted the villagers of Millthorpe to warn them of the 'Homogenic Comrades ... morbid appetites, naked dancing, corruption of youth, paganism and socialism' in their midst, their neighbours closed ranks around them. Today, Millthorpe is a pretty commuter village still proud of its adopted son. He's the main attraction on the laminated history board by the village phone box:

> Edward Carpenter [was] the celebrated reformer, poet, philosopher and gay rights pioneer ... His mission was a form of simple living; he eschewed the city and embraced the elements. He threw open the windows and threw off his clothes in an effort to cast off the curse of respectability. He wanted to reunite people with the landscape.

Carpenter makes me feel like a terrible frump. So did George when I first read his diaries. 'I hope he's left a bit of that magic dust around the place,' I wrote in my journal, but seven years on, I really don't. Rarely was it magic, more often a dubious application of power, and though there is so much to applaud in Edward Carpenter's life, perhaps it was the same there, on a far greater scale and scented with mysticism. When disciples came, they were often steered into pleasuring the prophet. In the 1960s, American writer Gavin Arthur recalled visiting in the mid 1920s, when he was in his twenties and Carpenter was turning eighty. Encouraged to have sex with Carpenter, for 'a young man's electricity is so good for recharging the batteries of the old', he did. After orgasm ('I could feel my young vitality flowing into his old age'), he 'fell asleep dreaming of the seminal smell of autumn woods'.

The next morning, Carpenter told Arthur about visiting America in his thirties and meeting his guru Walt Whitman, then nearly sixty. The grizzled old poet had insisted that they sleep together as 'a physical and spiritual expression of comrade love'. A lifetime pattern was set. 'Comrade love', all manly and heroic and equal, sounds so appealing, but it is almost always deployed only by those who, by dint of class, status, age or money, inhabit the superior rank; for them, the imbalance is a key component of the erotic charge.

E. M. Forster wrote in his diary: 'I want to love a strong young man of the lower classes and be loved by him and even hurt by him'; for Joe Ackerley, who also beat a path to Millthorpe, he 'should not be effeminate, indeed preferably normal; I did not exclude education but did not want it'. The homophobic homosexual is such a hoary cliché, and that's what offends me the most. Embarrasses me too, recalling the snap answer I gave many years ago when a friend asked me, 'What *is* your type? I've never been able to work it out.' Without even thinking about it, the words shot out: 'short, skinhead, looks like he might beat me up'. That is no one's definition of liberation.

According to Sheila Rowbotham's biography of Edward Carpenter, for all the noble aspiration to be rid of jealousy, and fine words about freedom and comradely love, the household was frequently deluged by difficult, occasionally dangerous emotional cross-currents. And for all his stated modern egalitarianism, Carpenter was never averse to snapping back into his residual persona, the landed Victorian gentleman.

As with George, me too at times, his formula for seduction – and whatever transcendental robes we swaddle it in, formula is what it is – became curdled by repetition into something lifeless and cold, vampiric even. And ultimately quite sad: a young journalist came to worship Carpenter in his final years and was dismayed to find 'a feeble old man, beyond conversation, who coquettishly pinched my behind'. Some serial seducers try to frame their behaviour as a radical damnation of bourgeois norms, though in a world still so deranged by same-sex desire, two men loving one another, emotionally and physically, ever deeper for life: *that* is the rare and truly revolutionary act.

Perhaps I protest too much. A few people have visited Preds and me at Rhiw Goch and made the comparison with Carpenter and Merrill at Millthorpe, something we hold as a great compliment. My take on sex is filtered through the razor-sharp rocks of dysmorphia; what do I know? Men's sexual locomotion can be so straightforward – an on/off button, basically – that contact between two, three or more may well have no emotional downside. If it hurts no one, then why the hell not?

In my first three years in Wales, before meeting Preds, it was not hard to find sex. Excitement at having made the move I'd so long dreamed of gave me wings, and propelled me out to meetings and classes, concerts and parties. One of the catalysts for moving had been getting online, and realising that my work was now portable. So too a rural love life: the dial-up Internet connection in my granny flat by the sea pinged with messages from chatrooms, and I soon had a roster of afternoon regulars, including a chapel organist, a single father of four and a farmer. Finding physical satisfaction was a cinch, but not so real fellowship, until I went to the wedding where I met Reg and George. I hadn't realised how much I'd missed easy gay friendship, and neither, I think, had Reg. I promised to go and visit them at Rhiw Goch soon.

That autumn, I went to another party. It was mushroom season – palpably so in the dark chaos of a Machynlleth flat. A friend pointed out Preds to me, and offered to introduce us. The music was loud and everyone was wrecked; Preds has absolutely no recollection of this first meeting. I followed up the party encounter by becoming more of a regular at the wholefood shop where he worked. Though we clumsily flirted over the yeast extracts, we both had boyfriends to nudge out of the picture before we could do anything about us. That there was an 'us' was so immediately obvious, a feeling both dizzily exciting and strangely calm, that getting together felt like removing the tiniest blockage from a stream and letting it flow along its natural channel. I was thirty-six and had only ever managed to hold down a relationship for a few months at a time. He was twenty-eight, with only a marginally better track record.

We did the early-relationship stuff: lusty exploration and pretending to be keen on each other's hobbies. Preds feigned enthusiasm for a spring swim in a mountain river, and managed to psyche himself up to follow

me by jumping off a ledge into the freezing flow. As I floated below, I caught – and will never forget – the look of bottomless panic that convulsed him as he hit the water, and genuinely worried that I'd killed him. We stopped trying so hard then, instead flowing fast into the life mapped out for us a century earlier by Edward Carpenter:

> Two people, after years, cease to exchange their views and opinions with the same vitality as at first; they lose their snap and crackle with regard to each other . . . If something has been lost in respect of the physical rush and torrent, and something in respect of the mental breeze and sparkle, great things have been gained in the ever-widening assurance and confidence of spiritual unity, and a kind of lake-like calm which indeed reflects the heavens.

FOURTH QUARTER

The Element of
EARTH

❖

The Season of
WINTER

❖

The Direction of
NORTH

❖

PEREDUR

EARTH

The day is fading; the year too. As a thin wind whips in from the north-east and the afternoon pulls in its shawl, we are finally gathered and ready to scatter the ashes of Reg and George at the top of the field, by far our most infinite view. Filling the northern horizon is the galleon of Fron Goch, bronzed by withered bracken, southern Snowdonia's two great mountains at its shoulders: the coronet of Cadair Idris to the left, the cone of Aran Fawddwy to the right. There's an uninterrupted view across the valley to the *noddfa* stone and to Darowen village, where they first found sanctuary, over woods and hills and solitary cottages and farms. Beneath the brow of the field, all that can be seen of Rhiw Goch are roofs – slate, tin, pitch, asbestos – and a couple of chimneys. From one, woodsmoke climbs into the thermals, where crows and kites wheel as they keep a beady eye on us. Through the bare branches of the trees along the drovers' track, there is the diagonal gouge of the Dylife mountain road, George's racetrack powering its way to the heavens.

Although the funerals had been back in the summer, the two urns of ash weren't delivered to us until November. The undertaker – father-in-law of Preds' childhood best friend, inevitably – had handed them to me and then stayed for a chat; all well and good, although I'd felt queasy about the etiquette of dumping the two heavy urns on the ground, so continued to grip them close to my chest, making my arms go numb and my back ache. Preds was out, and when the undertaker finally left, I was suddenly alone, and *so* alone, with our dead fairy godfathers in the hush of dusk. I took Reg and George into the house for the final time. The obvious place to stash them for the time being was the front room, Reg's last bedroom, the laying-out parlour of old.

A few weeks later, here we are, a dozen of their closest friends and neighbours, ready to strew them to the four

winds. We're all a little nervous, wanting it to be respectful and fitting, but unsure how to achieve that in a claggy field in December. I suggest we take turns with each of the urns, sprinkle a little of their contents as we share a memory or thought, first of George, then of Reg. All goes well enough until someone slips mid scatter on the wet

soil, and fistfuls of grey dust billow out of the urn, catch the wind and plaster us all. It is just what we need. Solemnity gives way to spluttering, and then hysterical laughter, our shrieks fusing with the cawing of crows and whistle of the wind. As we descend to the fireside and a farewell toast, the clouds of ash swirl in the evening gloom and settle on the cold earth.

From the top of the field above, we can see the summit of Preds' family farm, where fifteen years earlier they scattered the ashes of his father, Baldwyn. Another fifteen years before that, it was with his dad that Preds first saw Rhiw Goch. Although their farm is only three miles away, there was rarely any reason to pass this way, a shortcut to nowhere, but on that summer day in 1981, his dad had business nearby and took – as he often did – his youngest child with him for the spin and good company. These days, the hedgerow trees are low and scythed back for the winter, but then the steep holloway from the village below was a tunnel of foliage.

'Green lanes', my grandmother called them; on our regular tours of the Warwickshire countryside, dropping in on village churches and the occasional pub, she was always happy to go out of our way to show me a new one or drive us down an old favourite. They felt safe and secret, ways into a land lost in time and beyond normal rules. You never knew quite where they'd take you. Emerging from the tunnel, blinking like moles, you might just glimpse forever.

That day, Preds did. He remembers his father driving steadily up the hill with the light flitting through the canopy of trees, then popping out of the tunnel to see an old stone house on the bend at the top. On its front wall were a dozen pots of bright red flowers, wafting regally against the fresh whitewash of the house. The six-year-old boy drank it all in, and with the same surety as the deathbed note in *Howards End*, a destiny was cast.

Reg's pelargoniums: his last floral hurrah, but his first too. Having only moved in the previous autumn and inheriting a wasteland of a plot, he knew that an instant pick-me-up, for them, their guests and the garden, would be a seductive fanfare of scarlet across the threshold. It worked its magic: '*such* a pretty house! Your loveliest yet!' wrote a regular from Liverpool in the visitors' book.

The fairy-tale appeal is eternal, yet bespoke. Once when I gave my address to the doctor's receptionist, her response was immediate: 'Oh! The Beatrix Potter house! I've always *loved* that place.' This was not entirely welcome, since I have long loathed the twee anthropomorphism of Beatrix Potter. One of my earliest memories is of my Birmingham grandmother taking me to a ballet performance of *Mrs Collywobble's Teapot* or somesuch, and being so traumatised by the prancing, outsized frogs and rabbits that I howled and hollered until my little head felt fit to burst. Finally accepting inconsolable defeat, poor Nana spirited me out of there to a chorus of shushes from the better-behaved families.

Aged twelve, I too was hypnotised by a rather different version of the house. For most of the long summer holidays of 1979, the Boomtown Rats' 'I Don't Like Mondays' was number one in the charts, the video playing every week on *Top of the Pops*. It begins with a long camera shot, zooming in slowly towards an isolated white house on a green hillside, and ends with the same shot in reverse, as we pull gradually away. Its stark purity seared into me, and I was forever searching it out, the place of my recurring dream. It was, I knew, in Wales.

Yet the song is all about a school shooting, the first of so many in modern America. In the opening and closing frames of the video, we are looking at the distant white house through a twisted thicket of thorns and barbed wire, an ominously dark filter across the shot to emphasise that if there are dreams to be had here, they will be jet-black nightmares. When we are taken supposedly inside the building, we find it full of dead-eyed robot children chanting in unison. It is a vision intended to be terrifying, apocalyptic. To me, though, the Boomtown Rats' white house on the green hill was as beguiling as a butterfly, and its lustre never faded. My promised land was an image ripped from post-punk nihilism, while truly dystopian terror came from Beatrix Potter. It turns out they amounted to the same thing.

On paper, however, Rhiw Goch is nothing special. A modest, undistinguished eighteenth-century farmhouse, with a Victorian kitchen extension tacked on to the side, it was built out of stone hacked from the bedrock, a flaky grey rubble bound together with crude mortar. It is low-slung and Methodist plain. The rooms are diminutive, dark and difficult for anyone over six feet. In the weekend property sections' hierarchy of avarice, it lags far behind the country rectory, the cliff-top redoubt or even its northern cousin, the chunky Snowdonia farmhouse that appears to have grown from its rock.

The house's transfiguration comes from the setting, from being, in the words of a ragtime hit that George might have heard in a youth hostel common room before the war, 'a little white house on a little green hill (where the red, red roses grow)'. The combination is hardwired into our palette of desire, and never more so than little Welsh white houses on little Welsh green hills.

There are good views of Rhiw Goch from all angles and heights, but none as archetypal as that from the field opposite, with the humpback of Fron Goch framing us from behind. This is the fantasy white cottage against a fleshy green backdrop, the house from the children's stories, the one we drew in primary school, tongues protruding from our mouths in rapt concentration as we carefully crayoned the curl of smoke rising from the chimney. The lair of trolls and fairies, it is the house that Reg continued to draw for the rest of his life; the one that Preds draws now.

It has been a recurring trope of artists for two hundred years. Though earlier landscapists like J. M. W. Turner, William Sawrey Gilpin and Paul Sandby came to Wales to capture the classical subjects of castles, abbeys and ruins, humbler dwellings began to creep into the compositions. The Georgian taste for the Sublime gave way to the more sentimental yearnings of the Victorian age: the fusion of hearth and home, nature and man, God and Empire in the proud and solitary stone cottage teased from its harsh surrounds.

No mere landscape, this was painting as moral narrative, and in Wales, its chief promulgator was the artists' colony at Betws-y-Coed that emerged from the summer holidays of Birmingham landscapist David Cox in the 1840s. As well as rustic hovels rendered in syrupy tones, Betws gave Cox his most successful painting, *The Welsh Funeral*, so popular that he continually repainted it for the rest of his life. It sealed the mid-Victorian image of Wales, with its black-shawled peasants huddled beneath the mountains to mourn a little girl. The Betws school lasted decades and attracted artists from all over Europe, though hardly any from Wales itself. The colony's viewpoint was that of the privileged outsider, George Borrow's *Wild Wales* in oils.

To the enduring gaze of the colonist, the twentieth century has added its twin, the hiraeth-heavy art of the Welsh exile. John Elwyn, David Jones, Augustus John and Cedric Morris all conjured variations on this eternal theme; on a 1928 painting trip to Gower that produced a stack of stout cottages and lush hills, Morris wrote in a letter to his lover Arthur Lett-Haines back in Suffolk, 'I realise now that all my painting is the result of pure nostalgia and nothing else – I thought I was homesick for England but not at all – dirty grimy little market garden – it was this I wanted.'

The heirs of David Cox (and Beatrix Potter) can be seen in winsome abundance on the walls and postcard racks of commercial galleries across Wales. Pithier English artists – the likes of Graham Sutherland, John Piper and John Knapp-Fisher – came too, and deconstructed the eternal cottage, while keeping its iconography intact and loaded. Of all the outsiders captivated by lonely Welsh houses, most haunting is the work of Belgian artist Valerius de Saedeleer, who was displaced near Aberystwyth throughout the First World War. Most of his green hills are white with snow, under the sulphurous skies of a winter dusk. Each solitary cottage, often locked in a girdle of pitch-black trees like megaliths from another world, is muted and sombre, though a faint hint of light – a candle? a fire? a reflection? – draws the viewer in. In contrast to the heroic crags of Pembrokeshire, Gower or Snowdonia, the stars of de Saedeleer's works are the sullen, swollen humps of mid Wales, wrung out and dark with foreboding.

In *The Poetics of Space*, philosopher Gaston Bachelard quotes the poet Rainer Maria Rilke on 'seeing night for the first time' when he spies 'the lighted casement of a distant hut, the hut that stands quite alone on the horizon'. Although accompanied by two friends, the sight makes him feel cosmically alone; as Bachelard writes, 'we are hypnotised by solitude, hypnotised by the gaze of the solitary house; and the tie that binds us to it is so strong that we begin to dream of nothing but a solitary house in the night'.

Any time between dusk and dawn will do. It is then that the low-grade rubble of our lonesome house reconfigures itself into the walls of an ancient citadel, its lights dancing down the centuries, and all the merrier for the enveloping night. Coming home at any time is a relief, but none so heart-felt as after dark on a winter evening, catching the first faint glimmer through the trees half a mile up the lane, and watching it swell into a beacon, as warm as it is bright.

On the first night of February, we celebrate Imbolc (Gŵyl Fair y Canhwyllau, Candlemas), the festival that marks the climb out of winter. It is a brief and tentative celebration, one of snowdrops and newborns, and of candles guttering in a steely breeze. I like to beef up its presence by turning on all the lights in the house and outbuildings for a few minutes, and retreating to the top of the field to admire the blaze. We stamp our feet on the cold winter soil, where the ashes of Reg and George are mingled. The quick and the dead, we earth ourselves as one.

*

The light is fading, and dark snouts emerge to sniff the twilight. It is badger time. They come from all directions: up through the tree roots along the drovers' track, out of gaping holes in the floor of the beech wood, from behind ramparts of freshly dug soil in the quieter corners of the sheep pastures, out of tunnels under banks of bent thorns. A badger – *mochyn daear* in Welsh, 'earth pig'– is always bigger than expected. Beefier too, as dear old Taff, our late sheepdog, found to his cost one evening when he was bloodily beaten by one he had startled. Their squeals sliced through the dusk like blades.

Badgers are bigger too when you hit them. Driving back from the cinema one night, we rounded a corner on the lane and caught one briefly in the headlights before smacking it full-on. It lay twitching on the tarmac, still fighting. Without a word, Preds slammed the car into reverse to finish it off. The bumps as the wheels ran over it again were sickeningly substantial. We were both shaken, but to many round here, we'd done something positive, as badgers have become the unwitting front line in the latest war between farmers and almost everyone else. It was one less badger to be rooted out and shot; one less to be lured by lamps dancing on the hillsides after dark; one less to be thrown on to the road.

As with so many rural issues, tackling bovine tuberculosis by culling badgers has cemented the argument at its polar extremes. Some say it is the only answer and that they must exterminate every last one of them, others that it has no effect whatsoever, and that none should die. Websites, campaigns and selective statistics confirm that both positions are entirely correct, while science suggests that the truth lies buried in the no man's land in between: the territory where most of us live, but whose voice struggles to be heard above the din.

Badgers are only the latest front in the countryside's rumbling civil war between those who work the land and those who don't. 'Admonition is given by men who do not understand the occupation of the farmer,' growled Scottish agriculturalist Henry Stephens in *The Book of the Farm* (1841), a sentiment that has only grown with time into a dogged hatred of being dictated to by desk-bound townies. That they hold so many of the purse strings only makes it stick even deeper in the craw, and since the European referendum of June 2016, this belligerence has hardened even further.

While this has happened in most walks of life, there are very particular flavours here, the bitterest that so many upland sheep farmers voted to leave the EU and are now terrified that they were the proverbial turkeys voting for Christmas. In the sweet summer evenings leading up to the referendum, I heard the chorus time and again from farmers in the lane, how fed up they were with the prodnoses and paperwork, how 'Brussels' was now paying them to dig ponds on land that their grandfathers had been paid to drain, and where was the sense in that? Any caution – that Westminster or Cardiff would prove just as hock-deep in red tape as Brussels – was a squeak in a storm.

Before badgers, it was foxes. When the hunting ban became law in 2004 and 'BAN BLIAR' [*sic*] was daubed in white paint across local lanes, it made little difference here: our hunts are far from the stereotype of hollering hoorays in red coats. Instead of horses, there are battered vans driven by grizzled old fellas with walkie-talkies. My tune has changed since I was a teenager, when I dabbled as a hunt saboteur. I've seen the dead lambs with their throats torn out, and the bloody carnage in bird coops, our own included. I can't even begrudge those who work such long and lonely hours their sport, the sporadic days of comradeship and shared purpose.

Since the referendum, farmers are feeling more cornered than ever, and so shout even louder. This last year or two, there has been a shrill new note to the hunts: it sounds at first like a full-throated war cry, though if you listen closely enough you might catch within it an existential howl of despair, even self-recrimination for decades of dependence, of being rendered increasingly soft on the teat of the state. Many are convinced that it is a death rattle, the sound of the half-empty glass finally drained completely. Though the fear is real, it should be remembered that there is a particular kind of ear that hears that in almost everything.

We all hear what we choose to. There are those who care passionately about sustainability, whose ears are tuned like bats to the slightest ebb in birdsong or the buzz of bees, but who remain stone deaf to the fragile language and culture all around them, and unable or unwilling to make the connection. To them, solutions are plain. Get the sheep off the land, rewild, reforest, reroute the rivers, the future in artisan food and green tourism. Farm subsidies, they say, are rewarding failure and poor practice, and should go. Yet there have been subsidies to hill farmers of one sort or another since the 1930s. If left to the blunt cudgels of capital, most of our local farms would be out of business within a few short years, the land abandoned, built on or turned over to leisure. Like Native Americans or Aboriginal peoples in Australia, the Welsh could be reduced to squatting their own land and culture. It is not badgers or foxes that are being kept at bay, but this insatiably ravenous, well-spoken wolf.

He's been sharpening his teeth for a century or more, eyeing up these hills and seeing only emptiness. The gossamer threads of community, culture, language and history criss-crossing every field and stream remain invisible, and it is the Sisyphean task of the villagers to highlight and defend them. Through the 1960s, as revolutions swept the globe, in this rocky corner came the radical act of repopulation. In buying a farm down the road at a time when the future of marginal Welsh agriculture seemed even bleaker than it does now, Preds' parents placed themselves on the front line.

Though they had grown up only twenty miles apart, north of here in the mountains around Bala, they first met at a dance, and discovered common cause in the politics of Plaid Cymru. The 1963 flooding of the nearby Tryweryn valley for another Liverpool reservoir had changed everything; it was clear that despite unanimous objection, the villages and farms of the Welsh-speaking uplands were very readily drowned. And not just under water, but conifer plantations, military bases, nuclear dumps, even bricks and Brummies: a 1966 government report recommended building a massive new overspill city in mid Wales, but the aftershocks from Tryweryn killed the plan stone dead.

Compared with many of our farming neighbours, Preds' family's fifty years on the land is a heartbeat, though the same pressures weigh, and none greater than the impulse to pass it on intact. After his father's death, Preds gamely tried to shoulder the responsibility, but his tenure collided with the 2001 outbreak of foot and mouth disease that clamped the countryside shut under a fog of suspicion and paranoia, and that did for him. His brother, far more fluent in the language of agriculture, then farmed it until a few years ago, when he emigrated to South America. Though

Preds' mum, other brother and sister and their families all still live in various houses around the farm, there was no one to work the land, which is now rented out. It was a tough decision, riddled with unexpected guilt and sadness. Perhaps one of his seven nephews and nieces growing up on the farm will want to take it on, but even a temporary break in the chain, which has effectively removed them from first-hand experience of the job, makes this just a little less likely.

In the sixties, as Preds' parents were launching their new life, the tenant farmer up the road at Rhiw Goch was Len, one of the first out of the industrial West Midlands into the area. With his donkey and cart, he seemed initially to be an extreme exponent of the nascent back-to-the-land movement. Farmers chuckled to themselves and watched, waiting for the inevitable grand failure. It never came. Instead, he showed an unexpected empathy with the rhythms of the land and, coupled with a capacity for hard graft, became a well-remembered local character. It helped too that he soon upgraded from the donkey, acquiring some of the latest machinery that he was always happy to share. He brought the first muckspreader into the district, a huge boon to those who previously had had to do the job by hand, and with his nippy modern tractor he would plough everyone's otherwise unreachable slopes.

In such a lonely business, the communal activities, the days of pooling labour and resources around the farms, each in turn, are always the best part. As a youngster, Preds loved the sheep shearing: the broiling summer sheds, air full of fleece, noise and the hot stench of sweat and lanolin, the slap-up meals, high teas and laughter.

Even better was the haymaking in their meadows along-side the Dyfi, ending with a mass plunge in the river to rinse off the dust and calm the horsefly bites. Reg caught the tail end of this, too, helping his farmer friend Iorwerth and his family to gather the hay. Photos from that golden summer of freedom – back in Darowen but yet to take possession of Rhiw Goch – show Reg beaming as he forks bales on to the cart. They are images of such apparent timelessness, though the clock was ticking loudly: within a couple of years, everyone had turned to silage, and hay-making was history.

For Geraint, a retired farmer from across the valley whose family have tended the land since the seventeenth century, shearing days were always fun and sunny, though hay-making was occasionally punctuated by accidents caused by the fearsome Bamford side rake, an unwieldy contrap-tion of seven spiked wheels that would rotate wildly as it was tugged behind his father's first tractor. There were days of communal tail docking and potato lifting too, but his childhood favourite was threshing day, with two of them every winter. Seventy years on, he still remembers 'the excitement of hearing the *thump-thump* of the tractor gradually coming closer, and the hustle and bustle of shunting the thrashing box into place in the stackyard'.

In his life, Geraint has seen all the big changes: the com-ing of tractors, electricity, the telephone and mains water; the end of walking the sheep down to the long-closed railway station four miles away and thence to market, and taking the cattle to their winter fattening grounds in Leicestershire the same way; the gradual disappearance of churning your own butter, the egg rounds, the ritual slaughter of pigs to be shared between neighbours.

Mutual dependence between farmers hasn't vanished, though it is scant today by comparison. Mechanisation has played an inevitable part, but so too has monoculture. Well within living memory, the friable, slightly acidic soil of these farms sustained different grasses, corn, barley, oats and rapeseed, sheep, cattle – beef and dairy – horses, donkeys, pigs, geese and chickens, potatoes, turnips and swedes. Now it is almost all sheep, with a smattering of beef cattle. There are over ten million sheep in Wales, four times the number at the end of the Second World War, and over three times the number of people. Even farmers admit that it is too many.

It was having to kill an injured sheep that finally did for farmer Preds. Remembering how his dad used to do it, he first tried slicing its neck, but couldn't find the main artery and ended up in a bloody wrestle with a frenzied ewe. It took a stone slab to finish the poor thing off, and with it any notion that he could follow his father. In matters of the earth, his talents were manifestly elsewhere.

He has transformed Reg and George's suburban garden of rockery and roses, itself spun out of a workaday field, into a thing of wonder. In their final years, Reg put nearly all of his effort into maintaining the front garden, the one seen from the road. Preds has quietly reversed that, and though the front is lovely, his instinctive inscrutability keeps the best tucked out of first sight. Even there, and for all the hours he spends crafting and plotting, the challenge is to make the gardens appear only lightly touched. Not for him the egotistical stamp of the showman-planter, nor the coercion of a garden into delivering an annual orgasm of triumph. The pleasures keep on coming, a serial pageant of colour, texture, scent and views, even as the year winds down to its nadir.

Like the solitary lantern that both accentuates and offsets the long hours of gloom, his winter garden glows soft and still. Winter aconites, sweet box, hellebores, crabapple and witch hazel whisper their colour, before crocuses and snow-drops shine a strengthening light towards the coming spring. On the walls of the old pigsties, mats of succulents in royal purple and scarlet echo the bark of birch and dogwood. The mahonia, one of the first shrubs planted by Reg and George, is now a sturdy twelve-foot adult; its yellow candles of winter flowers perfume the crisp air and pull in the first bees. In the run-up to Christmas, usually on our shared birthday, he'll bring in the green: holly, ivy, mistletoe, even rosemary and pine, and a week later dig up some slender leeks for the big festive lunch. We have even learned to like kale and chard, the winter veg garden's other thin pickings.

Preds' favourite mornings are when the earth is solid, the air silent and the sun shallow as it catches the frost glinting across his beloved 'cloud hedge', a long and sinuous box below the orchard, faintly redolent of a Henry Moore sculpture. No other moment in the year feels as spacious or calm, nor combines so potently two of his visual loves: hedges and low sunlight. He loses hours checking for box blight, and waits impatiently for Derby day, when tradition has it that you can give the bushes their first clipping. Much loved too are the yews, the evergreen that never comes indoors with the other festive foliage, so deeply rooted is its association with death. It is a paradoxical death, though, one that has life and longevity at its core. Though the tree is so poisonous that precautions need to be taken even to work its wood, it is also by far the oldest living specimen found here; some churchyard yews in mid Wales are five thousand years old, far preceding the Christianity that usurped them. Yew's vivid green, even on the dimmest day, is the promise of returning vitality, and its clippings and bark are latterly being used to create a drug that fights cancer.

Although I'm sure Reg knew almost immediately that Preds was the one, the one to love and lean on, the one most worthy of their beloved home, watching him in action in the garden was the clearest confirmation. He saw death and rebirth beginning to fuse as one, and a very familiar inner strength that found its expression visually, but rarely in words. He was fond of me, I know, but without Preds I'd still be in my slate terrace in the old quarry village, and plummeting headlong into the pits of winter. Reg saw in Preds an instinctive genius for garden and home that would take what he and George had done and let it soar. That Preds and his family were from just down the lane clinched it. Reg could grant him his dream, our destiny, on his own soil.

WINTER

Our first year, as the nights lengthened, we massively overprepared for the coming winter. With steep hills on the lane in both directions, it was clear how easy it would be to get snowed in. I had thick-tread winter tyres put on my van, invested in some chains for extra measure, replenished the piles of grit on the verge and filled the freezer. In early November, the first snow settled on the mountain peaks, and I braced myself. By Christmas, the lower, closer hills had been dusted once or twice: just a matter of time. By Easter, I was still waiting. An entire winter came and went, with not a flake of snow and only a few mild frosts.

The second winter finally produced the goods. Midway through January, the snow blew in from the north-east and swaddled us in its cold cwtch. We were again prepared for a siege, and settled in contentedly. Being cut off by snow upends normality and bends the rules; anything goes. We ate cheese toasties and biscuits for breakfast, chased down with a brandy; went sledging and walking;

lit fires in every stove and cosied in for the evening, relish-ing the sensation of being on holiday at home, and happy for it to last. The next morning, a council gritter came through and broke the spell, turning the snow to dirty slush and a fairy-tale landscape to the old familiar.

Snow fell as early as November in Reg and George's first few months at Rhiw Goch. The kitchen range and living room stove were yet to be installed, and it hurt:

> As we left [a friend's in a nearby village] at 11.30pm there was one flash of lightning, one roll of thunder and all the lights went out. Back home in heavy artillery of thunderous, pelting hailstones. The road thick with them – like ice. All lights out when we reached home. Cold milk, cold bed, just COLD.

Their greater test also came in the second winter. It started to snow in early December 1981, and continued for months. 'Central heating keeps us and the house reasonably warm', wrote George, 'but the cold seems to seep through more each day.' His main worry was that the postman couldn't make it, cutting off his fix from the book clubs. As Christmas drew nearer, the weather worsened, with tempestuous blizzards: 'the wind gained in strength gradually and the snow is being blown everywhere'. Drifts piled up against the front and back doors ('Quite like a horror film!') and the electricity came and went. After a 'calm night but steady snow':

> Scene of Devastation in the light of day. Three conifers blown down cross bridleway to Bryn-y-Brain on our triangle of land (in front of the gate), also completely blocking the lane the dead ash tree! The road to Melinby-rhedyn just around the corner from us is completely blocked by snow 10 ft high! Likewise the road down to Talywern is impassable with deep drifts. The last vase of roses picked about a week or more ago are beginning to wither ...

Later. There is a Landrover abandoned in the snowdrift on the road towards Melin abovementioned. I saw a tractor shoveling snow away from it. Reg and I walked on top of the hedgerows!

Two days later, a tractor with snowplough attached got through, and they were able to get out for the first time in eight days ('Shopping in town – 20 pints milk!'). Having turned sixty-five only a few weeks earlier, George was relieved to be able to collect his pension and 'letters and 2

parcels from the P.O.' There was enough of a thaw to allow Christmas B&B guests to arrive and depart, but the snow and ice roared back in the New Year. With Reg ill in bed but no guests to worry about, George revelled in the quiet of being cut off once more, loving the 'brilliant sunshine on gleaming white icing-sugar landscape'. The sharp air sent his spirits soaring, as did a rendezvous with Daniel.

This was the first time that he really noticed the young man. In their early days at Cefn, the only neighbours that George had much liked were Daniel's parents in the old cruck house that had so excited him. 'A very nice person,' he'd noted in his diary when Dan's mother Pam first called to see them, and invited them to lunch. That midweek date in February 1975 was the first time that Reg and George had met her son, then seven years old. Home-schooled in a remote, 500-year-old farmhouse, and with no siblings, it is unsurprising that George found him 'very strange for his years (Christopher Robin? – an "old fashioned" boy)'. As Daniel himself puts it now, he was 'a country lad' who 'loved playing in the forests and streams, and catching fish with my hands'.

Seven years later, Christopher Robin had blossomed into Billy Elliot; he was now a boarder at the Royal Ballet School, though the blizzards had prevented him from returning for the new term. Pam and Dan were also cut off a mile away but with a houseful of provisions; she sent him to meet George halfway with 'a haversack of food: 2¼lb topside £2.50, Tin ham £1.00, 2 loaves 90p, Tin tuna 50p, Powdered Milk 60p'. George was enchanted, and invited Dan to come and play, as if he too were a teenager kicking his heels and waiting for the thaw. Over the week that they were all marooned, Daniel walked over to see Reg and George almost every day. Under the diary page heading of 'FREEZE UP CONTINUES', Wednesday, 13 January 1982: 'Danny came over for the day. Met him halfway to show him the route through Esgair Gadwyth. Chicken for lunch – Reg's special! Danny enjoyed it, "Do you have meals like this every day"! Walked part way back with him at 4pm.' Though their mutual adoration was to grow on sun-baked bike rides and beaches, I like that its seed was planted beneath thick snow.

The only comparable winter we've experienced here is 2017–18, when we were cut off numerous times over four long, snowy months. The fun wore perilously thin, though it had started with such excitement. Three weeks before Christmas, the first flurries arrived, sending me higher into the hills in search of more. Walking over the tops, there were three different skies fighting for dominance: to the north, a dirty yellow colour, alarming and post-apocalyptic; to the east, a ripe, creamy glow lifted straight from the snowy hills and magnifying them; and in the south, a purer and more sepulchral white that lent the hills a brilliance, as if they were sculpted from bone china. *Eira mân, eira mawr* goes the saying – 'after a light snow flurry comes the heavy fall' – and from the top of Bryn-y-Brain I watched it unfold. Dark clouds, pregnant with snow, steamrollered in so slowly and heavily that they crushed everything in their path. By the time I reached home, we were in the middle of a white-out that continued all day and night. There was no council gritting lorry through this time, or anything else save for one old Land Rover filled with grinning farm lads that skidded by late the first evening. Sliding down the lane below us, their headlights ricocheted off the trees and scythed through snowflakes still piling down from above.

The next morning, a Monday, all thoughts of work, of any adult responsibility, evaporated in the half-moon glow of an icy dawn. Up came a lean sun, only days from its low point, before bellowing with joy as it flooded another 'gleaming white icing-sugar landscape'. Again, there was no staying indoors. The snow was perfect: over a foot deep, dry and powdery, yet with enough internal adhesion to stack high on tree branches and coat the windblown side of their trunks, or to compact flawlessly into snow-balls, snowmen and toboggan runs for a couple of middle-aged men on plastic sheep feed sacks. Our new sheepdog Fflos, just over a year old and a snow virgin, bounced with glee, especially after catching her first – and, very quickly, second – squirrel. All day, I walked and walked, keen to see each one of my favourite trees in its fleeting guise as a Ravilious woodcut: torsos and limbs half black, half white, a medieval memento mori of good

versus evil. The display peaked through a long, luxurious sunset of gold, scarlet and the deepest indigo, the tree skeletons standing keener against every successive shade until only the stars were left to lead me home.

Being snowed in for a while is a scarce treat, as it brings so much that matters into sharper focus. The washed-out, bilious green of winter is sweetened into plump, pillowy whites studded with shards of liquorice black. Field furrows, hill shapes and tree outlines that we've overlooked a thousand times shyly reveal themselves. The lanes, though rarely busy, fall silent and spellbound. Animals edge closer than ever to us, leaving paw, hoof and claw prints as an interactive map of their world. Humans come nearer too: instead of a blurry wave through a windscreen, neighbourliness reasserts itself in impromptu visits at the end of bracing walks, when a nip of something strong and warming is acceptable at any hour. Time goes back in its box.

The brilliance of that blue day was amplified by the knowledge that it was winter's rare exception, not its rule. Normally, whole weeks can slide by where the sun never appears, and my eyeballs ache for lack of light. The short days shuffle past like pensioners in a bus queue, grey and downtrodden, all life sucked from them. Over Christmas, you'll often hear broadcast a fantasy Welsh winter lovingly evoked in a radio essay or drama. The soundscapes are all of crunching snow, cracking twigs and crackling fires, rather than the more truthful acoustic of slithering shit and mud, incessant wind and driving rain, the distant howling of restless sheepdogs. On that one brilliant snowy Monday, there will have been enough photographs taken to fill the calendars and Christmas cards for years to come, the visual incarnation of the same half-truth. It is – literally so – a white lie, but one in which we all cheerfully conspire.

The snow's timing was perfect. After falls and flurries in February or March, the sight of daffodils flattened by a white blanket can be oddly discordant – uplifting and depressing in the same instant. This snow, in the run-up to Christmas, worked a treat in sprinkling over everyone a genuinely festive mood. Most years, by the middle of December, Christmas already feels like an out-of-control avalanche, hurtling downhill and taking everything with it. You try and focus on other things, keeping the monster at bay, but it will have you.

Reg and George became masters at not just taming the festive monster, but pickpocketing it as it roared by. At Cefn, they received a letter in early October 1974 from Mary and David, a couple of teachers in Yorkshire: 'We have had a strong recommendation for your boarding house and wonder if you are open during the Christmas period?' They hadn't planned to be, and Reg – on whom most of the work would fall – was thoroughly intimidated by the idea. He felt that, as people had such high expectations of Christmas, he could only fall short. George saw the potential for charging extra, and talked him round. It was a resounding success, for everyone: 'Our first Xmas in the country and the first Xmas paying guests,' wrote George. 'Also my first Xmas not working for almost 30 years. Wonderful not to have to go out to the hotels over Xmas taking photographs!' Meanwhile, a mile and a half away, on the other side of the ridge to the north of Cefn,

XMAS
DAY
1983

there was another first Christmas taking place: the new-born Peredur, a week old, was brought home to the family farm.

Mary and David became Reg and George's most loyal customers over the next couple of decades. They returned in the Easter holidays of 1975, and came again that Christmas, by which time the price had nudged up from £30 for the two of them to £37. At the beginning of the following December, Reg and George moved to Penhempen, immediately decorating and furnishing the first guest bedroom in order to host them again for Christmas. The next year, they were not alone, as all four bedrooms were full over the holiday. Mary and David came most years, and to all three houses; as David put it, 'It turned into an almost annual tradition, and something we eagerly looked forward to at the end of what was always a long and exhausting autumn term was the tea and sympathy round the cosy log fire. We just loved it.'

Their Christmas visit was something that Reg and George came to anticipate just as fondly. 'We simply gelled,' says David – over long walks, the King's College carol service, books, food and fireside discussions. George would record a radio play – *Blithe Spirit, The Importance of Being Earnest* or something similar – for Christmas evening, after they'd had their turkey dinner. They became friends more than customers, though there was never any such thing as mates' rates at Rhiw Goch. Ten years after paying £30 for the full festive experience, the charge was £150, and they always gave a tip on top.

*

Nowhere is it more obvious than in the Welsh countryside that Christmas is only a patina of religiosity over an aching need to mark the dark point of the year. Here, it is the lights that count, distant pinpricks and flares to puncture the bottomless black. Almost everyone makes the effort to light their windows, walls or trees, even their garages, gutters or barn, as if the collective surge of current will be enough to jump-start us into spring. Some attempts are doomed. There's a 1970s bungalow alone on a nearby moor that looks even more terrifying under a colourful jangle of Santas and sleighs, and never more so than when suddenly glimpsed through a rain-lashed windscreen on a filthy night.

Up go the lights, and in comes the green – still a cottage industry here. At Machynlleth's weekly market there's an old boy who sells bunches of Herefordshire mistletoe, together with home-made wreaths of yew and holly. According to Preds, he's looked exactly the same age for forty years. Ten fields away is a family farm of licensed moss-gatherers, who fashion it into festive arrangements with lichens, holly and ivy, some for market in the big English cities. On the lane between us is Cae Clippiau, the only field kept by the family who first bought Rhiw Goch when it passed out of estate hands after the war. They planted it with Christmas trees, cropping a few dozen every year for sale in local lay-bys.

My jobs are to identify useful greenery in the woods, brew festive spirits and make cards – though my digital efforts are a faint echo of Reg's hand-drawn epics, bespoke to their recipients, that would keep him busy for a whole month. Preds crops the evergreens and transforms house

and garden into fairy tableaux of earth, fire and light. My love of tat and tinsel is roundly ignored, although I am allowed to hang one bauble on the tree, invariably in the wrong position. One tradition is that we make the Christmas cake together, in memory of our butter-fingered flirting fifteen years ago, when I bought my ingredients from the wholefood shop where he worked at the time. It was a large and expensive cake that year, as I had to keep going back for more.

Though neither of us had yet declared our hand, we both had relationships to end first, so our anniversary falls in mid January, easily the least conventionally romantic time of year. Not so the first one, though, which was cute enough to have been scripted by Hollywood. It was the night of the Mari Lwyd ('Grey Mare'), a Welsh wassailing tradition to mark the pre-Gregorian-calendar New Year. A growing crew of singers, some in traditional dress, hops from pub to pub parading an elaborately decorated horse's skull. At each stop, they swap topical songs and banter, growing ever rowdier as they go. The evening finished with scores of us on the street outside the final pub, circle dancing in the frost to a band and twmpath[7] caller. As he hollered and we twirled, steam rising off us like bullocks, the heavens softly opened and thick snow began to fall.

Another festivity operating on the old calendar is plygain, from the Latin *pullicantio*, 'the cock's crow', a traditional all-night Christmas carol service that's now transplanted into a more manageable couple of hours on a weekday evening in the New Year. Unlike the Mari Lwyd, a custom

[7] A Welsh version of a barn dance.

imported from industrial south Wales, plygain's heartland is here in Montgomeryshire. The service is distinguished by its carols, some unique to particular localities or even families, and that they are sung unaccompanied, by all ages and in all combinations, from soloists to small choirs. The sound is haunting, especially in a candlelit church, and the process mysterious; singers emerge silently from the congregation, perform their piece and then melt back into the shadows. Even St Tudyr's, our plain little parish church, comes alive for plygain. Afterwards, there is tea and sandwiches, quiche and cake down in the community hall a couple of miles away. As with all Welsh social events, whether a whist drive or a funeral, the provision of high tea is a fiercely competitive sport. Many plygain performers sing in numerous different churches at this time of year, and every village fights for their hospitality to be the best.

When Reg and George were first at Cefn, a hundred yards from St Tudyr's, they attended a Christmas service, but it is the only church in the district that still conducts its services entirely in Welsh, and they weren't minded to return. I much prefer it, since my Welsh is not sufficient to be bothered by tiresome liturgy, and I can just bathe in its earthy intonation. With the Christmas Eve service and the plygain, my festive season is now bookended by attendance at church, though no service will ever be quite as memorable as my first.

It was our first winter in Rhiw Goch. I'd wanted to go to plygain, but Preds was having none of it. However much I tried to frame it as a precious cultural artefact, or a way of meeting neighbours we hadn't yet encountered, or a chance to hear some dulcet singing, he couldn't get past the idea that it meant going to church, and that wasn't something he was going to start now. His upbringing was commendably – and, for Welsh hill farmers in the 1970s, unusually – irreligious; his parents braved many raised eyebrows by attending neither church nor chapel. In our early days together, he didn't even much like visiting churches when we were travelling, something I've always loved.

Alone, then, I decided to do it the old way by walking to plygain along the *wtra* – a Montgomeryshire dialect word for an ancient, sunken lane – that links us to the village, a steep mile and a half away. It was a clear, cold night with a full moon, but I underestimated how long it would take, and ended up having to scamper the last half mile. By the time I reached St Tudyr's, the heat from both exertion and anxiety was pouring from me; the singing had started, but there was no way I could burst in sweating and steaming quite so sumptuously. Instead, I sat on the stone porch step to cool off in the long moon shadows of the graveyard yews, eavesdropping on the service to the accompaniment of owls.

*

Central to Christmas at all three of Reg and George's Welsh houses were log fires, the nub of desire for every rural runaway. On first landing in Wales, I had eighteen months in my granny flat with only a hissing gas fire for warmth, and though both my summers there were idyllic, I could not have done a second winter. Contracts were finally exchanged on the old slate terrace house in mid November; I had my first hearth in the nick of time.

Fire maintenance was a winter job that George took great pride in: chopping and stacking the wood, drying it out, bringing it in and getting it blazing in the living room, where B&B guests ate and relaxed. So many of the entries in the visitors' book mention the fire, and it was one of the most vivid of Daniel's memories: 'They swore by [the Jøtul stove], and they had it perfect; knew to keep it going overnight, so they were always snug in that room. I never remember it being cold. It's a very special type of warmth too – it has to be wood.' Even later, towards the end, this was still true. George would be in his armchair by the fire, dozing and drifting, smiling politely and offering occasional gnomic assurances of his well-being. The warmth was womb-like, the room a sanctum of twilight against the uncharted depths beyond.

Only now do I realise what an incessant task that cosiness was. Close the door on the living room for just a couple of days, and it is as cold as a tomb. When the house lay empty for five months, between Reg being moved out in November and us arriving at Easter, winter had seeped into the marrow of the place and left it cryogenically frozen. Old stone houses leach heat, especially those that have resisted the lure of PVC windows, whose slate and tile floors pack down the damp earth, and whose walls comprise boulders, shale, rubble and pockets of musty air. You start by accommodating the chills and draughts, then get strangely used to them and expert at calculating precisely the combination of bath, bed, whisky, thermals, blankets, hot water bottles, fire and Aga needed to offset them. Before long the point is reached where other people's airtight homes, with their consistently even swelter, sealed windows and overheated floors, become quickly unbearable and leave us gasping for breath.

In his book of essays, *The Rub of Time*, Martin Amis gleefully disinters the corpses of Iris Murdoch and her husband John Bayley. He warns his American readers that they will not understand this sort of ultra-English literary couple, living in childish squalor and proud of it. As illustration, he tells Bayley's story of a large pork pie that was bought but then vanished into the detritus, never to be seen again: 'The kitchen ate it,' notes Amis, one eyebrow arched as high as it will go. Of the couple he wrote, 'They're the kind of people who like being ill, and like getting old, who prefer winter to summer and autumn to spring. They want rain, gloom, isolation, silence.'

This is clearly anathema to the sun-soaked Amis, but to me it rang ice-chimes of accord. I couldn't quite say that I *prefer* winter to summer, but neither could I say the opposite (though I can empirically state that, yes, I prefer autumn to spring). After the dark decade of winters in my last house, Rhiw Goch has had me reappraise the season radically, and find that it fits. I appreciate its introversion and stillness, the digging deep, its literal sangfroid. I like its clear sightlines and uncluttered horizons, even its muted palette. When the prevailing complexion is grey, and for months on end, the eye soon learns to focus and feast on the tiniest nuance: the tinctures of purple, pink or gold that briefly smudge the damp sky at either end of the day; the distant fields and hilltops that blush suddenly with sunshine and go out; the firework burst of starling murmurations catching the light as they turn as one; the rainbows and sun-shafts from the hand of William Blake; the long, low beams that rarely last, but while they do, pierce the very core; the equally elongated shadows pointing outstretched fingers towards the night.

So many winter pleasures are all about light, in the season when it is most strictly rationed. That is perhaps the point, that only by walking deep into the darkness can we even see, let alone absorb, the most fragile glimmers of contentment. Very few real pleasures come as floodlit or foghorned as our garish culture demands. More prosaically, dark, long winter nights – outwith the Christmas period – are joyously antisocial. No one is going to be popping round unannounced on a foul January evening; it is entirely safe to be in pyjamas by six and bed by nine. 'We love the winter / It brings us closer together,'[8] I bellow along with

---

[8] From the chorus of *The Masses Against the Classes*.

the Manic Street Preachers, and if the sentiment seems too cute, it is only the cosier flip side of the urge for 'rain, gloom, isolation, silence'. If those are commodities that alarm you, best keep away from rural Wales, where all are found in abundance, and often all at the same time.

On moving to Rhiw Goch, it is possible that we embraced a little too readily our own inner winters. Even after seven years here, we're still both younger than George or Reg ever were in this house – something we need sometimes to remind ourselves of. This is not retirement, nor a retreat from the world, nor a genteel coasting down the years to the final sunset. Things though have changed, as they should. A dwindling of some fiery forces, libido especially, is unquestionably welcome: like 'being unchained from a lunatic', as numerous observers, all the way back to Socrates, have had it.

The house has helped nudge this along, its atmosphere always cosy over racy. We've installed a small wood-burner in the parlour, and heat that for the evening rather than the larger living room opposite. That now stays resolutely arctic, as does our bedroom above. Backing on to a barn and with a window that's open even on the harshest of nights, the bedroom in winter is the coldest room in the house. While perfect for burrowing deep into the bed's feathery clouds, it is not much conducive to anything else. There is none of James Baldwin's *Giovanni's Room* about it, a seamy Parisian pit where 'affection, for the boys I was doomed to look at, was vastly more frightening than lust'; more – much more – the bedroom described in the first words of Bruce Chatwin's *On the Black Hill*: 'For forty-two years, Lewis and Benjamin Jones slept side by side, in their

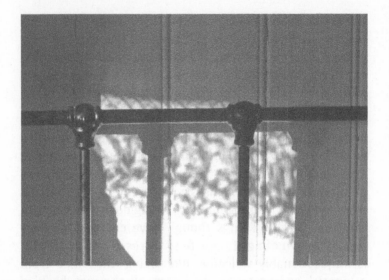

parents' bed, at their farm which was known as "The Vision".' The twins' room, we are told, is 'always dark and smelled of lavender and mothballs'.

We are so quickly on the climb out of the darkness. By the time January arrives, less than a fortnight after the winter solstice, there is already extra wattage in the daylight, even on a grey day, and an appreciable few minutes more in which to get out for a walk at sunset. The rule of thumb is that there are two more minutes of light every day, so more or less quarter of an hour with each passing week. It is keenly felt, far more so than the opposite, the almost imperceptible shortening of the days through July.

As the Christmas decorations come down, nature festoons its own, in catkins, buds and the first snowdrops. The dawn chorus inches earlier and swells each day with new participants; the skies thicken with wings. Out in the fields, the tupped ewes, tattooed like dockside hookers by the ink-pad around the ram's neck, are swelling too. February arrives, and they are all taken to the sheds, in preparation for lambing. For a few eerie weeks, the land is empty and holding its breath, pregnant with anticipation and getting ready to give birth to another infant spring.

NORTH

On the longest night of the year, when darkness plumbs its deepest, stand square-on to the frontage of the house – so facing north – and there, sitting low over the roof, will be the Plough. Our best-known star cluster, the first we learn to identify as children, lies at a rakish angle: tilted downwards and to the left, so that the blade of the plough (or pan of the saucepan, if you prefer) is aloft, the two stars at its far edge pointing as they always do to Polaris, the North Star. For this brief midwinter lull, the two stars at the other end, the butt of the handle, point straight down our central chimney. The year holds its frosted breath, and this earth, the airy heavens and the fires below pass in fleeting alignment.

The absent element of water came in torrents of hail and rain in the days running up to our first winter solstice. As it's also the week of our joint birthday and Christmas too, we decided to throw all the occasions together in celebration, and add another by calling it the long-awaited housewarming party. The guest list quickly escalated to far more than the house could hold, so we cleared the big barn, hired a fearsome gas heater to take the chill off it and built a massive fire pit in the garden. As darkness fell, the clouds and wind finally evaporated to leave a pin-sharp sky brimful of tiny pearls, and we partied through the long night. Preds' aesthetic connection with the place, seeded thirty years earlier when he passed by with his father, had flowered fiercely, and as the year paused and took stock, so did I. It was staggering to see how far we'd already come, how infinite was the promise of more, and how palpable the goodwill towards us from friends and neighbours, old and new.

If only those moments could be banked for insurance purposes, to be plucked from the vault when most needed. Darkness, so readily offset by fire and fairy lights, by love and laughter, can creep inwards like a fever. Mostly, the glow of a solitary lamp through the winter is just about enough, though sometimes, when restlessness and fury are scratching my innards, I open the door to take the dog out before bed and the night punches me in the solar plexus. I can hear trees crashing in the wind, feel the rain lashing me from all sides, but can see nothing, an impregnable black wall over which there is no escape. My mind's eye instantly – and so very selectively – conjures the brightly lit streets before Wales, the city pavements pounding with the heart-beat of thousands, the pubs, clubs and cafes spilling life on to wet tarmac that ripples with reflected neon. That is who I am, my brain thunders, not this, not here, *not ever*.

Such moments will always ambush me, but they pass. There are many, many more nights when I welcome the dark, and slip into its caverns as light as a leaf. To live somewhere so unafflicted by light pollution is a luxury, especially on nights as still as the stiffest brocade and silver-tinged by the moon. Animal shapes flit across the fields, trees teem with eyes unseen, and what at first seems to be silence unfurls into a patter of scuffles, snuffles, hoots and whistles. Some nights, the anticipated five minutes for the dog stretches into an hour's walk, across familiar green contours rendered suddenly incognito and recast in iron and pewter. The dog is a-quiver with instinct, head down and scurrying after scents that criss-cross through the shadows. When she checks back in with me, her eyes and nose are glistening fit to light us to morning.

On a cloudless night around the full moon, its intensity is sometimes exhausting, a nocturnal version of those baking blank summer days that leave me overexposed and itchy. Walking in the moonlight, especially last thing, can be far too much of an ice-white adrenaline shot, and though going to bed with its pale gaze filling the room is a treat – my moment as a Brontë hero(ine) peeping through a moonlit casement – to have any chance of sleep I have to turn my back on it.

The loveliest phase of the moon is when it begins to wax from new, and is first visible as a thin sliver in the twilight. By the time darkness has fully fallen, and your eyes have accustomed to it, if you look hard you will see the earth-shine, a faint reflective glow of our planet on its satellite, the 'old moon in the young moon's arms'. These are the nights too of maximum starlight, the real bonanza of remote rural life. In a city, even under the clearest skies, only a handful of the brightest stars manage to puncture

the galvanised glow, and they look drawn and sickly, mere whispers of a presence.

Like stars that expired countless years ago, our ancestors still shine in the dark country cosmos. Reg loved to sit out on a still evening to stargaze; his kindly spirit and gentle curiosity are never closer than when I'm doing the same. George preferred the flares and fireworks of the night sky, the super-moons, eclipses and meteor showers, but most of all the Great Comet of 1996.[9] It first appeared at Rhiw Goch on a Friday night at the end of March; 'see you again in 17,000 years!' he wrote in his diary, though it came again the following Wednesday ('bright in the firmament!') and throughout the next couple of months.

[9] Actually two: Comets Hyatuke and Hale-Bopp.

The comet fascinated him and fuelled an increasingly cosmic outlook, one coddled over chats with cute hippies on cycling days out, and simmered in his sci-fi paperbacks. It inspired him to write poetry for the first time in twenty years, celebrating its blaze through 'the chill dark, still-dark night', and hearing in it

> This do the Wild Ones say:
> 'Keep us Earth Mother, GAER [Gaia?], for today,
> We the Dark Ones, we the Wild Ones,
> Keep us now for aye.'

The cold war had ended, the new millennium was hurtling our way and New Agery was everywhere. They both embraced it to some extent. Once a year, Quaker neighbours would hold an al fresco meeting in their meadow, to which Reg and George were always invited. Although Reg's fondness for candles and incense made him wary of the Quakers' oatmeal ways, he loved the pregnant silence of the meeting, often interrupted only by birdsong, and the convivial picnic that followed. This being the 1990s, there'd be a circle dance as well, into which he would gamely hurl himself. That was a literal step too far for George: 'Reg danced, I watched,' he noted drily one year.

George's altogether more solipsistic doctrines were of manly athleticism, the sanctity of cycling especially, but also more general precepts of fresh air, stirring landscapes, strength, sun and – if possible – sex. In another poem from the comet year, the Anglican God of his childhood has shape-shifted into the lightest of deities, and the worship is mutual:

This day a butterfly touched me, fluttering by –
As I lay, lonely,[10] naked to the sky –
Gold-glazed my body to the sun on high
Gold-touched by a butterfly –

Touched by God, touched by His Butterfly
Touched by a Guardian Angel . . .
The wings of Heaven enshroud me
In the wings of my butterfly.

A rectilinear English God and the nature spirits of wild Wales grapple most sinuously in the poetry of Gerard Manley Hopkins (1844–89), always one of George's favourites. Hopkins, a fellow Londoner, came to St Beuno's college in the Vale of Clwyd to train as a Jesuit priest, their emphasis on celibacy and asceticism a major pull from his childhood Anglicanism. So extreme was his dedication to purity that seven years earlier, he'd foresworn writing poetry as too decadent and even burned all his works to date. St Beuno's changed all that. Faith and the ancient rocks of north Wales fused as one, provoking a poetic outpouring from Hopkins, much of it inspired by the euphony of the Welsh landscape, and the language woven through it.

'Lovely the woods, waters, meadows, combes, vales / All the air things wear that build this world of Wales,' he wrote in 'In the Valley of the Elwy', a river below St Beuno's. Although the next line – 'Only the inmate does not correspond' – hints at the eternal Romantic haughtiness towards the Welsh, ignorant of the sublimity of their setting, he

[10] In George's handwriting, I cannot be completely sure whether this word is 'lonely' or 'lovely'.

learned enough of the language to read its poetry, and came closer than perhaps any English writer to replicating its rhythms, particularly the 'consonantal chime', as he put it, of the strict metre system of cynghanedd.

As part of his final examinations, Hopkins gave a sermon in which he conflated the geography of the Holy Land with that of north Wales, the fertile Vale of Clwyd doubling up in shape, size and significance as the Sea of Galilee. This 'act of spiritual geodesy'[11] was aided by the presence of so many Welsh villages named after their chapels. A map dotted with settlements like Bethania, Bethesda and Bethlehem, Nazareth and Caesarea only inflamed his ideas that this was indeed the Promised Land – though there was also a far sharper warning in the nearest biblical village to St Beuno's: Sodom, only two miles away.

Central to Hopkins' poetry is the idea that the sensual and the ascetic are in perpetual synthesis *and* conflict. Though his chastity was devout, it was infused by the green swell of lost love, for a young man who had drowned in 1867. For someone like Hopkins, a dead nearly-lover is far more appealing than a live one. Ardour remains unsullied by reality, and every throb can be fine-tuned into the purest of elegies. In this, and in his annexation of Palestinian geography, he embodies mid-Victorian sensibilities, an age besotted by the death knell, by spirits and sprites, while simultaneously proclaiming a muscular Christianity that held the Holy Land to be as British as Kent.

To Hopkins, to George, and to so many before and since, though profoundly moved by the landscape and language,

[11] Damian Walford Davies, *Cartographies of Culture*.

Wales as a sacred repository existed only in counterpoint to benighted England. They could not see it on its own terms. In everything, it was 'chiefly developed by English energy and for the supply of English wants', as an 1866 editorial in *The Times* had it. That had concerned Wales's substantial mineral deposits, but as in the rock beneath, so in the heavens above.

Hopkins' arrival at St Beuno's in 1874 was also presaged by a spectacular comet: in his journal he wrote, 'I felt a certain awe and instress, a feeling of strangeness, flight (it hangs like a shuttlecock at the height, before it falls), and of threatening.' Ten years earlier, on his first trip to Wales, another comet had worked its way into his poetry and into his passion for Welsh skies, day and night. Fastidiously observant of the movement of galaxies, his appreciation of darkness was matched by a love of its concomitant quiet:

> Elected silence, sing to me
> And beat upon my whorled ear,
> Pipe me to pastures still and be
> The music that I care to hear.

Silence is as rare and precious a commodity as a truly dark sky, and only more so today. Almost no one, even in the countryside, is free of the hiss of traffic somewhere in their soundscape, the starkest proof of our Faustian pact with the car. I know that the irony verges on hypocrisy, for living at Rhiw Goch makes us painfully dependent on driving, but the divine absence of road noise here is the luxury I'd find hardest to give up.

Whether ramping up the volume or clamping on the headphones, noise is increasingly used as a way of exerting our boundaries and boosting our beleaguered sense of privacy. I hear it in our urban visitors, fizzing fortissimo for hours after they arrive, or when we go down to the beach and see carloads of tourists bursting on to the sands. Take away the perception of threat and the need vanishes. When E. M. Forster first visited Millthorpe in 1913, his constant bright chatter was met by Edward Carpenter's gruff instruction: 'Oh, do sit quiet.' He did, and liked it.

When we first moved here, we regularly talked late into the night of plans and possibilities for our new life. Most revolved around continuing the conviviality of its days as an alehouse and guest house. George's diaries bubble with the constant comings and goings, the daily merry-go-round of neighbours and a phone forever ringing. That would also be more of the same for Preds; his old house in Machynlleth, where he lived when we first met, had been a melting pot and party central for years, its doorbell the most overworked in town. We talked of gatherings, festivals, conferences, workshops; of people and chatter and shared inspiration hatched under the stars.

It hasn't worked out like that. Moving here, to my first house with no immediate neighbours, I remember telling people that I couldn't wait to crank up the music to full blast. Now that I can, I rarely do. We love throwing parties, or hosting friends and family, but we have both become hooked on the astringency of darkness and silence, and nudge guests that way too ('Oh, do sit quiet'). Most need little encouragement, and not only due to the gathering misanthropy of middle age. So shrill and bloated is our time, so swamped by empty words screamed at full volume, so obsessed by its own reflection, that this, its absolute antithesis, is the most urgent form of *noddfa*, of sanctuary, for now.

*

Fifty yards up the drovers' track, a heavy frost has caused a vertical shelf of stone to shear off the rock face, cascading downhill and splintering as it goes. The new slates are uniformly an inch or so thick, and starkly dichromatic. The sides that had previously faced outwards remain the same dusty brown; the newly exposed edges gleam sharp and dark grey, perfect rock pencils for doodling. Under a light scattering of snow and with the tree tunnel above stripped of leaves, deep winter is the best time to see the bones of Rhiw Goch: the three small quarries up the track that were plundered to build it.

You can tell the order in which the farm was constructed from the quality of the stones and the workmanship. The oldest barn, the original dwelling for people and animals, is rough and uneven, edged and cornered with the biggest boulders, some a few feet long. The house that replaced it was built in stages. In the smaller barn on the other side of our bedroom wall, there is a clear divide between an original building and a later extension. The older work again uses the biggest stones, infilled with the precision of a jigsaw puzzle; the newer is much more of a jumble. Even more slapdash is the Victorian kitchen extension at the other end, full of roughly mortared gaps and knobbly protrusions.

This is mudstone slate, a hard but brittle sedimentary rock that breaks easily along its many fault lines. In most of mid Wales, it is overlain with assorted grits, the residue of historic seabeds. It all adds up to wispy soils and stony fields, but with little to be usefully quarried on any serious scale, at least not for the rock itself. The minerals within were a different matter. This countryside is pockmarked with holes, often speculative commercial ventures that led nowhere and left investors smarting.

On the largest-scale Ordnance Survey map, the 25-inch-to-a-mile series that was completed for this district in 1885, amongst the wells and woods, streams and fields, one label leaps out: *Stone*. Tucked by a brook in an obscure wooded gulley, it seems an odd thing to mark and map. Unlike the Carreg y Noddfa standing stone, the label is not in the Gothic typeface that indicates something of antiquarian interest; it is simply a *Stone*, alone. I went looking for it, but drew a blank. The next time I was walking that

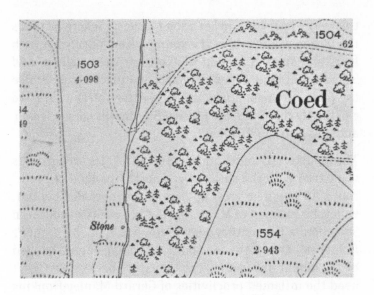

way, I searched again and spotted a rounded mossy hump down by the edge of the stream. Peeling off a little of its greenery revealed a sandstone boulder, about ten feet in diameter and five feet high. Not for the first time, I whistled in wonder at the perfectionism of Victorian cartographers.

Hiding in plain sight: that erratic rock, left high and dry twenty thousand years ago by retreating ice floes and now steadily vanishing into the camouflage of the wood, is an irresistible metaphor with a glorious soundtrack. There it sits, lumpy and awkward, clearly not the same as the surrounding rocks; small wonder that it tries to melt into the background. We would have left it there, a perpetual teenage woebegone, were it not for John Grant, the troubadour of middle-aged outsiders. Whenever I pass this way, I hear his howl of a song 'Glacier', where he takes the frozen wasteland of the young queer, 'paralysed with fear', and spins it around to extol the 'deep valleys' and 'spectacular landscapes' carved by our glacial pain. Praise the gods, we have a new anthem. After thirty years, we can finally thank the 'Smalltown Boy' for his comradeship, and kiss him a fond adieu.

The mudstones, shales and grits of mid Wales are upstarts compared with the rocks to our north, the land of Preds' roots. Although he grew up here in the more mellow Dyfi valley, he is a man of Meirionnydd, the county of southern Snowdonia. His mother's home town is Bala, his father's Dolgellau – two grey-stone bulwarks of Welshness fringed by the mountains from which they were hacked. You don't need the inflamed proclivities of Gerard Manley Hopkins to feel north Wales's growling force. The evidence is everywhere: ancient igneous crags piled high like gods made manifest; the vast gouges in their flanks from which the most exquisite slate was blasted and split; the glittering seams of copper, silver, manganese and pyrites, even gold.

It's more than money, for this is the original place, the nub of nations, the home of the most elementary DNA on our island. When the British carved up geological time with the same imperial hauteur as the African savannah, the first three of the six divisions – Cambrian, Ordovician and Silurian – were named after the rocks of Wales. In an age at first scandalised by the concept of evolution, many preachers fused geology and Genesis, equating the six eras with the six days of the week taken by God to build the world, so placing the Welsh squarely in the Garden of Eden.

Even when Darwinism became an accepted orthodoxy, Meirionnydd's old rocks could still pull off a dazzling show of primitive spirituality. In the last great Welsh religious Revival of 1904–5, a tiny chapel at Egryn, above the coast near Barmouth, became the epicentre of a phenomenon. Whenever local farmer's wife Mary Jones preached, the winter sky was said to erupt in lights: sudden flares, ghostly shimmers, exploding balls of phosphorescence, in all colours.

Stories in the local press soon spread, bringing journalists from London to see for themselves. Their reports all followed a pattern: utter incredulity, awful journey, super-stitious peasants, saintly Mary, and then '*bang!* I saw the Egryn lights!' No complete explanation has ever been found; offers include will-o'-the-wisps, fireflies, marsh gas, the Northern Lights, St Elmo's fire, the planet Venus, lighthouses, trains, cars, and that the chapel lies on an active geological fault in an area full of metal mines. What-ever the combination, mass hysteria played its part, too. Though the Revival emptied pubs, it filled the North Wales Asylum at Denbigh: over a quarter of the 1905 admissions were listed as suffering from 'religious mania'.

The story of the 'Merionethshire Seeress' is now forgotten by all but the most diehard Forteans; that of her earlier local namesake only grows by the year. In 1800, fifteen-year-old Mary Jones of Llanfihangel-y-Pennant near Cadair Idris was so desperate for a Bible in Welsh that, having saved for six years, she walked twenty-six miles barefoot across the mountains to buy one in Bala – an action that precipitated the foundation of what is now the global Bible Society. Her story was not published until 1879, fifteen years after her death, but has travelled the world since, mutating to fit every era, culture and agenda. In today's north Wales, religious redemption is eclipsed by the no less sacred linguistic element, that *yr iaith y nefoedd* ('the language of the heavens') is a rocky, lonely path, but one that leads to glory.

It fits, too, a contemporary soft-feminist agenda, and not before time. Despite Wales being such a matriarchal society ('the Italians in the rain'), its women have long been almost invisible in public life. Though there had been a couple in the fifties and sixties, when Preds was born in 1974, Wales had no female MPs at all; Ann Clwyd was elected ten years later and she was alone until the Blair landslide of 1997. For all their fame, neither Mary Jones makes it into the 1959 *Dictionary of Welsh Biography*, a 1,200-page doorstop of a book produced 'under the auspices of The Honourable Society of Cymmrodorion'. Indeed, of the 285 entries under the surname Jones, not one is female. In our copy, the only 'Mary Jones' is handwritten in looping script on the inside cover: Preds' maternal grandmother, of 'Gelligrin, Bala', to whom the book originally belonged.

As in life, so too in the sepulchre of death, for equally absent in Welsh town squares are statues of women that are neither Queen Victoria nor some saccharine archetype of peace or home. After an anguished debate, inevitably conducted while peering through the wrong end of the telescope, it was announced that a new development outside Cardiff Central station would be crowned with a statue of an actual Welsh woman. A competition was launched to establish who that would be, which was won by Betty Campbell, the country's first black head teacher in the 1970s.

Though there should be a woman crowning every town centre, I'd also suggest an immediate addition to the pantheon of Welsh statuary: a vast totem of a Welsh Mam, on the scale of the *Angel of the North*, to be placed, sleeves rolled up for action, at the nation's omphalos. (Where that might be would doubtless provoke another furious parochial argument; I'd go with it replacing Machynlleth's fussy, feudal clock tower.) On Mothering Sunday, youngest sons of all ages could dance around it, a giant ma-maypole garlanded with ribbons of apron strings that they will never, ever lose their grip of. At its base, a plaque of the finest slate, inscribed with a quotation from the autobiography of actor Emlyn Williams:

> I shall never grow up, or old, but shall lie on the grass for ever, a mummy of a boy with nestling in the middle of it a nameless warmth like the slow heat inside straw.

As with me, the most enduring influence on Preds came from his mother's mother. His memories of her double kitchen at Bala – one part farmhouse tradition of Rayburn, sofas and tantalising aromas, the other a cool post-war American diner decked out in floral patterns – set standards and ambition for the rest of his life. Her cosy parlour with its roaring fire has been lifted to Rhiw Goch, even down to the same curtains, still in good nick over half a century after she bought them in Chester. Her beds are replicated too: soft, pillowy islands of cool linen and hot water bottles, the *sine qua non* to darkness and silence. Deep sleep is one of Rhiw Goch's greatest gifts to its visitors.

Mary Jones, Nain Bala, was a model matriarch, running a busy mixed farm, fully immersed in community life and at the heart of her large family. Every year, she made the Christmas puddings for all five of her children's own families, each tailor-made to their favourite recipe. Even breaking a rib as she hauled them out of the Rayburn one year failed to dent the schedule. All fifteen of her grandchildren would also receive an individual present and a jar of home-made toffee, though Christmas Day itself was the one day of the year when she and Taid, Preds' grandfather, would shut the farm door and receive no visitors.

This is the oldest country. Up from their farmhouse, a rocky track known as *y stryd*, the street, and believed to be Roman, was famous for its fossils, whole walls of them chipped out by urbane Victorians and carted off to London and Cambridge. Down in the depths of Bala Lake, Llyn Tegid, the largest natural body of water in Wales, lurks the gwyniad, a prehistoric cousin of the salmon that is found nowhere else and is never caught on the line. Read the gravestones in any churchyard around Bala and you'll be struck by the longevity of its inhabitants, with nonagenarians and centenarians far from rare even in the Victorian era. Into this century, Nain and Taid Bala celebrated their seventy-fifth wedding anniversary and died a few years later aged ninety-eight and a hundred and one. (Taid, on receiving his hundredth-birthday telegram from the Queen: 'Oh, why did she bother?')

No one does a funeral better than north Walians: even the drabbest village *tabernacl*, frowning pebbledash against a slate sky, explodes into celestial colour when hundreds – and it almost always *is* hundreds – gather to raise the roof

in radiant mourning. At her parents' funerals, Preds' mother, their eldest, ensured that I was alongside the family with all of the other spouses; it is never spelled out or made anything of, but that has been her unwavering policy since we first got together. It is the Welsh way, as is the serious baking rivalry that kicks in for the lavish funeral tea afterwards. At Nain's funeral, I was on my fourth slice of bara brith when I said to the auntie who had baked it that it was a treat I too liked to cook. 'What's your recipe?' she fired back. I told her. 'That's not a bara brith,' she sniffed, 'that's a tea loaf.'

For somewhere so historically popular with visitors, north Wales is well practised at hiding its best. To Reg and George, it was the destination for one touring holiday, and in his seventies, George was a regular on the gruelling annual eighty-mile cycle challenge that headed to Bala over Bwlch y Groes, 'the Pass of the Cross', the second-highest of all Welsh roads and dizzier even than the Dylife route. Theirs was only ever the tourist trail, though: castles, more castles, big houses and steam trains. When writing the *Rough Guide* in the 1990s, I liked to believe that I dug deeper, but it was only further down into the same exposed seam, that version of Wales so carefully minted for outsiders. Being part of a local family has nudged open doors that I'd never have noticed otherwise, portals buried like glints of gold in the bedrock. And the passwords for entry will forever be in Welsh.

The spectacular Bwlch y Groes mountain pass was the route usually taken by Preds' parents when they went to visit Nain and Taid. The journey also passed his father's childhood home, in the first village on the River Dyfi as it surges down off the mountain. Though his other grand-father died before Preds was born, his name, William Thomas, remains etched in the glass above the front door of his old shop; he was a celebrated craftsman, north Wales's champion rake-builder, his portrait in the National Museum.

Between there and Bala, the road climbs vertiginously, reaching a gradient of 1 in 4. Preds remembers regularly being sent with his sister and brothers to fetch water from streams to help their overheating Ford Escort as it wheezed its way uphill. Though he loved visiting Nain and Taid, he always preferred the journey back, particularly cresting the top of the pass, seeing the lush green of the infant Dyfi valley open out ahead, and hearing the mud-stones of the middle-lands calling him home.

PEREDUR

One frosty night in 2004, as our new relationship ripened, I made Preds watch a television programme about the experience within families of middle children. Somehow I'd gleaned from the listings that it would be a paean of praise to those like me, number three of five, who had slipped unseen through the middle of turbulent family dynamics. It was anything but. To my horror and Preds' hilarity, a succession of experts outlined how resentful and damaged middle children often are, stunted emotional runts forever craving attention. Fortunately, the painful truth was blown aside by an observation that has become a cherished punchline in our lexicon. Proffered by a cheery American psychologist as he talked through the different positions in the family unit, he came to the youngest child: 'And as for little Schnooky, well, *he's Schnooky*! He can *never* do wrong.'

Even the earliest Peredur was a textbook Schnooky. In the Welsh early-medieval tales known collectively as the

Mabinogi, Peredur is the youngest son of Efrawg, the Earl of the North, though his father and older brothers have been killed in battle. To protect her baby from the same fate, his mother hides him away in the forest, where he is allowed the company only of 'women and children and quiet contented types who could not or would not fight or wage war'.[12] So sheltered is the boy that when three knights appear one day, Peredur does not recognise their armour or weaponry, and asks: 'Mother, what are these?' 'Angels, my son,' she replies.

For Preds too, the dark days of childhood were few. He was too young to recall the night their house burned down after a squirrel chewed through the electrics, though someone once let slip that the baby was the last to be rescued: *that* he does remember. Far worse for the princeling were the only two occasions his mother had to defy him. When he was three or four, she had to trick him into the doctor's surgery for an inoculation; his sense of betrayal sparked a lifetime's phobia of injections. Then, on a family trip to London a few years later, knowing that she had exactly one hundred pounds cash in her handbag, he couldn't fathom her refusal to buy him a sit-on train set in Hamleys, price tag £100. But the worst day of all is straight from the *Mabinogi*, when the realisation hit him that no matter how hard he tried, he would never grow up to be a robin redbreast. Until then, he'd been happily certain of this as his destiny.

It is a tidy fit. Regularly voted Britain's favourite bird for its Christmas card cuteness and warbling song, a robin is

[12] Translation by Jeffrey Gantz (Penguin Classics, 1976).

brave, loyal and feisty in standing its ground. 'The defence of territory is a robin's life,' says my grandmother's bird book, celebrating

> this chest-puffing individualist whose tameness . . . is a tribute to the British character. On the Continent robins are shy birds, keeping to deep woodland; but in Britain they are bold enough to dog the footsteps of a gardener who might turn over a worm or two for them.

A melodious creature of the soil, a bold but tame individualist, a splash of colour when it is most needed, yet with the calculating mindset of a warrior: no wonder the robin was Preds' role model.

Sometimes I look through a window and spot him outside, digging or clipping, his brow furrowed in concentration, and then notice the birds hopping around him or settling on nearby branches for a better look. Nearby, the cat will be keeping a watchful eye too, as will Fflos, our latest dog. Particularly in the morning when he's out there in his hooded brown dressing gown, I'm reminded of those glutinous icons of St Francis of Assisi sold in Catholic tat shops, the avuncular monk serenaded by gambolling creatures and with a smiling chorus of birds on his shoulder.

Preds as St Francis: Reg would have melted at the sight. Francis was his very favourite saint, and he had quite the collection of knick-knacks to prove it. When he and George went to Assisi in 1965, he spent days visiting every church, basilica, well, shrine and cloister, and remembered them always. In one of the side chapels of the Chiesa Nuova, built supposedly on the saint's birthplace, they stumbled upon a swarthy young friar fast asleep in a pew. He woke, and after chatting for a while took them for a coffee, and for the rest of their stay became their tour guide. For Reg, already in the most heavenly of dolly-daydream states, it was as if the saint himself had been reborn.

We went to Assisi a few months after they had both died in 2011. I was keen to light a candle for them in one of the churches, and aghast to discover that in the basilica, the cathedral and the Chiesa Nuova, votive candles had been replaced by tacky little electric versions that light up only when a two-euro piece is dropped in the slot, like a pub fruit machine. When we finally found a quieter backstreet church that still used real candles, lighting one made me cry with relief, and sadness. A circle was closed.

Preds' animal husbandry isn't always quite so Franciscan. One day, he came home with four white doves that someone had been getting shot of, and built them a set of nesting boxes on the inside wall of the big barn, around the narrow slits that were once its windows. After a fortnight of keeping them behind grilles to become acclimatised, he let them loose, and for a few weeks revelled in their soft coos and photogenic flutters around the garden. Then one day, silence. They'd flown, who knows where. A few days later, I was walking Taff in the wood below us. In the green evening gloom, I saw a patch of ghostly white on the path ahead. Drawing nearer, I realised that it was an explosion of dove feathers, like the chalk outline of a murder victim on a city pavement.

Deep in the vaults of Welsh-language TV station S4C is footage from a mid-1980s magazine show of a young Preds enthusing about his pet peacocks. For his birthday, he'd chosen a peacock as his main present, and the following year a peahen. Unsurprisingly, they produced a cluster of pea-babies, more than his mum could cope with. She made him place an advert to sell them in the local newspaper, which was seen by a TV producer who hotfooted it over to film Montgomeryshire's youngest livestock tycoon. In the interview, Preds told how his babies had all vanished one day, and that his mum had refused to go out looking for them 'until *Dallas* had finished'. Though mortified to have her trashy TV tastes revealed to the nation – and *in English!* – she instantly forgave him, as she always has and always will.

This was spelled out to me very clearly when we first started dating, by one of his dozens of cousins. She took me aside to warn that his mam is the kindest woman she knows, but that she is a tiger – her word – and if anyone causes grief to her cubs, especially the baby of the brood, they will reap the full force of her fury. I'd already worked out that there was no room for error in starting a relationship with Preds. If I cocked it up, as I had with such tedious predictability before, I'd have to leave the area, and fast. I had to be absolutely sure, more so than I'd ever been about anything – and to my great surprise, I was.

Even Sosej, their farm collie, was the perfect mother. Every year, she'd get pregnant and, shortly before giving birth, disappear into a deep hole in the earth that she'd dug for her confinement. A few weeks later, a scatter of fat puppies would waddle out of the burrow, blinking in the daylight, followed by an exhausted mam. Her behaviour cemented in Preds' mind the way a dog should be, and created an unanticipated cultural hurdle when we first got together. He couldn't believe that my mongrel Patsy had free rein of the house, for dogs live outside, not by the fire, and certainly not on the sofa. Two dogs later, he has come around, and spectacularly so, to my sissy Saxon ways.

As Joe Ackerley had it in his best-known book, *My Dog Tulip* (1956): 'Unable to love each other, the English turn naturally to dogs.' George and I, perhaps Reg too, nod in shame-faced recognition. Towards the end, Reg's plaintive diary entries, berating himself for being unable to care for George at home, take a sudden, wistful turn: 'Saw our darling George. He is ok looking happy. Wish he were liveing at home and we had dogs,' he wrote, a week before a massive stroke took him away too. Since arriving in Bournemouth in 1949, George had always had at least one canine familiar. The last of the long line, a feisty little terrier called Willy, was put down in September 2005, aged seventeen: 'Reg buried Willy in the garden next to Molly's grave – side by side – heart broken,' wrote George.

We were regular visitors by then, usually with Patsy. Reg was always keen that she should come too, as a way of bringing George out of himself for a while. A large and boisterous rescue dog, rarely still for a moment, she'd sit meekly by his chair, and be fussed over by a beaming George for as long as he wanted. It only made it clearer how empty Rhiw Goch is without a dog, but from fear of a new one outliving them, they had decided there could be no more after Willy, despite assurances from a few of us that they'd be looked after if need be. The decision was a typical tenet of their generation's proud self-sufficiency, but torture too. Is there any

chapter of life more in need of a dog's uncomplicated adoration than its finale? Happily, after George had been moved out and Reg was left there alone, a wild cat from a nearby farm appeared one morning and moved in. They were the closest of buddies, Reg and Puss, but the minute he went, so did the cat, never to be seen again.

*

When do you know that the future has arrived? There were so many signs, some hackneyed and slushy, others unexpectedly leftfield. None echoed with such piercing clarity as the most caustic of all, a conversation down the village pub in our first few months together. A group of us were discussing suicide. 'There's a hell of a lot of it in my family, going back generations,' said one friend, jabbing his rollie into the overflowing ashtray. 'Mine too,' said Preds. 'Not in mine, I don't think,' I said. Without skipping a beat Preds replied, 'Yes, well, that's because it's your family that makes other people kill themselves.' A shaft of light burst through the clouds.

They kept coming. After watching the television programme that gave us the concept of Schnooky, he pointed out something that had never quite swum into focus for me: that although at home I had been the over-looked middle child in a crowd of half- and step-siblings, in my other family – to my mum and her parents in their warm world of books and lasagne *al forno* – I was youngest of two, the little prince. Even if for only a few weeks every year, I too wallowed in Schnookydom, made all the cosier by its infrequency and harsh contrast with my regular life.

Helping me to see this was in his self-interest too; otherwise we were doomed, like all my relationships before. To build a life together, and a home new to us both, would require radical new ways, but the roots were all there. Our home would be soft and yielding, comfortably frayed and upholstered by light and colour: both palace and playpen for two princelings and their brood. That is the mission, even if it comes at the cost of worldly adventure, erotic charge or conventional notions of career. We could take Murdoch and Bayley's wintry English taste for 'rain, gloom, isolation, silence', and add to it the lot of the Welsh Schnooky, Emlyn Williams' 'nameless warmth like the slow heat inside straw'. This was always Reg's way, too, as he was a Schnooky grandmaster, and with an equally challenging initiate.

Soft, too, is the setting. The lattice of connections in Welsh-speaking Wales remains invisible to many, like a mesh of spider silk in the grass that is only glimpsed as the long, low rays of sunset glint off its strands. Once noticed, though, you marvel at its strength and see it clearly as a safety net that stretches for miles.

In the wrong moment, or the wrong hands, such comfort can also be claustrophobic; perhaps both simultaneously. It is, for instance, a common complaint amongst Welsh-speakers that they rarely see themselves reflected in wider cultural discourse. True enough, though there is no shortage of their own mirrors. When we watch Welsh TV, Preds invariably subtitles it with reminders of whose cousin, son, neighbour, lover, mother or difficult ex it is currently filling the screen. I grew up in an anonymous English town of fifty thousand people; were it a few dozen miles west and this side of the border it would easily be in the top ten largest places in the country. Through the whole of my childhood I can only remember seeing my town, or anyone from it, on the telly perhaps half a dozen times.

The deal here is different. When my instinct is to behave like my bookish grandfather, whose standard response to the doorbell was a heartfelt 'Oh, why can't they just leave us *alone*?', even before knowing who it was, I know that will not do now. The lattice hums with phone calls, unannounced visits and the scamper of the next generation of princes and their attendant courtiers: sisters, mothers, grandmothers, aunties. It took some getting used to, and still does.

There is an old saying that while an Englishman's truth is a straight line, a Welshman's is a circle or curve; a Roman road scything imperiously through the landscape regardless of locale or context, versus an ancient lane meandering around the contours. So it proved ten years ago, when Preds and I had our shittiest quarrel yet, an implacable gulf between our different versions of fact. Because the disagreement involved his family and the farm, it escalated horribly and came close to sinking us. The menfolk, me included, grew increasingly sour and silent, leaving his mam and sister-in-law to sort it out with a dexterity supped in their mothers' milk.

Marry into a local farming family and there are two languages to learn: Welsh and a largely voiceless code of glances and grunts. The Welsh is easier; there are at least evening classes for that. The silent language of ancestral osmosis is far trickier to grasp, especially for someone as word-dependent as me. When we first got together, I regularly nagged Preds about his 'failure' – by my definition – to have come out to his family. It presaged, I feared, an internalised repression, a shameful – if exquisitely decorated – closet from which he – we – could never escape until he made the formal announcement. But he never came out, because he was never in. A little boy so comfy in his choice of *Ideal Home* magazine over the *Beano*, and asking for a peacock for his ninth birthday, has no such surprises in store.

It's amongst his family that my Welsh gets its most rigorous workout, and although occasionally deafness and ignorance leave me feeling adrift in the crowd, there is no sound within these walls more fitting or hopeful than a babble of Welsh in tiny voices. Preds is a different man too in his mother tongue: younger and lighter, more animated. Even his physiognomy softens.

Some of his feistier cousins, those dug deep into the old rocks of the north, occasionally jib us that the primary language of our relationship is *yr iaith fain*, 'the thin tongue': English. Though the answer is clear – that no matter how good my Welsh gets, his English will always be better – it can make us feel indefinably guilty. In recompense, he defaults to Radio Cymru in the car and kitchen (if the broadband is working), and teaches the puppy only Welsh commands, while I massively overcompensate elsewhere. At one Gŵyl Fron Goch, the annual community get-together in a farmer's barn, I was asked to compère proceedings, including a discussion of the area's history with some of our elders. Taking one look at the crowd gathered to hear them, including so many faces new to the area, the participants switched straight into English, handling the unaccustomed words with the same polite daintiness as the Sunday best porcelain. I, meanwhile, got wrapped in linguistic knots attempting to simultaneously translate myself, Katie Boyle in a cowshed.

At home both in the middle and on the margins, Preds has long been a one-man bridge between our contrary communities and cultures. His house in town introduced so many who would never have otherwise met, and fused them together with tea and cheap red wine. Every time I went there, I'd never be quite sure who I might find at the kitchen table: an ardent Welsh nationalist deep in conversation with a black Brummie; an old farmer playing peek-a-boo with children called Rainbow and Gaia; a pillar of the chapel laughing with a couple of lesbians. We spent our first Christmas Day there; in a silent echo of his grandparents' farm in Bala, it is the only night I ever remember when the doorbell didn't ring.

His short-lived business on Machynlleth's main street widened the net even further. When we first got together, he was thinking of opening a shop to sell the kind of things he'd been obsessing over for years: fabrics, lighting, artwork and household trinkets, new, recycled and (to my eyes) straight from a skip. He was brilliant at that side of it, but less so handling the waifs and strays who drifted in, hauled themselves up on to the bar stool by his counter and stayed for hours, pouring out their problems: the lot of the kindly gay shopkeeper in any small town.

Occasionally, I'd fill in for a few hours if Preds was else-where, sourcing stock or running his nephews and nieces around. *Ding!* would go the bell over the door as one of his regulars bowled in at the end of her shopping expedition, to be confronted by me glowering behind a newspaper. 'Isn't Preds here?' she'd ask, peering hopefully into the back room. *Ding!* the bell would sing again as she'd leave seconds later, pondering which cafe to try instead.

The one regular he never minded seeing was Reg. Preds' shop coincided with the freedom of Reg's penultimate years, when George had given up driving and Reg could get on his glad rags, take a taxi into town and make a day of it. Unlike too many of the shop's habitués, sucking in the light and pulsing out only a nebula of gloom, Reg glittered on that bar stool like a box of jewels, holding court and swapping gossip with everyone. Not only was he with the man who had unlocked him, it revived the fondest mem-ories of his own years in retail, a lifetime ago, before Preds was even born.

When the shop limped to an eventual end, leaving a town full of widows, Preds looked for new ways to guerrilla-plant seeds of beauty in his home turf. Rhiw Goch rode to the rescue there too. During Reg's final winter, when he'd been forced from the house only days before an Arctic blast swept in and froze it rock solid, plans accelerated for us to buy the place and help pay for any care needs ahead. That February, with everything up for grabs and me in a predictable tizzy, we went to a grand wedding in London. Love was in the air; so too the first winks of spring, and as we nipped outside for a smoke, and contemplated the chaos about to engulf us, he silenced my frets with a kiss,

whispered, 'I promise you, I am going to build us the most beautiful home *ever*', and kissed me again. The thaw was instant, total.

Only weeks later, we were moving in. Our first impromptu guests were some old friends of Preds' who'd been passing and noticed our car outside. After spiriting them on a tour of house and garden, one of them turned to me, her eyes shining, and laughed, 'This is what Preds has been training for all his life.' She was right. I'll still sometimes struggle to see – *believe* – that I am a part of it; my soil is thinner and far more readily dispersed by the wind. If the worst happened, Preds could easily carry on here without me, but probably not the other way round. It was the same for Reg and George. Penny cajoled them into a civil partnership to give Reg security, but it was George who would never have coped had he been left alone, even before his dementia.

The old place will one day swat us aside too and embrace new hopefuls, wide-eyed with anticipation. Our ashes will mingle in the damp earth with those of Reg and George, weeds will lick the walls and fill the cracks, my pool will grow stagnant. Who will those hopefuls be? I am certain that the spirit of Rhiw Goch will endure; the spirit of sanctuary and deep conviviality, but also of *yr hen lanc*: literally 'the old lad', but best translated as 'the confirmed bachelor'. The Welsh phrase winks exactly the same euphemism as its English equivalent, though far scruffier, its fingernails packed with dirt.

Yr hen lanc was the spirit of the unmarried Anwyl brothers who lived here for decades after their mother's death in the 1860s, their maid a Chicago gangster's grandmother. The spirit, too, in the 1960s of Len the last farmer, the renegade Midlander who became a cherished local: another bachelor-and-mother combination, and with a friend across the valley who he'd invite over by flying bedsheets from the washing line. That too of the solo Buddhist monk who rented the house at its nadir in the 1970s, keeping it notoriously filthy; of Reg and George, of course, who nursed it back to a clean bill of health; and of us. On foul winter nights, I hear whispers too of that poor young son of the farm, driven by unknown demons to calculate which branch of the ash tree opposite was sufficiently sturdy to take his weight, to kill him.

Every parish had its *hen lanc*, often living undisturbed, perhaps with his special friend, his brother, blood or otherwise. His twin, even, sharing a bed and a midwinter birthday, their old farm neatly bisected by the frontier between Wales and England: *On the Black Hill* redux. For some Welsh boys, such a life would never be enough, their extrovert creativity so turbocharged that it could only blast them into lifelong exile. At least that is no longer the only option force-fed misfits by court and chapel; there is now choice. Though it often feels that progress is stalling, the revolution over the last half-century in notions of gender, sex and sexuality is real and massive; it lives in the fields and hills just as happily, and just as unhappily, as it does in the streets.

Rural Wales has always embraced *yr hen lanc*, and the definition is becoming ever more generous. As it grows in confidence, it's to be hoped that another dictum of Welsh masculinity shrinks in consequence. *Angel pen ffordd, diafol pen tân* ('an angel on the highway, a devil at the hearth') is a chillingly perfect six-word portrait of those men we all know, whose effusive handshakes freeze into iron fists the second they pass through the front door. What tacks a man that way? Many factors, but none surely more disastrous than a fundamental schism in his sexual geology.

In a landscape so apparently static, the tectonic plates of change grind slowly and invisibly far beneath our feet, manifesting only occasionally as the eruption of individual beacons. Like solitary lamps on a December night, they make a disproportionate difference in the countryside: 'I muse at how its being puts blissful back / With yellowy moisture mild night's blear-all black,' wrote Gerard Manley Hopkins. Their light travels unexpectedly far, reaching eyes that may never be known as they scan for even the faintest distant glimmer as confirmation that there is life out there, that all will be well. Reg, George and I have all borne that light, but had to carry it many miles from the darkness that spawned us. The clearest beacon is the one that has burned here constantly, nurtured and maintained by its tribe, that of our quiet revolutionary.

*

The circle turns and the light scatters in new and unexpected directions. As Laurence Scott points out in *The Four-Dimensional Human*, these days the glow in the window of the solitary cottage may well be the Internet router chugging along, at once further atomising an already scattered population while also helping a lonely farmer find love. Even rural Welsh broadband will eventually improve; for now, our neighbours panegyrise its paucity by listing 'a digital detox' as one of the main selling points of their new holiday barn conversion.

If the uncharted cosmos of the fourth dimension will inevitably bind us in further to the wider world, the three dimensions of our physical terrain remain reassuringly impenetrable. Our steep, twisting lanes and blind corners, so easily blocked in winter but tricky enough all year round, mean that large-scale development is impossible. Even those for whom this is potentially a downside, the farmers especially, are quietly resigned to it. They know the land with such intimacy and, like their forefathers, are adept at thinking laterally as the challenges roll continually around. Although agriculture, marginal highland farming especially, is often portrayed as close to extinction, they take the long view and have seen it all before.

The older farms, in the same hands for centuries, are our lodestars. The rest of us – whether in an ex-farm, converted barn, old mill, village terrace or lead miner's cottage – whirl around them: we come, we go. After fifty years as Rhiw Goch's nearest and dearest neighbours, but only three as ours, the time came for Penny and David to sell up and consolidate their life back home in the south. Plans were accelerated, as they often are, by sad circumstance: David had a serious stroke. Even in the panic and sudden urgency to sell, Penny dropped neither her standards nor her *noblesse*. The grand old house went on the market with an estate agent who pitched it squarely at downshifters and holiday-home hedge-funders. Quite a few came to have a look, and every time, Penny asked them outright whether they were '*at all* homophobic', before going on to explain that the nearest neighbours are a 'quite wonderful!' gay couple who she would not have cold-shouldered by anyone. Some potential buyers were quite nonplussed by this, she told us with a gleam in her eye.

Her daughters were horrified. 'For God's sake, Mum, you need to sell up, and fast. It's not your business who buys it,' they told her. Of course it was, though, as it always should be when selling a house, an old one especially, that you love. ('To them Howards End was a house: they could not know that to her it had been a spirit, for which she sought a spiritual heir.') Being mindful of the brevity of your custodianship, that you are only a footnote in its long history and never the other way around, means that passing it on correctly is your last great duty to the place.

As it was, Penny's blunt question actually sealed the deal. Just as winter was biting, and the chances of selling the house started to retreat towards the following spring, along came an American looking for a radical new life. Her only fear was that the countryside, the Welsh countryside in particular, would prove to be stiflingly conservative. An unexpected grilling about homophobia was her green light to go for it, enough of a sign that all would be well. She was in there by the second week of January, and the umbilical link between our two houses has been steadfast ever since. Though we miss Penny and David, the new neighbour has slotted in perfectly. Of course she has: with family heritage in the Sicilian gangs of New York, she brings home the ghosts of Murray the Hump, William Bebb and the many who went in the other direction and died of hiraeth.

The ghosts are gathering now, on the lane outside, ready to join our New Year's Eve party, its theme a celebration

of *yr hen lanc* and his eternal greenwood. The boys of
God's Own Country are swapping sheep husbandry tips
with local farmers. Walt Whitman is cracking waspish
asides at the hearth and being doted on by Edward Carpenter, their lustrous beards silhouetted by firelight.
Supping a beer, George Merrill looks on, and contem-
plates a hairy threesome. Emlyn Williams and Ivor
Novello are camping it up in the kitchen, performing a
parody eisteddfod for the benefit of a bemused James
Baldwin: 'With a name like that, you're Welsh!' they keep
telling him. 'Slave name, baby, slave name,' growls Baldwin in response, before throwing a gap-toothed grin.
Edward Prosser Rhys nods and chucks in a few shy
suggestions.

In the parlour, Cedric Morris and David Hockney are hunched over art books and name-dropping loudly to a star-struck Reg. In the flickering shadows of the crow skull chandelier, Lord Montagu, his friends and the airmen are having the party of their wildest dreams, and no one cares. Down by the pool, under an eternity of stars, Joe Ackerley is helping his old friend E. M. Forster direct a remake of the skinny-dip scene from *A Room with a View*, starring a radiant George and some of his cycling club, who needed no persuasion. Tantalising bursts of sound erupt from the granary, where John Grant is tuning up for his slot in the cabaret, after the poetry jam between Hopkins, Housman and Auden. I catch Preds' eye and we grin at each other across the garden, dark and slumbering now but soon to be rocked awake by fireworks that will point the Plough towards a new year, its five hundredth at least over the householders of Rhiw Goch.

All time is now, for, like love, beauty and a Welsh truth, it is no straight line. Time loops and doubles back on itself, skips a beat, ducks for cover and then stretches out like a lizard on hot stone. We charge our glasses to toast Peredur in the *Mabinogi* as he sets out on his Arthurian quest to find the Cruc Galarus, the 'Mound of Mourning'. There, a serpent is coiled and waiting,

> and on the tail of the serpent there is a stone, and the virtues of the stone are such, that whosoever should hold it in one hand, in the other he will have as much gold as he may desire.

Cruc Galarus, Rhiw Goch: the Mound of Mourning is the Red Hill, the Hill of Blood. Peredur searches for the stone, and spots it across the way at the top of a starlit field. He knows it immediately: Carreg y Noddfa, the Stone of Sanctuary, squire of the district and midwife to outlaws and outcasts. Peredur has succeeded in his quest. The gold is his, though far more than coins, for there, say the *Mabinogi*, also lies 'the fairest river valley he had ever seen'.

That too is his: for now, for never, for always.

STANDING STONE (BARWON IN DISTANCE)

THANKS AND ACKNOWLEDGEMENTS

Writing *On the Red Hill* has been like building a three-dimensional jigsaw puzzle. Pieces came from all quarters: from Reg's paintings and notes, George's diaries and photos, their books and our memories, the countless nuggets of their lives that are still seen or used every single day at Rhiw Goch.

Many of Reg and George's old friends gave me crucial (and often unexpected) pieces of the puzzle, that didn't always fit in to the picture quite how I first imagined. Thank you to them all, and for the hours spent in their company in such happy reminiscence: Peter Prior in Bournemouth, Mary and David Cockman in Yorkshire, Daniel Gwatkin, Penny Glaister, Geoffrey Lloyd, Jonathan Pickles, Angela and Meic Llewellyn, Tom and Lisa Brown, Gwilym Fychan, Justin and Hem, Wyn, Geraint and Audrey Jones, Dave and Liz Butler, Geraint and Nora Wigley, Pauline and Dave Thorne, Sarah Gerrard and Janey Howkins, Nicholas and Claire Cann, Suzanne and Tony Penybont, Kim and Jeremy Yr Efail.

Countless conversations about this very special part of Wales helped frame the story. The richness of talent around here is extraordinary; thanks for eternal Bro Ddyfi comradeship to y teulu Tomos: Meg, Dafydd, Ceri, Mair, Ioics, Mabon, Gruff, Branwen, Mali, Macsen, Begw and Nanw; David, Charmian, Izzy, Ryan and the much-missed Ken; Meri Wells, Jane Lloyd-Francis and Georges, Alma and Andrew, Nick and Liz Fenwick, Owain and Fflur Fychan, Julia Forster and Tom Crompton, Nia Llywelyn, Jean Napier, Nicky Burgess, Jane Whittle, Allan and Enid Wyn Jones. Huge thanks to Diane and Geoff at the superlative Pen'rallt Bookshop for being our communal literary lynchpin.

Help in slotting some of the pieces together came from sleuths Sam Christie, Rachel Gibson, Fran Box and the historians of Steep, the irrepressible John and his guests at the Hamilton Hall hotel in Bournemouth, and the superb staff of the National Library at Aberystwyth. To get the ball rolling, I was fortunate to receive a Literature Wales Writer's Bursary supported by the National Lottery through the Arts Council of Wales.

Other pieces of the jigsaw came gift-wrapped from those often unlikely pioneers who have gone before: the countless millions who lived their quiet, stoic spans, as well as the more ebullient guests and ghosts who gather at Rhiw Goch at the end of the story. I came to understand afresh some favourite books and dramas, pieces of art and music, but also discovered many more that were entirely new to me (see *Bibliography and Inspirations*). Picking up on a queer theme in history, and even more so a queer rural or Welsh theme, is often just a momentary connection, a sudden flash of recognition in peripheral vision that can vanish altogether if you try and hold it up to too bright a light. We have to be experts at reading the shadows.

Confirmation that I was on the right path, and that there were other comrades on it too, snuffling around in the undergrowth, came in similarly fleeting glimpses, in particular of Francis Lee's viscerally muddy movie *God's Own Country*, Patrick Gale's TV drama *Man in an Orange Shirt*, Luke Turner's lyrical memoir *Out of the Woods* and Matthew Lopez's epic saga *The Inheritance*, where E. M. Forster himself was so joyously conjured back on to the stage.

I am especially indebted to friends who read drafts, gave advice and helped me shape the kaleidoscope of pieces into a clear(ish) picture: Jay Griffiths, Helen Sandler, Jane Hoy, Jon Woolcott, Pete Telfer, Matthew Gidley, Rachel Wilson and Noel Dunne. Julian Alexander of the Soho Agency (né LAW) steered me gently but firmly in all the right directions; editor Tom Avery was careful, considered, thorough and enthusiastic at every turn. He and the rest of the team at William Heinemann have been a pleasure to work with.

It's an honour to use short extracts from so many wonderful writers in the book. Songwriters too, notably:

- 'Green, Green Grass of Home' by Tom Jones; written by Claude Putman Jr.
- 'Londinium' by Catatonia; written by Mark Roberts and Catatonia.
- 'Go West' by the Village People; written by Jacques Morali, Henri Belolo and Victor Willis

- 'Smalltown Boy' by Bronski Beat, written by Steve Bronski, Jimmy Somerville and Larry Steinbachek.
- 'The Masses Against the Classes' by the Manic Street Preachers; written by James Dean Bradfield, Sean Moore and Nicky Wire.
- 'Glacier' by John Grant; written by John Grant.

Most of all, my love and thanks to my fellow dwellers at Rhiw Goch, both corporeal and ethereal. For all our funny little ways, we are a bloody good team.

www.mikeparker.org.uk
Twitter: @mikeparkerwales
Instagram: @rhiwgoch

BIBLIOGRAPHY AND INSPIRATIONS

In a house that has long creaked under the weight of so many books, they inevitably infused *On the Red Hill* more than any other artform. Those asterisked are my particular recommendations for further reading:

Ackerley, J. R.: *My Father and Myself*

*Ackerley, J. R.: *We Think the World of You*

Aldiss, Brian W.: *The Hand-Reared Boy*

Articulture: *Machynlleth Rocks: A Tour for the Untame*

Baldwin, James: *Another Country*

*Baldwin, James: *Giovanni's Room*

Bebb, W. Ambrose: *Y Baradwys Bell*

Bebb, W. Ambrose: *Lloffion o Ddyddiadur 1940*

Ansell, Neil: *Deep Country: Five Years in the Welsh Hills*

Brown, Michael: *A History of the Dylife Mines and Surrounding Area*

Caradawc o Lancarfan, translated by Nicholas Fenwick: *A Portrait of Machynlleth and its Surroundings*

Carpenter, Edward: *The Intermediate Sex: A Study of Some Transitional Types of Men and Women*

*Chatwin, Bruce: *On the Black Hill*

Cohu, Will: *Out of the Woods: The Armchair Guide to Trees*

Condry, William: *Exploring Wales*

Davies, John et al: *The Welsh Academy Encyclopaedia of Wales*

Davies, Russell: *Hope and Heartbreak: A Social History of Wales and the Welsh 1776 – 1871*

Deakin, Roger: *Waterlog: A Swimmer's Journey Through Britain*

Ford, Ken: *Assault on Germany: The Battle for Geilenkirchen*

Ford, Ken: *Assault Crossing: The River Seine 1944*

*Forster, E. M.: *Maurice*

*Forster, E. M.: *Howards End*

*Furbank, P. N.: *E. M. Forster: A Life*

Gale, Patrick: *A Place Called Winter*

Gardner, Don: *Vagabond Books of Mid Wales*, assorted

Gardiner, James: *Who's a Pretty Boy, Then?: One Hundred and Fifty Years of Gay Life in Pictures*

Gayford, Martin: *A Bigger Message: Conversations with David Hockney*

Godwin, Fay and Toulson, Shirley: *The Drovers' Roads of Wales*

*Green, Andrew: *Wales in 100 Objects*

Grey, Antony: *Quest for Justice: Towards Homosexual Emancipation*

Griffiths, Niall: *Sheepshagger*

Hartnup, Richard: *Gold Under Bracken: The Land of Wales*

*Hopkins, Gerard Manley: *Poems and Prose*

*Jones, Cynan: *The Dig*

Jones, Cyril: *Maldwyn (Cyfres Broydd Cymru)*

Lipscomb, Lt.-Col. C. G.: *History of the 4th Bn. The Somerset Light Infantry*

Llewellyn, Alun and Vaughan-Thomas, Wynford: *The Shell Guide to Wales*

Leeming, David: *James Baldwin: A Biography*

Louis, Édouard, translated by Michael Lucey: *The End of Eddy*

Machen, Arthur: *The Hill of Dreams*

Moore-Colyer, Richard: *Farming in Wales 1936–2011: Welsh Farming and the Farm Business Survey*

Morris, Jan: *Wales: Epic Views of a Small Country*

*Morris, Jan, translated by Twm Morys: *A Machynlleth Triad*

*Parker, Peter: *Ackerley: A Life of J. R. Ackerley*

Peters, Andrew Fusek: *Dip: Wild Swims from the Borderlands*

Roberts, Dewi: *A Powys Anthology*

*Rogers, Byron: *The Man Who Went Into the West: The Life of R. S. Thomas*

*Rowbotham, Sheila: *Edward Carpenter: A Life of Liberty and Love*

Rowley, Trevor: *The English Landscape in the Twentieth Century*

Sanderson, Terry: *Mediawatch: The Treatment of Male and Female Homosexuality in the British Media*

*Scott, Laurence: *The Four-Dimensional Human: Ways of Being in the Digital World*

Shopland, Norena: *Forbidden Lives: LGBT Histories from Wales*

Summerskill, Clare: *Gateway to Heaven: Fifty Years of Lesbian and Gay Oral History*

Thomas, R. S.: *Collected Poems 1945–1990*

Thoreau, Henry David: *Walden*

Todd, Matthew: *Straight Jacket: Overcoming Society's Legacy of Gay Shame*

Tremain, Rose: *Sacred Country*

True North: *Memories of Bournemouth*

Walford Davies, Damian: *Cartographies of Culture: New Geographies of Welsh Writing in English*

West, D. J.: *Homosexuality*

West, Elizabeth: *Hovel in the Hills: An Account of the Simple Life*

White, Edmund: *A Boy's Own Story*

Whitman, Walt: *The Complete Poems*

*Wildeblood, Peter: *Against the Law*

Williams, Raymond: *The Country and the City*

At the theatre, research and pleasure combined in excellent Birmingham Rep productions of Terence Rattigan's *The Winslow Boy*, Eugene Ionesco's *Amédée, or How to Get Rid of It* and Janice Connolly's *Stuff*; Lighthouse Theatre's funky take on Malcolm Pryce's *Aberystwyth Mon Amour*; Simon Armitage and Clive Hicks-Jenkins dark and silky *Hansel & Gretel*; David Ian Rabey's turbocharged *Land of My Fathers*; Terry Hands' full-fat version of Dylan Thomas' *Under Milk Wood*. Matthew Lopez's *The Inheritance*, his reworking of *Howards End* into a gay New York milieu, gave me two of the best nights in the theatre I've ever had.

In the cinema, *God's Own Country* was my runaway winner, a film that left me gasping with its uncompromising authenticity, especially next to its far more mannered contemporary, *Call Me By Your Name*. The media couldn't seem to cope with two queer rite of passage films at the same time; with some inevitability, it was the glossier but weaker one that garnered most of the attention. Other influential films included *A Fantastic Woman, Yr Ymad-awiad, Manchester by the Sea, Can You Ever Forgive Me?, Pride* and *Moonlight*. Wales is home to the LGBT+ Iris Prize for Film; one 2018 entry, Amy Daniel's short *Arth*, was largely filmed at Rhiw Goch. We're lucky to have two fantastic independent cinemas nearby, at the Magic Lantern in Tywyn and Aberystwyth Arts Centre; the latter is home also to the brilliant *Aberration*, a regular night of queer performance, curated by Helen Sandler, Jane Hoy and Ruth Fowler. They also programmed the first dedicated LGBT+ stage at the National Eisteddfod in 2018, which I was proud to compère.

In the summer of 2017, to mark the fiftieth anniversary of the partial decriminalistation of male homosexuality, the BBC ran a series of TV programmes under the masthead of *Gay Britannia*. It was fascinating, and the perfect accompaniment to writing this book. For too long, our history had languished in its little ghetto, but this broke it gloriously wide open and made it relevant to all. The poignancy of *The Man in the Orange Shirt* was only exacerbated on learning that it too was based on reality, in the hidden history of Patrick Gale's own family. Other highlights were the *Queers* set of monologues, a pet project of the divine Mark Gatiss, the archive pageant of *Queerama* and a superb dramatisation of the Montagu trial, *Against the Law*, based on the book of the same name by Peter Wildeblood. Reg and George would have been utterly blown away by it all.

Art is in the bones of Rhiw Goch. Preds' drawing and painting has exploded since we've been here, much of it inspired by the land and its shapes. The illustrations in this book are just a tiny fraction of his exuberant output.

Galleries and exhibitions that have inspired us both include the mid-century masterpieces of John Piper at Tate Liverpool; the mesmerising *Skin: Freud, Mueck and Tunick* at the Ferens in Hull; a double-bill of Sir Cedric Morris at the Garden Museum and the Philip Mould Gallery, both in London; Nikolai Astrup at the Dulwich Picture Gallery; Hilma af Klint at the Serpentine; Hockney in London and Paris; *Modern Couples* at the Barbican; the Artes Mundi in Cardiff, especially Bedwyr Williams' *Tyrrau Mawr*, a fantastical reimagining of a mid-Wales mountainscape; the installations and living sculpture of David Nash; Van Gogh and Edvard Munch in Amsterdam; *Waking the Witch* at Oriel Davies in Newtown; the unexpectedly glittery Andrew Logan Museum of Sculpture in the green hills of Berriew; and across Wales, *Curious Travellers*, exploring the stories of eighteenth-century visitors.

Exhibitions at the National Library of Wales in Aberystwyth are invariably excellent: recent highlights have included a lavish retrospective of photographer Pete Davies' work and *Tirlun Cymru*, a huge sweep through centuries of Welsh landscape art. Machynlleth is blessed with Y Tabernacl cultural centre, including the galleries of the Wales Museum of Modern Art. The standards there are the very highest, and never more so than in the ambitious exhibitions curated by Dr Peter Wakelin, or the creative Welsh anarchy of Pete Telfer and Culture Colony. Eternal thanks to the Lamberts for setting it up, and in fondest memory of Richard, the Captain.

There are so many places that helped this book. Edward Carpenter's Millthorpe is a fascinating village whose pride in its adopted son was deeply moving. Dorset was a joy to explore, and to connect with the sense of George and Reg's early days. George felt so close at T. E. Lawrence's Clouds Hill, and Reg at another National Trust property nearby, Kingston Lacy. They were with us too on trips to Paris, Barcelona and Rome, to Venice and Assisi, and throughout the English-Welsh borderlands, which they adored. I'm often asked where is my favourite place in Wales, home aside. It's impossible to say, but if forced to pick one, I would plump for a corner that never fails to works its magic, in any weather and at any time of year: the Dysynni valley, on the seaward side of the mighty Cadair Idris. There is no better walk than from Abergynolwyn, along the river and up to the gaunt ruins of the native Welsh castle, Castell-y-Bere, down into the hamlet of Llanfihangel-y-Pennant (don't miss the 3D cloth map of the district in the church vestry), and then climbing through the oak woods up past the waterfalls and into Nant yr Eira on the return leg.

As I say in the book, since moving to a place where I can blast music as loud as I like, I rarely do. All the same, *On the Red Hill* has been incubated by a spectrum of sounds: from George's favourite, Mahler, to one of mine, Melys. Weekday evening work has often been accompanied by the BBC Radio Cymru shows of Rhys Mwyn, Georgia Ruth, Lisa Gwilym and Huw Stephens. They are the finest intro to modern Welsh life, regardless of what languages you do or don't speak. Music needs no interpreter.

ILLUSTRATIONS

MAP AND QUARTER PAINTINGS
by Peredur Tomos

PHOTOS
by George Walton or Mike Parker, unless otherwise stated
or unknown.

Prologue
Machynlleth register office, February 2006
Reg and George, Battersea embankment, London, c.1952

*

Air

Red kites over Bryn-y-Brain
The old drovers' track, with Taff

Swallows on the wire, Cae Oddiar y Tŷ
Reg's bedroom in the parlour, 2010

Spring
Beltane morning, Coed Rhiw Goch
Lambs, Cae'r Dderwen
'We climb Ebbor Gorge from Wookey Hole', June 1938
'North Wales Tour', July 1939
Canvey Island camping, August 1939
Reg in army gear, March 1945

East
Reg and George at Cefn, 1975
Coed Esgair Gadwyth
From Bryn-y-Brain, looking east, morning
Carreg y Noddfa
Fron Goch and Rhiw Goch

Reg
Ordnance Survey benchmark, Rhiw Goch
Reg in Italy, 1965
Reg and his father Gus, Bournemouth, c.1955
George, Reg and friends, Bournemouth beach, c.1954
Robert Old window display, Bournemouth, c.1966
Artwork by Reg
Reg's portrait, Rhiw Goch

*

Fire
Crow skull chandelier

Party barn (by Emyr Jenkins)
Cinio al fresco
George at Penhempen, c. 1977
Sunset on the drovers' track, 9.30pm, Bryn-y-Brain

Summer
Beach frolics at Tywyn, 1983
Weightlifting selfie, Rhiw Goch, 1983
Barbed wire bunting, Cae Glas Isaf
Perimeter walling, Y Ffridd
Hawthorn on Bryn-y-Brain
Reg and George, Rhiw Goch, 1984
White foxgloves, Cae Oddiar y Tŷ
Hollyhocks, by the pigsties
Rhiw Goch advertising pamphlet, 1981

South
The Garret photographic studio, Bournemouth, 1950
Stanley in The Garret, 1950
George, Stanley and friends in The Garret, 1950
George's best-selling photograph, The Garret, 1953
Boys on the beach, Studland Bay, c.1954
Reg in Paris, 1954
Seville, Spain, 1957
George on Spanish beach, 1957
Stanley in Spain, 1958
Crossing the channel, 1961
Reg in Greece, 1966
Reg and George, Lake Como, Italy, 1965
Reg and George, Langdale, Cumbria, 1969

George
Stanley, 1944
George and army comrades, Northern Ireland, 1941
George in Somerset Light Infantry gear, 1944
George's parents and sister, Homerton, c.1938
'Hero-cyclist of Wales!', Rhiw Goch, 1983

*

Water
Nant y Gwinau
Swimming pond
Well in the oak wood
Rain-a-coming, Bryn-y-Brain
Walls of words, Rhiw Goch, 2018
One of the springs on Y Rhos

Autumn
Ash at Esgair Gadwyth
Fflosiffont
Autumn birch on the common
Chiselled graffiti, 1960s?, Owain Glyndŵr Institute,
Machynlleth
'In Oven George Dear'
Reg in the kitchen, 1982
Liberty caps, Cae'r Mynydd
Thorn hedge, on the lane

West
Ffrwd Fawr on the Afon Twymyn, Dylife
George on the ascent to Dylife, 1989 (by Ed Buziak)
Iron and spiders, Rhiw Goch

Gravestone, Tal-y-Wern
Capel Beerseba, Melinbyrhedyn

Michael
Quarry tiling, Rhiw Goch
Tal-y-Wern and Moelfre from Ffridd yr Hen Felin
Autumn morning over the beech wood
Face at the window, Rhiw Goch
In the pub, Esgairgeiliog, 2004 (by Pete Telfer)

*

Earth
Funeral tea, Rhiw Goch (by Peredur Tomos)
Moon on a cold tin roof
Light on a winter night
Ex-fox, Weirglodd Isaf
Taff under fire, Bryn-y-Brain

Winter
The big barn, the swallows' doorway
Icicle roof, the small barn
Coed Rhiw Goch
Christmas Day 1983
Christmas Day 2018
Wood and stone
Tongue-and-groove

North
Magpie and moon
Quarried bedrock on the drovers' track
A Stone, alone

Tal-y-Wern chapel graveyard

Peredur
Reg's robin
Fflos at the gate, Cae Bach
Man's best friend, Dorset, c.1963
Spider silk, Cae Pant
Peeping ahead
On Bryn-y-Brain
Ghosts are gathering
'Standing Stone (Darowen in distance)'